CELTIC
a Comparative Study

CELTIC

A comparative study of the six
Celtic languages:
Irish, Gaelic, Manx,
Welsh, Cornish, Breton
seen against the background of their
history, literature, and destiny

by
D. B. Gregor

THE OLEANDER PRESS

The Oleander Press
17 Stansgate Avenue
Cambridge CB2 2QZ, England

The Oleander Press
210 Fifth Avenue
New York, N.Y. 10010, U.S.A.

 British Library Cataloguing in Publication Data

Gregor, Douglas Bartlett
    Celtic. – (Oleander language and literature; vol.11).
    1. Celtic languages — History
    I. Title
    491.6'09   PB1015

    ISBN 0–900891–41–6
    ISBN 0–900891–56–4 Pbk

CONTENTS

LIST OF MAPS

LIST OF ILLUSTRATIONS

NOTE

By their own speakers the Celtic languages of Ireland, Scotland, and the Isle of Man are all called Gaelic (respectively Gaeilge, Gaidhlig, Gailck or Gaelg); and Gaelic they are, being originally one language, that of the Gaels. In a comparative study, however, it is necessary to distinguish them; and the study being in English, English usage is followed. Hence in the following pages, 'Gaelic' signifies the Gaelic of Scotland; and the language of Ireland is called 'Irish', a word containing the oldest name of that nation as still used in the name of the State of Eire and of its citizens, the Eireannaigh; while Manxmen speak, or rather spoke 'Manx' which the Irish themselves distinguish as An Mannanais.

* * *

TIR GAN TEANGA, TIR GAN ANAM

(Irish, 'A country without a language is a country without a soul')

HEP BREZHONEG, BREIZH EBET

(Breton, 'Without Breton, no Brittany')

CENEDL HEB IAITH, CENEDL HEB GALON

(Welsh, 'A nation without a language is a nation without a heart')

GYN CHENGEY, GYN CHEER

(Manx, 'Without a language, without a country')

TIR GUN TEANGA, TIR GUN ANAM

(Scots Gaelic, 'A country without a language is a country without a soul')

DEN HEB TAVAS A-GOLLAS A DYR

(Cornish, 'A man without a language has lost his country')

ACKNOWLEDGEMENTS

I am grateful to the following for permission to
reproduce maps and/or for other valuable help:

Mrs. Audrey Ainsworth, Secretary of *Yn Cheshaght
Ghailckagh*; Mr. Siôn Aled, Secretary of *Cymdeithas yr
Iaith Gymraeg*; Mr. Colm Ó Baoill, of the Department of
Celtic Studies in Aberdeen University (for his map of
Scotland in *Meascradh Uladh* and some lexical information);
Mr. George Broderick of Queen's University, Belfast, and
Editor of the Manx recording, *Chengey ny Mayrey*; M.
Pierre Denis, Maître Assistant à l'Université de Haute-
Bretagne, Renne; Mr. Alan Heusaff, General Secretary of
the Celtic League (for the maps of Scotland and Wales
in Mr. Keith Buchanan's article, 'Economic growth and
cultural liquidation', in the *Celtic Annual* of 1970, and
for a phrase in Breton); Mr. E G R Hooper of Camborne,
Editor of *An Lef Kernewek*; M. Ronan Huon, Director of
Al Liamm, Brest and Mlle. J. Queillé, a member of his
staff; Mrs. M.C. Killey, Assistant Librarian in the Manx
Museum, Douglas, Isle of Man; Mr. Cailean Spencer,
Secretary of *An Comunn Gaidhealach*; Mr. Gearóid Stockman
Editor of *An t-Ultach*; and Mr. Brian Stowell (for a
photocopy of chapter 4 of St. Mark's Gospel).

A Language has Died

(To the memory of Dolly Pentreath (1777) and Ned
Maddrell (1974), last native speakers of Cornish and
Manx)

The darkness grows behind the cottage-wall,
 at least for that still figure on the bed;
 the silence deepens and begins to spread
throughout the room as 'twere a velvet pall,
muffling the breath that struggles for recall:
 a silence all unearthly, full of dread
 and nameless horror, such, one might have said,
that all around a curtain seem to fall.

That silence shall be evermore unbroken,
 those sweet notes nevermore be understood.
O do not die! Let something yet be spoken!
 Say something, anything - delirious rave!
O do not die! O think what goes for good:
 you take with you a language to the grave.

1. THE CELTS.

The historian Ephorus (*fl*.350 B.C.), whose now
lost work supplied later historians with much of their
material, divided the known world among four great
peoples: Ethiopians, Indians, Scyths, and Celts. His
criterion of greatness may not have been the same for
all, but what they had in common, at least for the
ancient imagination, was the extent of their territory.
This happens to be true of the Celts: wherever the
inhabitants of the Roman Empire looked to the North,
from the Atlantic to the mouth of the Danube, they saw
Celts; and if they did not see them, they were told it
was so by Herodotus (2,23), who has the Danube rise
among the Celts and (forgetting the Rhône) flow right
across Europe from the Pyrenees to the Black Sea. If
this authority was not enough, there was the statement
of Aristotle (*Meteor*.1,13) to the same effect and calling the Pyrenees "a mountain in Keltike". This agrees
with our earliest reference to the Celts, namely the
statement of Hecataeus (*ca*.540-475 B.C.) describing
Massilia (Marseille) as "a town in the land of the
Ligurians bordering on the land of the Celts (Keltike)";
which location explains why Hannibal encountered them

on his march through the Pyrenees and Southern Gaul to
Italy, as Polybius (*fl.*150 B.C.) states (*Hist.*3,40).

If they went westwards, sooner or later they
would meet Celts and have confirmation of Herodotus'
further statement, that there were Celts outside the
Straits of Gibraltar, i.e. on the west coast of the
Iberian Peninsula. This, however, was to be confirmed
by Rome's own great philosopher-scientist Posidonius
(*ca.*130-46 B.C.). He had visited the area and found it
inhabited by a people calling themselves *Celtici*,
whose place-names often end in the Celtic root - *briga*
("Height"), as is pointed out both by the later geographer Pomponius Mela (*fl.*A.D. 50) and by the polymath
Pliny the Elder (who died in the eruption of Vesuvius
in A.D. 79). North of this people there was another,
whose name many years of bitter fighting, culminating
in the famous siege of Numantia in 133 B.C., had impressed on the Roman mind: the Celtiberi. This name,
which was coined by Greek colonists from Massilia
settled in a trading-post (Emporion), now known as
Ampurias (north of Barcelona), referred to Iberians who
had intermarried with the Celtic inhabitants of the
Iberian highlands into which they had penetrated in the

seventh century B.C.

The union of the two stocks, which produced what
Diodorus Siculus (who lived under Augustus, but fortunately copied out much of Ephorus) called the bravest
of all the Iberians, can hardly have been confined to
the area where it finds linguistic recognition.
Indeed, the theory of an Iberian (Mediterranean)
element in the Celtic physical constitution has long
been advanced as the only explanation of the fact that,
whereas for the ancients the Celts were a tall, blond
people (like the heroes of early Irish prose epics),
the modern world distinguishes them from northern
Germanic peoples by the absence of those very features.
Certainly, as the Celts moved out from their heartland
in Central Europe, they must have found an indigenous
population and mingled with it: and in fact the
measurements of excavated skulls indicate a mixed race.
These previous inhabitants may have been the descendants
of the megalithic people who covered Western Europe with
huge monuments like Stonehenge hundreds of years before
the coming of the Celts. It remains odd, however, that
the physical features of the submerged substratum should
have finally predominated; and one can only assume

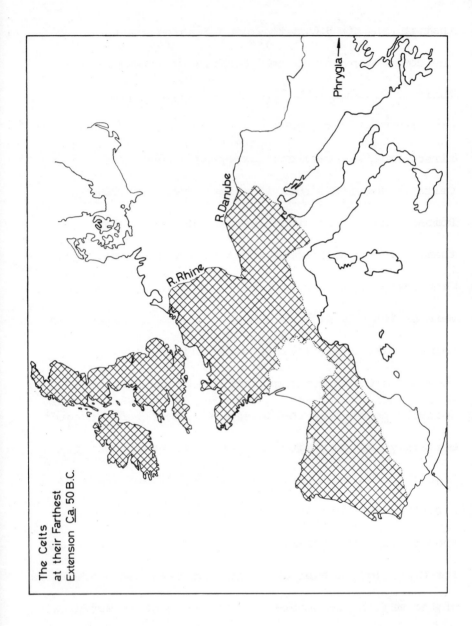

The Celts
at their Farthest
Extension <u>Ca.</u> 50 B.C.

R. Rhine

R. Danube

Phrygia →

that the Celtic invaders were far from outnumbering
the conquered peoples and were accompanied by few of
their womenfolk.

As a matter of fact, although one of the world's
first explorers, Pytheas of Massilia, had distinguished
Celts from Germans early in the fourth century, the
Romans were not always careful to differentiate between
them. It is still disputed, for example, whether the
Cimbri and Teutones[1], who tried to invade Italy and
were eventually defeated by Marius in 102-1 B.C., were
Germans or Celts. The names of the Cimbric leaders
look Celtic[2]; but Strabo, the Augustan geographer,
(4,196), calls them both *Germani*, and they were
certainly in the territory now known as Jutland when
Augustus in A.D.13 wrote his *Res Gestae* and Tacitus *ca.*
A.D.98 his *Germania*. There is a solution that allows
them to be both: if *Germani* be taken as a tribal name
for Celts living east of the Rhine, this would explain
why the Belgae claimed to have originated in Germania
(Caesar, *B.G.*2,4,1) and above all why the historian
Dionysius of Halicarnassus (*fl.*20 B.C.) makes Germania
a part of Keltike extending from the Rhine to the
Hercynian forest in Bohemia.

If the numerous tribes which made up the Germani had another collective name, it has not come down to us; but the Celts had the best of reasons for knowing that their neighbours belonged to a different stock, because it was the movement of these hordes which started off their own. About 900 B.C. some event such as a climatic change increasing the rainfall led a Nordic people to seek more favourable territory in the south. The Celts fell back before them from their home on the Upper Danube and by 500 B.C. had occupied "Spain" and "Gaul" with the exception of the south coast west and east of the Rhône inhabited respectively by Iberians and Ligurians; and soon afterwards they moved on into the "British Isles". About 400 B.C. they invaded Italy, either from Gaul, as Livy thought, or from the Danube, which would account for their earliest contact's being with the Etruscans, whom they drove out of the area on both banks of the Po to create what became known as Cisalpine Gaul. The Romans failed to halt them, and if the Gauls had not been more interested in plunder than in territorial conquest, they would have held on to Rome and not been bought off with a sum of money. Another group reached Apulia, but again made

no attempt to settle, being content to serve in the
army which Dionysius I of Syracuse sent to help Sparta
against Thebes in 368.

It will be noted that the Romans now start speaking of Gauls, not of Celts; and although there is no
doubt that linguistically the Gauls were Celts, i.e.
that Gaulish was a Celtic tongue, it is not absolutely
certain that the two names are interchangeable. For
Polybius apparently they were (2,17), and Caesar
actually says (1,1) that *Galli* is the Latin for *Celtae*.
The same distinction is made by Strabo (*Geographica* 4,
177), writing some thirty years later. It has even
been proposed to see in the two names the distinction
between the blond and the dark Celts of which we have
already spoken. Generations of school-children have
scratched their heads over the opening sentence of the
De bello Gallico; but the real puzzle is not the best
translation of *omnis*, but why the Belgae and the
Aquitani should apparently be denied the name Celt.
In the case of the Aquitani the answer is simple:
with the exception of one tribe, the Bituriges Vivisci,
at the mouth of the Garonne, they were "different in
physique and language from the Celtae and more like the

Iberians" (Strabo 4,176 and 189,2); and in fact it is
tempting to call them Iberians outright, because their
race would then bestride the Pyrenees as the Basques
do today[3]. (This did not deter Augustus from later
adding 14 Celtic tribes from south of the Loire to
their 20 or so to form a new Province.) The Belgae,
on the contrary, are shown to have been Celts by the
Celtic names of their tribal kings (e.g. Divitiacus)
and of towns such as Mediolanium (cf. Mediolanum, now
Milan, in Cisalpine Gaul)[4], and by the obviously
Celtic character of their immigrants into Britain, who
extended westward as far as Bath. Strabo indeed
(4,176) allows only slight linguistic differences
among Gauls outside Aquitania. The real key, however,
is the difference between Celti and Celtae. For
Caesar the Celtae were only one part of all the Galli
(and Augustus removed even their name by making them
part of Gallia Narbonensis), and it may well be that
the generic term "Celt" came from the first contact of
the Greek colonists of Massilia with their neighbours,
the Celtae[5]. Similarly, from Gallia Narbonensis, the
name "Gallia" was extended to the whole country, including even Iberian Aquitania.

If we now look eastwards, surely a Roman could move into the Hellenic world and not find himself among Celts? No; the Celtic drive southwards down the Italian Peninsula was paralleled by another one *ca*.350 B.C. into the Balkans and Greece. The movement of the Celts had directly or indirectly triggered off an irruption of Illyrian Triballi into Macedonia in 376-5 B.C.; and in 335 Alexander the Great decided to make a pre-emptive strike against them. Among embassies he received on this occasion was one from the Celts (presumably those in Istria), which resulted in a treaty of friendship. Strabo thought an anecdote worth relating here: over drinks Alexander asked the Celtic envoys what they feared most, confident that they would say, "You," but the reply was, "Nothing, short of the end of the world". "Braggarts!", muttered Alexander after their departure[6]. Celtic raids into Illyria and Thrace continued during the Macedonian Wars of Succession, and in 280 a Celtic chieftain with the interesting name Belgios or Bolgios defeated a Macedonian King, Ptolemy Keraunos. The following year saw their invasion of Greece under Brennus (the same name as their leader against Rome,

and clearly a royal title, unless the Welsh for 'king',
brenin, is a coincidence). Once again we have a Battle
of Thermopylae, the turning of the Pass, the disunity
of the Greeks, and an abortive raid on Delphi, saved
by a timely thunderstorm; but the Gauls were defeated
as thoroughly as Xerxes' Persians, thanks chiefly to
the Aetolians, who discovered for the world the valuable secret that Gallic hordes were no match for
determined guerrillas. The remnants of the Gauls
withdrew to Thrace, whence one band settled at the
confluence of the Save and the Danube, where under the
name of Scordisci they routed a Roman army in 114 and
raided as far as Delphi again, before providing two
Roman generals with triumphs in 112 and 106, the
latter ending a four years' campaign and memorable for
the monument called after the victorious general
Porticus Minucia, where corn-doles were distributed in
Rome during the early Empire.

There were still plenty of Celts left east of the
Rhine as far as the Weser and north of the Danube as far as
the Main: the Boii, for example, who gave their name to Bohemia
(Boio-haims) and Bavaria (Boio-varia), as later to Bologna
and Boulogne (Bononia); and the Bastarnae, variously called

Celts or Germans, but expressly said by Livy (40,37,7)
to be related to the Scordisci in language and customs.
Nor must we forget the Celtoscyths, since the name
will remind us of the Celtiberi and the Celtoligurians,
and indicate the capacity of the Celts to impose
recognizable characteristics on any people with whom
they mingled.

Surely the Celts will not have overflowed into
Asia. How could there possibly be room for them among
the Bithynians, Lydians, Phrygians, Pergamenes, and
other nations which had occupied Asia Minor for
centuries? Yet after the third century B.C. a Roman
could hardly move far into Phrygia without coming up
against a people of vaguely familiar appearance, and,
if he had ever been in Gaul, recognizing the cadences
of their speech, as St. Jerome did in the fourth
century A.D.[7] Inquiry would show that these were the
descendants of three Gallic tribes, of which two, the
Tolistobogii and Trocmi[8], had not taken part in the
invasion of Greece, but had advanced through Macedonia
and crossed the Dardanelles, where they were later
joined by the third tribe, the Tectosages. The crossing had been at the invitation of King Nicomedes of

Bithnyia, who was embroiled in a struggle with the
King of Syria; and he now enrolled all three tribes
in his service. Asia Minor being in no condition to
offer resistance, the Gauls enjoyed unlimited oppor-
tunities of plunder, until in 275 Antiochus met them
in battle with a squadron of elephants specially imported from India, and inflicted a severe defeat.
Nicomedes then settled the Gauls in northern Phrygia,
where they formed an independent State powerful enough
to exact 'protection-money' from the kings of Syria.
The Greek for 'Gauls' being *Galatai*, the country became known as Galatia, and as Kingdom and Province
later played its part in Roman History (sometimes
providing Rome's enemies, Pyrrhus and Carthage, with
mercenaries, sometimes helping Rome, as against
Mithridates of Pontus) and in St. Paul's missionary
journeys. The other name for them, *Gallograeci*
(Livy 37,8,4),indicates the formation of another hybrid
people.

An advantage for posterity in the presence of
Gauls in Phrygia is that the Pergamenes who fought and
tamed them possessed sculptors who could portray them
in bronze statue[9] or stone relief and thus show us

what a Celt looked like, at least on the battle-field.
We see the smeared, long hair, and the athletic frame,
and can well believe Strabo when he says (4,199), that
any youth whose waist-line exceeded a certain figure
was punished. The trousers[10] which they are often
described as wearing indicate an original abode in a
cold climate. As for the material objects surrounding
them, excavations, particularly of chieftains' graves,
show the earlier migrants to have been carriers of the
so-called Hallstatt Culture (700-500 B.C.), and the
later ones of the La Tène (500-50 B.C.). They had
evolved a characteristic art in gold, metal, and stone,
to the high quality of which numerous finds all over
Europe testify; and there were certain classes who
could write either in the Ogam script[11] or in the
Greek letters picked up from the Greeks of Massilia
and used, not only by Gallic Druids (the legal and
religious class), but even in administrative documents
like those brought to Caesar from a Helvetian camp
(*B.G.* 1,29). Other educated classes were the *vates*
(Irish *faidhe*) or seers, and the bards, who combined
the functions of royal panegyrists and genealogists.
How far literacy extended downwards is not known, but

according to Diodorus 'some' would throw letters on

to the pyres of the dead for them to read.

We have seen the Celts spreading from the Upper

Danube westwards to the Atlantic, southwards to a

line from Milan to Ravenna and the Save, and eastwards

to the further borders of Phrygia; but they had been

moving northwards too.

Notes to Chapter One

1. The word is cognate with Irish *tuath* 'a people'
    (Old Welsh and Breton *tud* 'people') and reached
    Latin via Gothic *thiuda*, Old High German *diota*
    (*deutsch*). Cf. the Teutoburg forest, where in
    A.D.9 the Romans lost their chance of romanizing
    Germany.

2. e.g. Boiorix, the King of the Cimbri (Plutarch,
    Marius 24,4 and Livy, *Epitome* 67), where *rix* is
    the Celtic of *rex* 'king' (Irish *rí*) and *Boio* is
    clearly connected with the Celtic tribe of the
    Boii. On the other hand, the other leader,
    Teutoboduus, is made a Teuton by Florus, who
    flourished under Hadrian, and a Cimbrian by
    Eutropius (*fl*.A.D.370). For the suffix *-boduus*,
    which is certainly Celtic, cf. the Irish war-
    goddess *Bodb*, the Irish word *buaidh* 'victory',
    and our Queen Boudicca. Cf. too the Marcomannic
    king, Maroboduus, where the prefix *Maro-* is also
    Celtic (Irish *mór*, Welsh *mawr* 'great'). But the
    prefix *marco-* is germanic, meaning 'border-
    country': cf. *Ostmark*, *Markgraf* 'Marcher-Lord'.
    The Celtic cognate is *bro*. Perhaps we should
    rather connect *marco-* with the Celtic word for
    'horse'.

3. Cf. J. Whatmough, *The Dialects of Ancient Gaul*:
    'It seems improbable that the Keltic language

was ever spoken in Aquitania, but Iberian instead'.
In an earlier work, 'Some lexical variants in the
dialects of ancient Gaul' (in *Studies presented
to D.M. Robinson*, Vol. II, p.482, 1953), he re-
marks on the 'curious feature (of) the number of
lexical agreements between Aquitania and Belgica',
a striking confirmation of Caesar's opening
sentence referred to above.

4. R.S. Conway, *Prae-italic dialects of Italy*, points
    out that the correct ending is -*lanum*; otherwise
    Milano would be called Milagno.

    The syllable *lan* may represent Irish *lán*, W. *llawn*
    ('full'), with lost P as in Latin *plenus*, or
    possibly its cognate is Latin *planus* ('flat'), W.
    llawr ('floor').

5. The root *celt* is variously derived from Latin
    celsus ('exalted'), Irish *ceilt* ('cloak') or
    Latin (*per*)*cello* ('I strike'). It is noteworthy
    that the father of the Gallic hero Vercingetorix
    was called *Celtillus* (Caesar, *B.G.* 7,4,1). Para-
    doxically, the Irish word derived from *Gallus*
    (*Gall*, plural *Gaill*) came to mean 'non-Celtic',
    'foreigner', whether Frank, Dane, or English
    (especially Protestant). Hence *Dun na nGall*
    'Fort of the Foreigners' (Donegal).

6. Strabo, 7,302; Arrian (consul under Hadrian),
    Anabasis, 1,4,6-8.

7. This stubborn adherence to their Celtic tongue
    annoyed the irascible Jerome. Why can't they
    speak Greek like everyone else?, he asked (*Comm.
    Epist. Gal.*). (Lord George-Brown could say he
    was in good company.)

8. Cognate with Caesar's interpreter C. Valerius
    Troucillus (*B.G.* 1,19,3), (where however some
    read Procillus), a name found in many inscriptions;
    with *Trogimarus*, and with *Trogus*, the Augustan
    author of a History of the non-Roman world, which
    has survived in Justin's Epitome. Ch.xliii of
    that work makes him a Narbonensian Gaul. The
    Celtic cognate may be Irish *truaigh*, W. *truan* (sad!)

9. Byron might or must have still referred to the
    dying figure's 'noble brow', even if he had known
    it was not a gladiator; but how many fine lines of
    English poetry would have been lost!

10. The Gallic word *braca* seems to be a rare example
    of Celtic borrowing from Germanic; cf. Anglo-
    Saxon *broc* (plural *brek*), Dutch *broek* (trousers),
    English *breech(es)*.

11. This script resembles the Runic in being composed
    of straight lines in varying combinations, and it
    probably arose in the 4th century A.D. from the
    use of notches on the wooden tally-sticks used in
    counting sheep. About 400 have been found, dis-
    tributed as follows: 40 in Wales (mostly S.W.);
    ca. 30 in Scotland (including the 27 or so in un-
    deciphered Pictish; 316 in Ireland (the probable
    land of origin); 6 in the Isle of Man; 6 in
    Cornwall; 2 in Devon; and 1 in Hampshire. (The
    O is long as in *home*; in fact, since the G was
    once aspirated in certain parts of Ireland, and
    therefore silent (*infra*), the sound would have
    been like that word with dropped H).

2. THE BRYTHONS AND THE GOIDELS

The earliest recorded inhabitants of the British Isles were the Priteni (or Preteni), who gave their name to the islands as early as 323 B.C., when Pytheas visited Britain and later referred to the Pretannic Isles. These are probably the people whom archaeologists believe to have brought a new culture from Central Europe to the islands in the Late Bronze Age (*ca.* 1000 B.C.). For reasons that we shall see later, the Irish name for them was *Cruithin*, the Welsh name *Prydyn*; and both these words were later used to mean the Picts. It is an irresistible deduction that these earliest inhabitants of Britain and Ireland were, therefore, Picts. Unfortunately, it is not so certain that the Picts were Celts.

Common Celtic, which had no letter P, had by this time split into two main 'dialects', according as, after learning to pronounce P, the speakers had kept it or changed it into Q. The P-Celts are known as Brythons (from the Welsh for the later Latin military name for Britons, *Brittones*); the Q-Celts are called Goidels (from the Old Irish for 'Gael' derived from the Welsh *Gwyddel* 'raider'). If the Picts were Celts,

to which 'dialect' did Pictish belong? The name
Priteni (whether or not the source of *Britanni*) indicates the P-Celts.

Under pressure from Teutons moving south and
already suffering from over-population in Gaul, as
Livy's story about the 4th century Ambigatus (5,34,
2-3 *abundans multitudo*) sufficiently shows, the Celts
began the migrations that were to end in the occupation of the British Isles. Since Irish is Goidelic
and Welsh Brythonic, it might be thought that the
first new wave, which would presumably go furthest
under pressure from those following it, was composed
of Goidels; but this traditional view has had to
yield to the evidence of language and the earliest
Irish annals. From these it is clear that the Goidels
were late, in fact, the last newcomers to Ireland. A
number of words for humble objects, for example, have
Brythonic features, and these must have been borrowed
in an early phase of Goidelic, i.e. from the people
whom they met in Ireland. Moreover, the Irish pagan
pantheon betrays a mixture of Brythonic and Goidelic
names: *Indiu*, the 'Great God', contains the equivalent
of the Welsh intensive prefix *en*, whereas *Dagda*, the

'Good God', is Goidelic in its use of *dagh* (W. *da*) as
a prefix (Modern Irish *deagh-*). Then among the names
of the peoples traditionally supposed to have invaded
the island in the earliest days (one group of whom,
the Tuatha De Danann ('Peoples of the Goddess Danu')
are clearly euhemerized deities), are the Fir-Bolg.
This name, once rendered 'Men of the Bags' and
variously explained, is now recognized as referring
to the Belgae, *Bolg* being here the Genitive Plural,
not of *bolg* ('a bag'), but of *Builg*, a tribal name
found in the *Historia Brittonum* of Nennius (A.D. 850),
and the phrase being simply a periphrasis for 'The
Builg', i.e. the Belgae[1]. For the phonetic variance
from E to O, one may compare the Celtic chieftain who
is called Belgius in Trogus (xxiv. 5,1) and Bolgius in
the second-century geographer Pausanias (x. 19,7).

These Belgae evidently represent the first wave
of invaders mentioned above, and legends suggest that
they came via Britain, as we should expect. They are
almost certainly identical with the Erainn, whom
Ptolemy, drawing on early sources, places in Southern
Ireland under the name *Iverni* (representing, as Welsh
Iwerddon shows, a Celtic *Euerni* and finally yielding

Hibernia). This must be the source of the name *Iris*,
which Diodorus uses for the island and which reappears
in German *Ir*, Dutch *Ier*, Danish *Irer* for Irishmen,
whereas English preserves the root only in that compound and in the name of the country as it is called
everywhere outside itself (*Ireland*; G. *Irland*; Dan.
Ierland), unless we count the discredited name for
the language, *Erse* (cf. the Dutch adjective *Iers*). In
any case, since the Old Irish name for the island was
Eriu, it is clear that *Erainn* means 'Men of Ireland',
and so the modern name of the Republic of Ireland goes
back to pre-Goidelic times.

Sharing Ireland with them were, among other
tribes, the *Laigin*, whose name (hidden now in that of
Leinster) is shown by the Welsh *Lleyn* in Caernarvon-
shire to be Brythonic. This suits their traditional
identification with the *Domnainn*; for these clearly
bear the same name as the Dumnonii of Devon and Cornwall, not to mention those of Southern Scotland (cf.
Dumbarton), a distribution which incidentally shows
that the Brythons conquered the Preteni over an area
as great as the later Roman province. Their invasions
from the Continent went on from the sixth century B.C.

down to Caesar's own day, when King Commius of the
Gallic Atrebates, having broken with Rome, fled with
his followers in 52 B.C. to Britain[2], whither the
Belgae had been emigrating throughout the first half
of the century. Thus for nearly 500 years the whole
of the British Isles except Pictland spoke Brythonic.

     Then came the Goidels. They must have come,
because Irish today is Goidelic; but where did they
come from, and when? One of the peoples whom early
Irish annalists count among their ancestors (and as
the conquerors of those mythical Tuatha De Danann) was
the Milesians, a name startling to students of Greek
history, but in fact unconnected with Miletus and
meaning the descendants of *Milesius*, which name was
the latinized form of the Irish *Miledh*, sc. *Easpain*
('Champion of Spain'), the nickname of a certain Golamh.
These descendants are supposed to have come from Spain
around 1000 B.C. There were indeed Celts in Spain, as
we have seen;[3] and the possibility of so long a voyage
across the Atlantic has to be admitted, because the
unknown author of a Greek poem amalgamating two travel
documents ('Periplous' or *Circumnavigations*) of the
4th and 2nd centuries B.C.[4] describes how travellers on

the tin trade-route between Tartessos and Oestrymnis

(Brittany)[5] were told by the Oestrymnians of their

exciting voyages in boats of sewn hides across the sea

to Ierne and Albion. On the other hand, if these

annalists could bring the Fir-Bolg from Greece, as

they did, a voyage from Spain must be equally suspect;

and it is more probable that they were influenced by

the similarity of the names *Iberia* and *Hibernia*. It

must be from Gaul that they came, just as the Fir-Bolg

(Belgae) did.

Were there Q-Celts in Gaul? Fortunately, there

is no doubt about that, because the tribe occupying

the area between the Rhône and the Rhine was called

Sequani; and furthermore the Druidic Calendar of the

late first century B.C. found in Sequanian territory

at Coligny (S.E. of Dijon) in 1897 contains the words

equos, *quimon*, and the month-name *Qutios*[6]. Their

neighbours, the Helvetii, may reasonably be supposed

to have been Q-Celts also, because Caesar puts them and

the Sequani among the Celtae (*B.G.* 1,1,2-4) and they

had probably been neighbours earlier in South Germany.

Why should these people emigrate to Ireland? There

was one very good reason for leaving Gaul between 58

and 50 B.C.: Caesar. The chiefs of the Belgic

Bellovaci sought sanctuary in Britain in 57 (*B.G.* 2,

14), and Commius, as we have seen, fled there in 52.

Now, when the Helvetii and various neighbours began

moving towards the western coast of Gaul in 58, the

total host numbered 368,000, of whom 92,000 were

fighting-men (*B.G.* 1,29). Assuming that most of

these latter were eliminated at the Battle of Armecy,

and knowing from Caesar that 130,000 surrendered, we

are left with 146,000 unaccounted for. They might

well have continued their trek westwards, but no

longer with the aim of stopping at the coast: what

they needed was a refuge, and Ireland would seem to

them with their faulty maps nearer than Britain and

certainly safer. Here then may be our missing Gauls[7].

Be that as it may, the newcomers called them-

selves *Feni* in the sense of free landholders, in con-

tradistinction to the *Aithach-Tuatha* or unfree clans,

among whom were the Fir-Bolg. They called their

language *Bélre Fene* 'the language of the Feni', a

name which came to stand for pure, archaic Irish. It

is strange that, if the Goidels had not occupied Ireland,

Q-Celtic might have vanished almost without trace,

and, as Professor Ó'Rahilly suggests (*op. cit.*p.52),

the solid block of Brythonic might have better

resisted English.

It is time now to follow the two branches in

their subsequent history.

Notes to Chapter Two

1. This identification was made independently by
    R. O'Flaherty in 1685 and Prof. T. Ó'Rahilly
    in 1935, *The Goidels and their predecessors*.

2. Frontinus,Agricola's predecessor as Governor of
    Britain and conqueror of the Silures in S. Wales,
    describes the stratagem by which he shook off
    his pursuers (*Strategemata* ii,13,11).

3. The Lusitani in the west of the country were a
    much celtized branch of the Celtiberi; whence
    the affinity of Portuguese with Galician and
    French.

4. Translated into Latin *ca*. A.D. 300 by one of the
    last practising pagans, Avienus, under the title
    Ora Maritima.

5. Cf. Pliny's Ossismi in Cap Finisterre (*N.H.* 4,107)

6. *Qutios*, however, also appears as *Cutios*. There
    is a full-size reproduction of the Calendar in
    the entrance-hall of the National Library of
    Wales. The Sequani also had a divinity called
    Sinquatis. Arbois de Joinville thought the lan-
    guage of the Calendar to be Ligurian.

7. T.Ó'Rahilly, *op.cit.*,pp. 23-27.

3. GOIDELIA

The Goidelic take-over of Hibernia was complete.
No pockets of Brythonic were left, and indeed the
Goidels spilled over into adjacent territory. In the
Isle of Man, as we shall see, they found the Brythons,
and in due course absorbed them so that the speech of
the whole island became Goidelic. Emigration to
'Scotland' came later, probably in the first half of
the 6th century, and here Goidelic was at first sand-
wiched between Pictish to the north and the Brythonic
of Cumbrian Strathclyde to the south-west. For some
reason the Picts faded out, allowing Gaelic to spread
northwards into the Highlands. Extension southwards
was hindered on the west by the stubborn survival of
Strathclyde, and prevented altogether on the east by
the advance of the Angles, who had supplanted the old
Brythonic kingdom of Gododdin. Thus fragmented, and
sharing 'Scotland' with Picts, Goidelic Scotti, and Angles,
Brythonia is clearly going to have a more complicated
story, until its component elements embark on their
separate careers. Then Goidelic and Brythonic
countries will have an equally tormented history.

4. BRYTHONIA

The survivors of the Brythons (the Ancient or
Roman Britons) are the Welsh; but for a long time
there was no single word in Latin for the part of the
Roman province now called Wales. Britannia was one
country and its inhabitants were Britanni; and these
words stood for an ethnic and linguistic unit more
accurately than does the modern legal term, 'British',
for citizens of Great Britain. Even the Picts, known
to the Romans as Caledonii from the name of one of
their tribes[1], though distinct in certain physical
features, can still be called Britons by Tacitus[2].

When the Romans withdrew from Britain early in the
5th century, romanization was far from complete and
was by no means uniformly distributed over the country.
For one thing, Britain had not been a single province
since it was divided into two by the Emperor Septimius
Severus, whose determined but vain attempt to crush
the Caledonians in 209 brought him farther north than
any Roman Emperor had ever been or ever would be.
Then, when Diocletian reorganized the Empire in 297,
it became four provinces, and again later five, when
Valentinian I, soon after 368, carved the province of

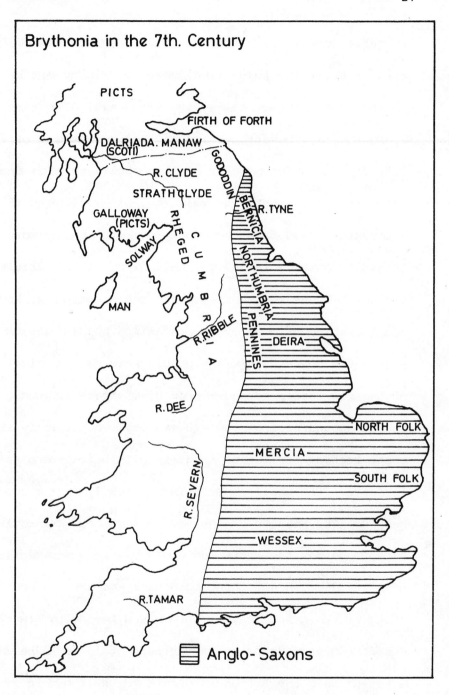

Brythonia in the 7th. Century

PICTS

FIRTH OF FORTH

DALRIADA. MANAW
(SCOTI)

R. CLYDE

STRATHCLYDE

GALLOWAY
(PICTS)

SOLWAY

MAN

RHEGED

CUMBRIA

GODODDIN

BERNICIA

R. TYNE

NORTHUMBRIA

PENNINES

R. RIBBLE

DEIRA

R. DEE

NORTH FOLK

MERCIA

SOUTH FOLK

R. SEVERN

WESSEX

R. TAMAR

Anglo-Saxons

Valentia out of it. (This may have been coextensive
with Wales). The population, however, was by now
romanized enough not to see the withdrawal of the
legions as a liberation; indeed they resented being
left to the tender mercies of the barbarians both from
the north of the Antonine wall (the Picts, Scots and
Attaccotti), and from the Continent (the Saxons and
Franks). Already in 367 the incursions of the former
had emptied the territory between the Antonine Wall
and Yorkshire of most of its romanized population outside a few towns. It was probably this desire for
protection that produced a crop of usurpers in Britain
in the second half of the 4th century; certainly they
spent much of their time fighting with barbarian
invaders: the challenger of Theodosius I, Magnus
Maximus (the Machsen of the *Mabinogion*), had to fight
hard to defeat the Picts and Scots before his own down-
fall in 388. In 407 three more usurpers arose in
Britain. When the last of them was defeated by the
Western Emperor Honorius in Northern Italy in 411, and
Honorius told the Britons "to look to their own
defence" (Procopius, *Hist.* vi.10), the Britons did just
that. Responsibility for law and order was taken over

by the chief men of the various *civitates*, called
teyrniaid by our Welsh and 'tyrants' by our Latin
sources. Hence arose the Kingdoms of Strathclyde,
Gododdin,and Rheged, of Elmet in what was later Yorkshire, of Demetia in S.W. Wales, of the Cornovii
(capital Wroxeter), the Silures (Caerwent), and the
Dumnonii (Exeter). The Anglo-Saxons who soon replaced
such new kingdoms in the eastern part of the country
were not only invaders, but defenders called in by
romanized Britons to protect them when Rome proved
unable to do so. According to Gildas, in his *De
Excidio Britanniae* of *ca*. 540, these Saxons rebelled
and had to be defeated, as they were at the Battle of
Badon in 450, by a king called Arthur, if Nennius is
to be believed[3]. Some of the Saxons whom Rome had
recruited into her legions may also have stayed behind;
but this too would have affected the eastern more than
the western part of the country, for a document describing the distribution of Roman forces throughout the
Empire and dating from *ca*. 425, the *Notitia Dignitatum*,
has no reference to any units stationed in the west of
Britain. This means that 'Wales' had been for many
years out of contact, not only with Latin speakers, but

also with Saxon legionaries; in other words, the
eastern and western zones were clearly marked off
from one another by race, language and religion.

At this date (the early 5th century) the indigenous language, called today Brythonic (or more
recently Brittonic), was still a relatively uniform
speech (Early British). A glimpse of it can be had
in the few words preserved by writers in Latin and
Greek: for example, the anonymous authors of the
Antonine Itinerary (A.D. 300), of the map of the
Roman Empire called the *Peutinger Table* (365), of the
Ravenna Cosmography (670, but based on an earlier
document), the *Notitia Dignitatum* mentioned above, and
of the *Geography* of Ptolemy (150). Such rendering
into an alphabet not designed for it was all the easier
in that the Italic and Celtic branches of Indo-
European had not then so far diverged from each other:
in phonetics, the short vowels and the long A were the
same in Latin and Brythonic; in morphology, Celtic
still had its case-endings. The disintegration of
Brythonic began with the break-down of law and order
consequent on the incursions of the Anglo-Saxons;
under such conditions a language is abandoned to the

uncontrolled caprice of the less literate. Thus

change, when it came, was rapid. Within 150 years

(450-600) Brythonic had split up into three forms

known later as Welsh, Cornish and Breton. One change,

however, was common to them all: they had lost their

case-endings.

The three new languages then embarked on their

several careers, passing through four phases of vary-

ing duration:-

	WELSH	CORNISH	BRETON
PRIMITIVE	6th-8th centuries	6th-9th centuries	6th-9th centuries
OLD	8th-12th centuries	9th-14th centuries	9th-11th centuries
MIDDLE	12th-15th centuries	14th-16th centuries	11th-17th centuries
MODERN	15th- centuries	16th- centuries	17th- centuries

For the primitive form of Welsh and Cornish (so-

called because the phase antedated written, literary

records), we rely on early Christian epitaphs of the

5th to the 7th century, inscribed in Latin with or

without the equivalent in Ogam. They represent a

fusion of Christian funerary custom originating in

5th-century Gaul (the dead man's name in the Genitive

followed by the word for 'son' in apposition), a pre-

Christian element (the name of the father[4]) and the

Ogam tradition (perpendicular script). We may quote

from one of the 5th century which can be seen in the

National Museum of Wales:-

SIMILINI
                    ('Of Prince Similinus')
TOVISACI

Here the last word is the Brythonic form of the term

used today for the Irish Prime Minister (Taoiseach)

and the Prince of Wales (Tywysog)[5].

Besides these inscriptions, certain early Latin

works contain words derived from Primitive Welsh:

the *De Excidio Britanniae* of Gildas, a *Life of St.*

Samson (*ca.* 620), Bede's *Historia ecclesiastica*

gentis Anglorum (731), and various *Lives* of saints

composed in Brittany between 869 and the 11th century,

but based on earlier material.

Some of the oldest words in Welsh are loans from

Latin, but the Brythons were more ready to borrow a

few words than to learn the whole language of the

occupying power. In a significant sentence Tacitus[6]

lets slip the information that the Britons 'refused to

learn Latin'; and if he is here referring to the

upper classes, it is hardly likely that the mass of

the people were more enthusiastic. Equally, when

Tacitus goes on to say that as a result of Agricola's

campaign of romanization Britons began to study

rhetoric, i.e. to seek real proficiency in Latin (a

statement confirmed by references in Plutarch and

Juvenal to rhetoricians in Britain[7]), it is still the

élite to which he is referring.

Rhetoric, though originally meaning the art of

effective speech, had, as the advent of the Empire

left no place for republican oratory, come to mean

literary style in general; and it may be presumed

that the students in these new courses of rhetoric

were those who wanted and needed to write. Such were

above all the ecclesiastical hierarchy, who needed to

be able not only to hold their own in debate with

their 'coepiscopi' on the Continent, when they were

summoned to Councils like that of Arles in 314 and of

Poitiers in 348, but also to communicate with them

and to address members of their flock in writing. One

such literary work is the *De vita Christiana* which,

whether by Pelagius or, as is more probable, by the

Fastidius to whom Gennadius of Marseille attributes

it, may be taken as an illustration of the kind of

Latin that could be written by those who had studied
rhetoric. An illustration of the opposite is provided by the literary efforts of Saint Patrick, the
Confessio and the *Epistula ad Coroticum*, where it is
only too clear that for him Latin was, as he called
it in the *Confessio* (9), 'a foreign language', into
which he was having to translate thoughts that arose
first in his mind in Welsh or Irish.

Where there are writers, there are readers, so
that these works are an indication of the spread of
Latin and therefore of literacy[8] among the Brythons.
It was not for the Irish Christians whom certain
phrases in the *Confessio* (42 and 51) show to have been
there even before his own visit as bishop or that of
his predecessor, Palladius, sent by Pope Celestine I
in 431, but for the Brythons that St. Patrick wrote;
and if Gildas included in his *De Excidio Britanniae* a
sermon aimed at Brythonic chieftains, he must have
known that they would understand it or could have it
translated. When, then, it is asserted that by the
time of St. Patrick's writing activity (420-450) most
Britons were Christians, including the populations of
Strathclyde and Rheged, and even, thanks to St. Ninian,

some of the Picts, we are being told also how far

Latin had penetrated Brythonic society. Some arch-

aeological evidence is relevant here: a 4th-century

ring from Silchester inscribed *Seniciane vivas in Deo*;

the mosaic containing a head of Christ at Hinton St.

Mary in Somerset; the Chi-Rho monogram in the

paintings of Lullingstone villa in Kent and on the

funerary slab at Whithorn in Wigtown (where St.

Ninian had arrived in 396) - all this suggests a

country-wide religion and hence that the place-names

Eccles and *Eccleston* may indeed be taken as proof of

the existence of an organized church (cf. W. *eglwys*,

from Latin/Greek *ecclesia*). Nor must we forget that

monasticism had already taken root in Britain: both

Patrick and Ninian may well have been monks[9]; the

son of the usurper Constantinus certainly was[10].

Moreover, we have in Pelagius a Briton who produced a

heresy that shook the early Church (the denial of

original sin and of the need for divine Grace), the

spread of which led to the despatch of St. Germanus to

Britain by Pope Celestine *ca.* 429. As this was done

on the appeal of British orthodox bishops, one can

imagine the heated debates that preceded it, and

wonder in which language they were held: Latin or

Brythonic?

None of this was enough to make Latin the lan-

guage of the home. What it might have become there,

is shown by the few scribblings that have survived:

the business-letter written by the son of one Calli-

sumus to Epillicus (two Celtic names) between 100

and 150 and found at Walbrook in London in 1953;

the Camulodunum (Colchester) inscription of *ca*. 230;

the numerous *defixiones* (curses) inscribed on leaden

plates; the epitaphs from South Shields and Carlisle;

and the dedication to the god Nodens from Lydney Park

in Gloucester. Here we see a Latin different from

the doomed language of cultured writing, which in

other parts of the Roman Empire prevented for centuries

the evolution of the vernacular; but a Latin which

itself was doomed not to evolve thanks to a factor

absent elsewhere in the Empire: the tenacity of the

indigenous population in cleaving to its own language.

We rejoice that Welsh survived where Gaulish perished;

but we cannot help wondering what this other Romance

language might have been.

Morphological elements (e.g. the Definite Article,

the Future Tense, etc.) would no doubt have evolved

as they did on the Continent, without the features

peculiar for special reasons to Rumanian, but possibly

closer to Carnic (Celtic) Friulan than to Italian.

Its syntax could hardly have owed anything to the

totally different Brythonic. It is from the phonetic

system of Brythonic that we can dimly see what might

have emerged when Latin words began to be used daily

on Brythonic lips.

In the first place, the Brythonic borrowings

show that Vulgar Latin or the ordinary speech of the

middle classes (halfway between slang and the literary

language) had phonetic peculiarities of its own in

Britain, due partly to the 'scholastic' nature of the

Latin taught to the élite which wished to learn it

in the class-room; and it was from these that Latin

filtered down. It was a more old-fashioned form of

Latin that would have evolved, with even the old

system of syllabic quantity preserved, and V still

pronounced as W long after it had become labio-dental

V elsewhere; whence Welsh *gw* as in *Gwener* (Friday)

from (*dies*) *Veneris; gwir* (true) from *verus*, - a

change which was effected by the eighth century (later

in Cornish and Breton). Secondly, there were idiosyncrasies such as the insertion of W between U and
another vowel (e.g. *destruo* was pronounced *destruwo*,
whence Welsh *distrywio* 'to destroy', and *posuit* 'he
placed' was pronounced *posuwit* (cf. W. *clywed*) which
produced *posiit* in some inscriptions). Even more
remarkable, the same W was inserted between E and O
and between E and U. *Leo*, for example, was pronounced
lewo, whence Welsh *llew* (lion), *oleum* became *olewum*
W. *olew* (oil), *deus* became *dewus*, W. *duw* (god; cf.
the Gaulish prefix *Devo-* seen in the name of the
Galatian king whom Cicero defended, Deiotarus). Thus,
if Brythonic had borrowed the word for boy, *puer*,
Welsh would have had a word like *pewyr*.

Again, Welsh *plwm*, from *plumbum* (lead) and *ffydd*
from *fides* (faith) show that short stressed U and I
did not become respectively O and E, as on the Continent; cf. Italian *piombo* and *fede*. (*Fedes* on a coin
of the Belgic usurper Carausius, who set up an Empire
in Britain in 286-293, perhaps shows his non-British
origin). The palatalization of *ti*, *di*, etc. also
seems not to have taken place in the Latin of Britain;
e.g. *ratio* and *diurnus* which evolve into *ragione* and

giorno in Italian, become in Welsh *rhaid* and *diwrnod*,
with unimpaired dental.   (The *od* represents the Latin
syllable *at* generalized into a collective suffix).
Similarly, L and N resisted palatalization, i.e. there
was no L *mouillé* as in French, and the group *li*
affected a preceding vowel instead (e.g. *solea* 'sole'
through *solia* became *seil* in Middle Welsh), just as
did the group *ni* (e.g. *cuneus* 'wedge', through *cunius*,
became *cỹn*).   Nor at first was there voicing of P,T,C
intervocally or before L and R, though later it
occurred in all Welsh words, whether borrowed or not.
It is significant too that L after A did not become U
as in French (e.g. *palf* from *palma*;   F. *paume*, and *mn*
remained unassimilated (e.g. *colofn* from *columna*; cf.
F. *colonne* and, this time, also Italian, *colonna*).

Apart from these specific peculiarities of British
Latin, which Celtic orthography enables us to identify,
changes in the pronunciation of Latin common to the
whole Empire, such as are reflected in the orthography
of British inscriptions, must also be taken into
account;   e.g. E for I (*ella*), N for Gn (*sinum*), S for
Ns (*libes*), D for T (*capud*).   There must also have
been sounds with which Britons could not cope;   e.g.

the group *nct* as in *sanctus* (holy), where the N was

dropped and the C pronounced as a fricative. (Hence

W. *Sant*, C. *Sans* must be an importation from Italy).

Thus the interaction of a specifically British for

of Latin and a specifically Brythonic form of Celtic

could have produced a distinct Romance language, as

different from French and Italian as they, thanks to

the specific qualities of Gaulish and the Latin of

Tuscany, were from each other[11].

It was not to be; and if we wonder why Latin

failed in Britain whereas it triumphed in Gaul, we

can only decide that, in the last analysis, it was

because Roman immigrants and Latin-speaking Britons

were too thin on the ground. The army can hardly

have been a source of diffusion, its soldiers being

drawn from all over the Empire, with a medley of

mother-tongues; so much so, that even to talk among

themselves, they may have found some Brythonic, picked

up from intermarriage or concubinage or general contact

a useful *lingua franca*. It is significant, for example

that some place-names are Brythonic, where the meaning

does not correspond to any physical feature existing

prior to the Romans; e.g. Durobrivae (Water Newton),

'the fort by the bridge'. But there was never a
Brythonic fort there. Cf. the other Durobrivae
(Rochester), where there was no bridge at its capture
in A.D. 44 (Dio lx.20), Cambodunum (Leeds), Moridunum
(Carmarthen), and Segidunum (Wallsend). Presumably
these places were first known by the name of the
military unit established there (cf. Castra Explora-
torum (Netherby) and Caerleon, *sc. legionis*), and
when the unit left, another name had to be found.
The initiative may have come from Celtic-speaking
auxiliary troops[12], but the implication is that
Brythonic was a much-spoken language in the army and
acceptable to the Roman authorities.

Against the immigration of Latin-speakers there
was the Channel, a greater obstacle then than it is
now, especially as it was imagined to be part of the
Atlantic: the stock epithet for Britons in the early
years of contact was 'ultimi', as though they were at
the uttermost bounds of the world (Catullus xi.11 and
xxix.4; Horace, *Odes* 1, 35,30; Virgil, *Ecl.*1,66).
Then, the unknown being subject to exaggeration, as
Tacitus pointed out in a reference specifically to
Britain[13], the Britons had been represented by their

poets and historians as a wild and inhospitable
people[14], and the country's weather was notorious
from the start[15]; and there were no vineyards. Above
all, there was no highly civilized region on their
doorstep, such as Gaul had in Gallia Narbonensis, which
had been conquered in 121 B.C. and thoroughly romanized
by the time of Caesar's conquests in the North. Thus,
whereas the Franks found themselves up against late
Vulgar Latin or embryonic French and lost their own
Germanic tongue, British Latin did no more to Anglo-
Saxon than lend it 24 words: the confrontation was
between Brythonic (Welsh) and Anglo-Saxon, and it was
Welsh which preserved its pristine purity, while Anglo-
Saxon was corrupted by Norman French into the *franglais*
that is the mother of English.

The Brythonia (as we may call it) which faced the
Anglo-Saxons in the 7th century covered a considerable
area (page 27). In the North there was the region called
Cumbria, extending from the Firth of Clyde southwards
and west of the Pennines as far as Preston. This was
composed of various principalities: furthest north in
the valley of the Clyde was Strathclyde, with its
capital Dumbarton (Dun Breatan) and its ecclesiastical

centre in Glasgow (where the Cathedral still bears the
name of its 'Welsh' founder, Cyndeyrn): then came
Rheged, bestriding the Solway Firth and reaching deep
into Cumberland, with Carlisle for its capital. The
region between Cumbria and 'Wales' was also occupied
by Brythons, apparently not organized politically. The
Cumbrian language seems to have been similar to Welsh,
as we would expect. Its three surviving words, all
legal terms, can be deciphered by comparison with
Welsh: *galnys* is Welsh *galanas* (enmity resulting from
homicide or the blood-money due therefor); *mercheta*
(cf. W. *merch* 'daughter'); and *kelchyn* (cf. W. *cylch*
'circuit'). It may even have had the Welsh LL, if THL
in the 13th-century Cumberland place-name *Polthledith*
is an attempt to render the sound, as it certainly had
been in the Book of Llandaff; and the syllable *gos* in
names such as *Gospatrick* and local terms in Galloway
such as *gossock* may well represent Welsh *gwas*(servant)
(cf. C. *gossel*). The Welshness of modern Cumbria survives in our own day in the use of 20 as a unit of
counting, and in the numerals which 'children still
repeat when they are counting out: *yau, tau, tethera,*
methera, pimp, sethera, lethera, nothera, dothera,

dick'[16].

East of Strathclyde were the Gododdin (Ptolemy's *Votadini*), inhabiting a country of the same name between the Forth and the Tyne, with Dun Edin (Edinburgh) as its capital, in the middle of a district known as Manaw.

It was in two of these princedoms that extant Welsh literature was born in the 6th century: with Taliesin in Rheged, of whose ruler Urien he sang in a still surviving elegy, and Aneirin (the court-poet of the Gododdin Prince, Mynyddawg), who describes for us a disastrous expedition mounted by the Prince around A.D. 600 against the town of Catraeth (Catterick), which, after belonging for a time to the Gododdin, was now in the heart of Saxon country.

Brythonia continued southwards through 'Wales' into Dorset, Devon, and Cornwall, with the same possibility of movement overland north and south which continuity of territory permitted, though in fact we hear of only one such contact, namely the expedition of Cynan Carwyn, King of Powys, to Cornwall, of which Taliesin sang. In 'Wales' itself the language had faced an unexpected danger. The Irish, who had been

settling in Wales ever since the 3rd century and
whose superior civilization had redounded much to the
country's benefit, were by the year 400 so numerous
that there was a real danger of their taking over part
of the country, as they did later in 'Scotland'. Indeed, an old Irish Glossary of 908 harks back to the
days when Crimthawn was 'King of Ireland and Britain
as far as the English Channel' [17]. A proof of these
Irish settlements in Wales can be seen in a stone of
the 5th century ploughed up near Wroxeter in 1967[18],
which bears the inscription: CUNORIX MACUS MAQUI
COLINE (i.e. in modern Irish *Cunorix mac mhic an
chuilinn*) 'Cunorix, son of the son of the holly-trees'[19];
and as the Welsh for 'son' was then *map* (today *mab*)[20],
it may be deduced that Cunorix was either the descen-
dant or actually one of the Irishmen who settled in
Wales in Roman times. The man who saved Wales for the
Welsh was their kinsman from Gododdin, Cunedda, who
around 400 came with his eight sons and an army, and by
settling between the Teifi and the Dyfrdwy himself and
distributing the area in the typically Celtic way among
his sons, arrested the goidelization of the country[21].
Irish, however, continued to be spoken in both S.W. and

N.W. Wales, as our inscribed stones show; e.g. the

name of that 'Protector' as he is called, the Vote-

porix already mentioned, who died in   550, appears

also juxtaposed in Ogam in the Goidelic (therefore

Irish) form *Votecorigas* (the C developing out of Qu).

These Irishmen embraced the externals of romanization

as readily as the Brythons: the father of Voteporix

himself bore a Roman name, *Aircol*, which is no other

than *Agricola* (a fitting name in a way, because the

great Agricola himself almost certainly had Gallic

blood in his veins); and an Ogam inscription was

regularly accompanied by a version in Latin (often

reflecting Brythonic pronunciation). Meanwhile around

them Brythonic had developed into (Primitive) Welsh

and south of them into (Primitive) Cornish.

Meanwhile too the Anglo-Saxons had been moving

steadily westwards and northwards. We have to imagine,

not the ruthless elimination of all Britons in their

path, as Gildas would have us believe, but either the

occupation of Brythonic territory abandoned by its

fleeing inhabitants or the by-passing of inoffensive

groups of Britons, who remained as distinct units until

absorption. Such *enclaves* are known to have survived

between the Thames and Luton, on the Yorkshire moors,
and in the Fens, where as late as the 10th century
there was a special punishment for killing a Briton.
There may have been some intermarriage, even in royal
circles; and certainly many Britons would be bilingual
in Welsh and Saxon[22]. The progress of the Saxons can
be traced by the distribution of Celtic river-names,
which are more frequent where the invaders were later
in arriving[23]. By the end of the 7th century continuous Brythonic territory extending from the Clyde to
the English Channel confronted a similarly unbroken
expanse of Saxon territory (Map on page 27).

Most northerly but last to arrive were an Anglian
people bearing a Celtic tribal name, the Bernicii (W.
Brynaich), who had thrust themselves between the
Gododdin and the sea to occupy finally the territory
between the Forth and the Tees. They had moved north
from the earlier kingdom of Deira, which included York
and that Catraeth which the King of Gododdin had by-
passed Bernicia to attack. Around 600, with the
marriage of Aethelfrith, the Bernician king, to the
daughter of the king of Deira, these two kingdoms united
to become the powerful Kingdom of Northumbria. South

of them was the rival Kingdom of Mercia which, under
King Penda (577-654), not only claimed lordship also
over the 'North Folk' and 'South Folk' of 'East
Anglia' and over the East Saxons of Essex, but also
extended its territory westwards towards the Severn.
South of these were the West Saxons of Wessex, with
the South Saxons of Sussex and the Jutes of Kent to
the south-east.

The first breach in this continuous Celtic line
came when the men of Wessex won a victory at Deorham
in Gloucestershire in 577 and thus extended their
territory to the estuary of the Severn. The Brythons
of 'Wales' were now cut off from those of Devon and
Cornwall, and by the time of Augustine's conference
with British bishops in 603 the Severn was regarded as
the boundary between English and Welsh. The next breach
came at the northern river-boundary, when in 613 or
616 the Northumbrians under King Aethelfrith won a
victory near Chester which brought them to the mouths
of the Dee and the Mersey. 'Wales' was now cut off from
Cumbria and Strathclyde except by.sea. That this was
not necessarily regarded as a permanent cleavage at the
time is shown by the reaction of Cadwallon, Prince of

Gwynedd, to an invasion by the next Northumbrian king,

Edwin, a fellow-Christian and a foster-brother, who

attacked Gwynedd and Anglesey in 620 and forced

Cadwallon to flee to Ireland. Twelve years later

'Wales' hit back: Cadwallon made history by allying

himself with a Saxon king, Penda of Mercia, and the

combined army marched as far as Doncaster and defeated

and slew Edwin(632). This was the end of Northumbria's

attacks on 'Wales'. but not of her military strength:

in the following year Edwin's son, Oswald, had his

revenge, defeating and killing Cadwallon on his way

back to Gwynedd. Northumbria now turned her attention

to the North: her king, Oswy (641-672) married the

great-granddaughter of the famous Urien, and Rheged dis-

appeared, to be followed soon by Gododdin. Saxonia was

now deep into south-east Scotland. Strathclyde, how-

ever, remained, and when Northumbria was crippled by

Viking invasions in the 9th century, the Brythons re-

occupied the central area of Cumbria and held it for

nearly another 200 years.

Following years saw Saxon penetration into Devon

and the loss of some border-territory south of the Dee.

The main danger now came from Mercia. Her king, Offa

II (757-796) had already taken over Northumbria and
much of the South, when in 776 and 784 he invaded
'Wales'; but he must have learnt something significant
from these invasions, because he later thought it no
waste of time and money to mark the boundary between
the two countries by the construction of a huge dyke
from the mouth of the Severn to near that of the Mersey
That it was not intended to be a military barrier like
Hadrian's Wall seems to be proved by its occasionally
favouring the Brythons in its choice of direction:
and indeed it never became a permanent dividing line
between the two peoples, for some of what was Mercia
east of the Dyke is today part of Wales[24].

   Territorial delimitation was complete; and although the territory was not a united country, it neede
a name. Foreigners, as usual, invented their own name
from the circumstances of their first contact. To
peoples of Germanic stock all former subjects of Rome,
whether Celtic or not, were known by words derived
either from the name *Gallia* or from the Gallic tribe,
the *Volcae*, namely *Wolch*, later *Wälsch* (renamed in
Anglo-Saxon *wealas*), which simply marked them off as
'foreigners'. This one word covered the speakers of

Ladin (Churwälsch) in the Grisons (now called Romon-

tsch), the Walloons on the Rhine (now francophone

Belgians), the Vlachs of what is now Rumania, and even

the Italians, whose country the Poles with their own

word *Włochy* are really calling Wales; and the Anglo-

Saxons naturally applied it to the Brythons confront-

ing them. The 'Welsh' themselves, however, called

themselves by the meaningful name 'Cymry', i.e.

'fellow-countrymen', a declaration of the unity that

eluded them[25].

With the fragmentation of Brythonia the component

Celtic elements go their separate ways alongside their

Goidelic neighbours; and we have now to see how the

six countries arrived at their present political and

linguistic situation.

Notes to Chapter Four

1.   Cf. *Caledonum aliorumque Pictorum* (*Inc. Paneg.
     Constantin.* 7,2), if the emendation is correct.
     Their capital was Dunkeld: 'Fort of the Cale-
     donians'.

2.   *Agricola* 29,3.

3.   This is not the place for a discussion of the
     historicity of Arthur.

4.   Cf. Matt.23/9: 'and call no man your father'.

5. Sometimes the Latin shows ignorance of Brythonic: e.g. the Genitive *Maglocuni* supposes a Nom. Maglocunus (and in fact Gildas has a Vocative *Maglocune*), whereas the syllable *cun* is part of the Genitive termination of *cu* 'dog' as in Greek; whence Modern Irish Genitive *con* from *cu*. The name, however, is a Welsh one: *Meilyg, Maelgwn*.

6. *Agricola* 21,2. *linguam Romanam abnuebant*.

7. Plutarch, *De Defectu Oculorum*, 412c, refers to a Greek rhetorician as visiting Britain at this time, and two inscriptions from York bearing his name show that he was attached to the military H.Q. (Dessau 8861). Juvenal xv.111.

8. Hence the paradox that most of our Gaulish inscriptions come from Gallia Narbonensis, the most romanized part of Gaul; i.e. Celtic was not yet a written language and anyone who wanted to write had first to learn Latin. There are no Brythonic inscriptions in Britain.

9. For Patrick we depend on implications in his *Confessio*; for Ninian, on deduction from his link with St. Martin.

10. Orosius, *Historia adversus paganos*, vii.40.

11. If we can imagine an earlier equivalent to the Strasburg Oaths, which marked the birth of French, i.e. a Brython and a Saxon swearing an oath of alliance against a third party, as Charles the Bald and Louis the German did against their brother Lothair in 842, a romanized Cadwallon, using the same kind of chancellery-language, might have sworn as follows on allying himself with King Penda of Mercia in 632:-

> Per amur dy Dew ed per salwament dy pobol
> cristiane ed dy nus tuts, dy yst di inawant,
> in cant Dew saber ed poder mi duna, sig eo
> salwerai yst mew fradre Penda, sig cum hom dy
> drieff sew fradre salwer debe, in ho che ill
> altertan face, ed cun Edwyn nul plegit nunche
> prendrai, che willy mewe a yst mew fradre Penda
> damnuse sî.

12.   as suggested by Prof. A.L.F. Rivet, who first
      pointed out the anomaly in his presidential
      address to the Roman Society on 5 June 1979.

13.   *Agricola* 30 *omne ignotum pro magnifico.*

14.   Horace, *Odes* 3,4,33 *Britannos hospitibus feros;*
      Tacitus, *Agr.* 11,5 *plus tamen ferociae Britanni
      praeferunt* . According to Dio Cassius (*ca.* 200)
      60,19 the troops of Aulus Plautius' invading army
      in 43 refused to embark, complaining that they
      were being sent 'outside the inhabited world';
      and he makes Boudicca (62,4) taunt Roman soldiers
      with not even knowing the island's correct name.

15.   Tacitus, *Agricola* 12,3 *caelum crebris imbribus ac
      nebulis foedum.*

16.   Iona and Peter Opie in the *Times Literary Supple-
      ment* of 14 July 1979,   p.799.

17.   Pembroke, being in Dyfed, whose dynasty claimed an
      Irish origin, was 'a little Ireland' before be-
      coming 'a little England beyond Wales', and St.
      David himself probably needed to speak Irish as
      well as Welsh and Latin. Cf. the Irish element
      in the *Mabinogion*, archaeological remains such as
      the Pillar of King Voteporix , Wales' only
      crannog (lake-dwelling), in Breconshire, and the
      Irish etymological element in *Llantwit* (*-twit* from
      Iltuath, Welsh *Illtud*), Brecon (W. *Brycheiniog*)
      from Brychan, a 5th-century Irish prince. It was
      against Irish raiders that the Romans built their
      forts at Segontium and Caergybi.

18.   *Journal of Roman Studies*, 1968, p.207.

19.   Sacred trees were part of Celtic religion. The
      tribal name *Eburones* (Caesar *B.G.* 2,4) and the
      mythological Irish hero Mac Ibar's both contain the
      root meaning 'yew-tree' (Modern Irish *iubhar* ,
      now written *iar* to reflect the pronunciation. Cf.
      W. *efwr* 'wild parsnip', Breton *evor* 'hellebore'
      and 'black alder'). There was also a Gallic place-
      name *Eborodurum*, surviving in Embrun in France,

Yverdon in Switzerland, and Brno in Czechoslo-
vakia.

The word *bile* in the name of the Pictish king
Bruce the Bile and the Gaulish place-name
Biliomagus means 'sacred tree'. For Romans too
the grove could be sacred (cf. Tibullus 3,3,15;
Juvenal 3,17; Horace *Odes* 3,22,1) and their
word for it (*nemus*) is found in Gaulish as a
prefix in many place-names; e.g. *Nemetodunum*
(Nanterre). Greeks, perhaps thinking of their
Dodona with its oracle of rustling oaks, derived
the word 'druid' from their word for 'oak', and
Pliny (16,249) thought the derivation justified
by the importance of the oak in Druidic ritual.

20. It is remarkable that Celtic developed its own
    word for 'son' (*mac*, *mab*). Meillet explained it
    as 'un mot du langage enfantin'.

21. Cunedda may have been commissioned for this task
    by Stilicho, the romanized Vandal general sent to
    Britain by the Emperor Theodosius in 399 to
    drive out the Picts, Scots and Saxons, and praised
    by the poet Claudian for doing so. Cunedda was the
    father of the Ceretic who gave his name to Cardi-
    gan and who may be the Coroticus to whom St.
    Patrick addressed an Epistle, rather than the
    Coroticus of Dumbarton.

22. Welsh borrowed a few words from Anglo-Saxon, such
    as *sidan* (*sida*, silk), *llidiart* (*hlidgeat*, gate),
    hosan (*hosa*, stocking), *dewr* (*deor*, brave), *cusan*
    (*cyssan*, to kiss), *tarian* (*targe*, shield, from
    Norse).

23. See the brilliant analysis in K. Jackson,
    Language and History in Early Britain, pp. 221-
    228. River names provide useful evidence also in
    Gaul: as they are mostly non-Celtic, the Celts
    came from east of the Rhine (Whatmough).

24. Monmouthshire (now, as centuries ago, Gwent),
    created by the Act of Union of 1536, extended
    eastwards beyond the old Dyke as far as the Wye.

Inasmuch as the Act itself declared the con-
stituent 'Lordships Marchers' to be 'within the
said County or Dominion of Wales' (a significant
terminology), it is clear that the old legal
formula 'Wales and Monmouthshire' was a misnomer
due, no doubt, to the irrelevant fact that in
1542, as a matter of administrative convenience,
the county was made part of the Judges' Circuit
of Oxford (as Chester was of the N. Wales Circuit,
without being lost to England!) Early in the 19th
century it could be said that 'no County of Wales
has so large a portion of it wherein the English
language is not understood'; and as late as
1867 there were monoglot speakers in some villages.
(Aneirin Bevan owed his name to a Welsh poet who
was his father's friend). In 1969 the British
Government promised that Gwent will always be
considered part of Wales, and that the phrase
'Wales and Monmouthshire' will never be used
officially again.

25. From *bro* 'country' and the prefix *cym* 'joint'.

5. WALES

The Mercians did not stop attacking the Welsh just because there was now a dyke between them; in fact, they slew King Rhodri the Great, who had given Wales a brief unity (844-848) and had driven off the Vikings. Back to disunity with the traditional division of the country among his three sons, Wales next found in Howel Dda (910-950) one who not only unified her, but codified her laws and guaranteed peace by doing homage to Athelstan, the king of what since 829 had been a united England. No Welsh prince however, could do what a Saxon king had done, though demonstrations of strength such as the success of Llewelyn ap Seisyll against the Vikings and of his son Gruffudd (1039-63) against the Saxons in Gwynedd showed what could have been achieved. Gruffudd did indeed make war on the English, as we may now call the Saxons, only however to lose South Wales to them. Three years later England herself tasted defeat at the Battle of Hastings.

Meanwhile the young Welsh language born from Brythonic around A.D. 600 had passed through its 'Primitive' phase and was in the phase that now for us is 'Old'. For this we at least have some written

records. Our earliest written text is a legal deed
called the *Surrexit-memorandum* which at some time in
the 8th century was written into the so-called *Book of
St. Chad*, a Latin version of the Gospels composed in
the same century. Before this, in the same book but a
little later in time, there is a brief note in Latin
recording the presentation of the Gospels to the church
of Llandaff and including some Welsh names (*Chad* 2).
The ninth century also yields the document known as
Oxoniensis Prior, which to proper names adds some
Welsh glosses both on a Latin text concerned with
weights and measures and (in a manuscript bound in
later) on Ovid's *Ars amatoria*. Proper names are what
we find also in the contemporary *Historia Brittonum*
of Nennius and in Asser's *Life of King Alfred* (*ca*. 890),
together with some Common Nouns in the former. Probably a little later is a Gospel-story in Latin verse by
Caius Vettius Juvencus (now in Cambridge University
Library), the manuscript of which includes, not only
some glosses, but two *englynion* in OW of three and nine
lines respectively. Glosses too are found in two other
MSS: the *De nuptiis Philologiae et Mercuriae* of
Martianus Capella (owned by Corpus Christi College,

Cambridge) of the 9th century, and the slightly later
De raris fabulis (the Bodleian's *Oxoniensis Posterior*),
the latter's having been written, to judge by the
orthography, by a Cornishman. Then at last, with the
10th century *Computus Fragment* (also in Cambridge
University Library), we have our first continuous
passage of Old Welsh: 23 lines about the calendar
(*ca.* 920). The only other piece of continuous writing
are some verses in the *De Trinitate* of Saint Augustine,
but their obscurity has not been helped by a careless
binder (1085-1091); otherwise, to the *Annales Cambriae,*
(end of 10th century), the *Lives of the Welsh Saints,*
and the *Book of Llandaff* (a collection of Charters of
ca. 1135-40) we owe nothing more than some more glosses
The inscribed stones of these centuries also provide
little more than Welsh names.

This stock of material reveals that in Old Welsh
there was no initial, and rarely medial, mutation;
that Y was not prefixed to 'impure' S; and that by the
end of the period the stress had shifted from the last
syllable to the penultimate. What it teaches about
pronunciation is less certain. Once again the Latin
alphabet was being used to represent sounds for which

it was not designed; and those sounds themselves had
been modified in the course of time without corresponding change in spelling. Thus, internal plosives
had evolved so that surds became sonants (P became B,
etc.) and sonants became spirants (B became V, etc.).
The name of the Irish king who ruled in S.W. Wales in
the 6th century, Voteporix[1], appears in the Genitive
Voteporigis on his tombstone from near Carmarthen;
but by this time the word would have been pronounced
Wodeborigis, with the G and final S much weakened on
their way to final extinction. Vowels too had under-
gone change: long A was no longer the same in Latin
and Welsh, so that "brother" was not *bratar*, as in
Brythonic, but *brawd*. Similarly, Brythonic *ei* (Latin
e) had become Welsh *wy* (e.g. *rete/rhywd* "net"),
Brythonic *ou* (Latin o) had become Welsh U (e.g. *ordo/
urdd* "order"). So too:-

Latin *au* became Welsh *aw* (e.g. *auctor/awdur* "author")
    "   *ae*   "   "   *oe* (e.g. *Graecus/Groeg* "Greek")
    "   *ue*   "   "   *awe* (e.g. *construenda/cystrawen*
                                     "syntax")
    "   *ui*   "   "   *ewi* (e.g. *ruina/rhewin* "downfall")
    " initial S became Welsh H (e.g. *Sabrina/Hafren* "Severn")
    "   "   V   "   "   Gw (e.g. *vinum/gwin* "wine")

All the above words (except *brawd*) are loans
from Latin; and such etymologies permit a glimpse
into the stage of civilisation reached by a people.
Thus, if we find no or few loan-words relating to
legal or political systems, we may deduce that in
both these fields the people had reached a certain
degree of sophistication. So it is with Welsh. The
earliest borrowings relate to military life (*castell,*
ffos, etc.), then to commerce (*aur*, *mesur*, *plym*, etc.)
and to daily life (*cegin*, *ffenestr* , etc.). Fewer than
a thousand words were borrowed from Latin by the
Brythons and "Welsh"; and the number seems even less
because of the phonetic disguise: e.g. *llafn* from
lamina (blade), *pebyll*[2] from *papilio* (tent), *ystafell*
from *stabellum* (little room). Of course, once we know
the phonetic code, we can recognize *vacuus* in *gwag*
(empty) and even *viridis* in *gwyrdd* (green), but we are
still surprised to learn that the typically Welsh *gwers*
(lesson) is nothing but *versus*[3] and that behind *gwyrth*
(miracle) lies *virtus*[4]; and though we may know that
the Romans called their men-of-war *naves longae*, we
pronounce the Welsh *llong* (ship) without realising the
connection, so typical is that Welsh liquid sound[5].

Whether any of these loan-words drove out a
native word could be established only if an exact but
rarer synonym had survived in one or more of the off-
shoots of Brythonic. Welsh, for example, has *call*
defined as "wise" i.e. as a synonym of *doeth* in the
dictionaries, and Cornish likewise can boast four
synonyms for its *doth*; but the Latin *doctus* from
which *doeth* derived must have conveyed some nuance
that was lacking in the native words; perhaps the
dubious notion that learned men are wise. On the other
hand, it is not clear why *pons* should have driven out
briva (bridge)[6]. Of the 27 words mentioned in the
previous paragraph (from *llafn* onwards and in note 5)
only 12 are found also in Cornish[7]; for the other
words Cornish either used a word of its own (e.g.*gorhel*
ship, *enclathva* cemetery) or later borrowed an English
one (e.g. *studya*, *müvya*).

The movement of manuscripts from Welsh monastic
communities to England indicates a friendly relationship between the Welsh and the Saxons; but with the
Norman invasion hostilities were resumed. The first
result of the defeat of the English in 1066 was the
appearance of Norman barons with their private armies

along the frontier (the Marcher-Lords). As they extended their power westwards, feudalism began to
jostle tribalism, and the Welsh princes had yet another source of disunity. Princes and barons had both
to be tamed by Henry II (1154-89), who cunningly
fostered quarrels among the Welsh princes, so that the
Marcher-Lords would not be needed; but the barons
were greatly helped by Prince Llewelyn the Great
(1197-1240) against King John, whose Magna Carta declared the privileges of the Welsh Prince and recognized the independence of his law. In return,
Llewelyn placed Wales in feudal dependence on the
English King, Henry III (1216-1272). The refusal of
his grandson Llewelyn ("our last Prince") to do homage
to Edward I in 1272 led to that King's invasions and
conquest of the country in 1282, a feat which seemed
to disprove his own earlier belief that the Welsh were
"untamable". Two years later the Statute of Wales
(or of Rhuddlan) made Wales a part of England. ("The
Divine Providence . . . hath now . . . transferred
under our proper dominion the land of Wales with its
inhabitants . . . ; and hath annexed and united the
same unto the Crown"). Llewelyn's Princedom became

six shires (the original Principality of the first

Prince of Wales), and his chieftain-allies were re-

placed by officials. The barons, however, remained;

and it was their tyranny which provoked the rising of

Owain Glyndwr, "an attractive and unique figure in an

age of debased and selfish politics"[8]. In 1404 he

was holding his own Parliament in Wales and calling

for independence, including that of the Church, which

had been merged in the English Church since the 12th

century. It was in the belief that the Lancastrians

in the Wars of the Roses were carrying on Owain

Glyndwr's struggle, that the Welsh helped Henry Tudor

to his victory on the field of Bosworth (1485), with

consequences for Welsh that we shall examine later.

Thus the son of a cousin of Owain Glyndwr became King

Henry VII of England. These years gave Wales her

reputation for military prowess and saw the Golden Age

of her poetry.

The new dynasty used its broom: in 1535, under

Henry VIII, Wales was united to England (not to Britain)

by an Act of Union, and received for the first time

representation in the Parliament at Westminster.

According to the Act there were two motives for the

extension of the earlier Statute: the continued
difference between England and Wales in laws and customs, and the continued use of Welsh as the language
of daily life. The Marcher-Lordships, of which there
were still over 100, each with its own court of law,
were replaced by Shires, and the "Great Session" (four
circuits with respective judges) gave Wales at last a
uniform system of justice; but just as Wales thus
became in a real sense a united country, its language
was dealt a mortal blow by the provision that all
legal proceedings were to be in English. From now on
Welsh history can hardly be disentangled from that of
England. In one field, however, Wales took an independent line: she rejected the Anglican Church in
favour of Methodism and Nonconformity, making the
Chapel almost the symbol of a properly Welsh community.
For, as the anglicization of the country proceeded, it
became possible to distinguish a Welsh Wales that clung
to its language and traditions.

Yet both groups lived side by side in perfect
harmony. This was partly because English-speakers
resident in the country were felt to be Welsh, and
indeed, however anglicized, thought of themselves as

Welshmen and Welshwomen, and sincerely believed it
possible to be simultaneously English and Welsh. Hence
even landlords, being Welsh and not absentee, never
provoked the violence seen in Ireland, even after the
evictions of 1868 in N. Wales. At worst, they could
be unpopular for not knowing Welsh and therefore suffer
defeat in county council elections, as happened
throughout Wales in 1889. Thus, when a proposal for
self-government for Wales was first heard in Parliament
on 11 March 1914, it was received with incredulity.
Incredulity too was what was widely felt when a
Nationalist won the Carmarthen seat in 1966; and since
then two more seats have been gained, and many county
councils taken over - not from landlords, but from those
who were once identified with Welsh interests and then
found wanting. The "venerable relic of the past", as
Gladstone called the language in 1873, has proved to be
the vigorous champion of the future.

Notes to Chapter Five

1.   Called Vortiporius, King of the Demetae, by
      Gildas.

2.   This word seemed to echo Umlaut-forms of the
      Plural, and so a Singular *pabell* was invented; cf.
      the converse procedure of forming a Plural *cyrff*

for *corff* from *corpus* instead of the natural
corffor.

3. Because *gwers* can also mean a period of time; cf.
German *Stunde* ("hour" and so also "lesson").

4. Cf. the obsolete Italian *far virtù* "to perform
miracles".

5. Other surprises are: *egwyddor* (principle: from
abecedarium, ABC being the 'first' letters);
athrylith (talent: from *intellectio*); *cybydd*
(miser: from *cupidus*); *cynnig* (offer: from
condicere); *cymell* (to urge: from *compellere*);
melltith (curse: from *maledictio*); *myfyrio* (to
study: from *memoria*); *mynwent* (cemetery: from
monumenta); *neges* (message: from *necesse*,
through the sense "affair"); *parch* (respect: from
parcere "to spare" through "to give value for");
pregeth (sermon: from *praecepta*); *priod* (spouse:
from *privatus*); *pwys* (weight: from *pensum*);
swllt (shilling: from *solidus*); *swydd* (office,
job: from *sedes*); *symud* (to move: from *summotus*);
ysgeler (wicked: from *scelera*); *ystr* (meaning:
from *historia*).

6. Cf. *Brivodurum* and the French town Briare.

7. Viz. (in the order of mention): *laun, stevel*
(later replaced by *rom*), *gwak, gwer, mollath,
negys, pregeth, pryas, pos, sols, soth, styr*.
(*Gwers* was used only in the sense of "verse").

8. G.M. Trevelyan, *History of England*, p. 212, (3rd
ed., 1948.)

6. CORNWALL

There was a time when Cornwall was known as West Wales, and if it had not been for the Bristol Channel, the promontory would indeed have been the real South Wales, the Dumnonii[1] would have played a part in Welsh history, and the fortunes of Welsh would have been very different. This, however, would probably have cost us the Cornish language, which evolved away from Welsh after easy contact between the two territories was lost in 577.

What put Cornwall on the map was its tin. Phoenicians and their colonists, the Carthaginians, were trading in Cornish tin as early as the fifth century B.C., and it was the desire of Rome to break into this monopoly that gives us our earliest example of industrial espionage. The Phoenicians had kept the source of their supply secret; and when the Romans one day followed a Phoenician fleet out of Cádiz, the crafty Levantine deliberately sailed into the shallows, wrecking both his own ships and those that were shadowing him, and was repaid the value of his cargo by a grateful country. The respite was short, however; for the consul of 97 B.C., Publius Crassus, after showing the flag in Lusitania and occupying Corunna (Brigantium),

himself made the crossing and, discovering that the
mines were shallow and the miners peaceable, opened up
the trade to Romans.[2] Diodorus (5,22) describes the
extractive process, commenting on the Cornishmen's lack
of xenophobia and their superior degree of civilisation,
both due to their contact with traders from the Continent and elsewhere. There was a time when Cornwall
supplied all Britain's tin, 13,000 tonnes being produced annually for several years down to 1913.

Mineral wealth, however, cannot save a community,
and the Dumnonii had no mountains to retreat into before the advancing Saxons. Whether or not Howel,
defeated by Athelstan at Boleit in 925 or 936, was the
last Cornish king (and some see a reference to another
king, Ricatus, on the Penzance Market Cross of *ca.* A.D.
1000), the Domesday Book (1086) shows all the major
landowners west of the Tamar bearing Norman or Saxon
names, which can mean only that the Celts were subordinate to an Anglo-Norman feudal class. In 1337 Cornwall
was made a Duchy, the Duke of which was to be the
eldest son of the English King; but for our purpose
the importance of this is the implicit recognition that
the Cornish constitute a distinct entity and that Corn-

wall could not be just another county. One reason

for this must have been that the language was still

being widely spoken even in east Cornwall, and that the

memory of Cornish kings, if not of King Arthur, had not

entirely faded.

For knowledge of this language in its primitive

phase we have little more than one inscription of the

7th century from Devon (to remind us that Cornish may

once have extended into Dorset[3]) viz. DATUIDOCI

CONHINOCI, where the first word represents what would

be in Welsh *Dedwyddog* and the second is a compound

word including the name *Henoc* found also in the

contemporary *Life of Saint Samson*. For the next

phase, Old Cornish, we are once again dependent on

glosses. The earliest monument of this is a group of

sixteen glosses written into a Commentary on Donatus

(an African sectarian bishop of 315), either not long

after its composition around 900 or possibly by the

author himself, once believed to be Smaragdus, an abbot

living near Verdun. Three more glosses are found in a

Latin version of the Book of Tobit of the 10th century;

and a little later than this are the marginal notes in

a Latin version of the Gospels called the *Bodmin Manu-*

missions because they record the freeing of slaves, most of whose names, like those of the witnesses, are Cornish, either correctly spelt (when the notes are in Latin) or phonetically adapted to Anglo-Saxon. Most abundant is the crop of glosses in a Latin-Anglo-Saxon vocabulary compiled by the monk Aelfric *ca.* 1000; for a hundred years later this was converted into a *Vocabularium Cornicum* by the substitution of Cornish words for the Anglo-Saxon. A few Cornish names also occur in the Domesday Book and in some Anglo-Saxon charters.

With no leaders, speakers of Cornish could hardly develop anything like a nationalist feeling. To be sure, we hear of rebellions on two occasions, but these were provoked by such universal motives as resentment at high taxation (1496), which may have had something to do with their support of Perkin Warbeck in the following year, and objections to a change of religion, when 6000 men crossed the Tamar and nearly reached London (1548) to present a petition to the King. It should be noted, however, that in this their objection is expressly based on the *local* ground of their being "Cornyshe men, whereof certain of us understande no

Englishe".

The difference between Cornishmen and Englishmen
is remarked on in the *Anglica Historia* published (in
Latin) by Polydore Vergil, the Italian who became
Prebendary of Wells, in 1534:   "Britain is divided into
four parts, whereof the one is inhabited by Englishmen,
the other by Scots, the third by Welshmen, and the
fourth by Cornish people";   and there are signs early
in the 17th century that, whatever the gentry felt
about anglicization, in the humbler ranks of the
population a sullen resentment was still burning.   John
Norden, author of *Speculum Magnae Britanniae*, noticed
"a kind of concealed envy against the English (and) a
kind of desire for revenge for their fathers' sakes",
and about the same time (1600) Richard Carey recorded
in his *Survey of Cornwall* that some of the inhabitants
would refuse to speak English to a stranger.

This sense of being different (which is such an
important factor in the survival of national identity)
was undoubtedly fostered by the extraordinary flowering
of literary activity in the preceding two centuries.
The anonymous writers (for we must assume more than
one) probably did not think of themselves as men of

letters, but they had a sound artistic instinct,

called forth by the practical motive of entertaining

the people with dramatized versions of the great

themes of Christianity. We have 9,780 lines from them

in pure Middle Cornish, a late medieval heritage which

many a more fortunate language might envy. Most of

these come from a trilogy of plays recounting the

history of the world (like that of the House of Atreus)

in three great events: the Creation, the Passion and

the Resurrection. These *Ordinalia*, as they are called,

had been preceded by the 250 trochaic stanzas of the

"Passion of our Lord", and they were followed in 1504

by the 4,568 lines of "The Life of Meriasek" (first

published in 1872 shortly after its discovery), which

narrated the life of the Cornish Saint through events

in Cornish and Breton history, and which is the first

work to bear its author's name (Dominus Hadton). A

hundred years later (1611) one Will Jordan wrote (or

copied) a play on the "Creation of the World", in

which, deliberately or not, the only English spoken is

put into the mouths of the devil and his demons. That

these works (some 18,000 lines of verse) are the

survivors of a much greater output, is indicated by

the discovery in the British Museum as late as 1877 of
41 lines of a Cornish play dateable to the early 15th
century.

The man who discovered this was Henry Jenner
(1848-1934), of whom it can be said that if there is
one man to whom the survival or revival of Cornish is
due, he is that man; and perhaps his greatest service
was to devise a unified spelling for the publication of
these texts. Thanks to this, Middle Cornish, which
had been the philologist's dream, ceased to be the
ordinary reader's nightmare, and could be chosen as the
form of the language to be revived. Thus the language being spoken today is not the direct continuation
of Late Cornish, grossly adulterated as it was by English, but represents a leap back over an epoch to the
pure forms of Cornish in its prime. This is a bold
step, without parallel in the history of linguistic
revivals; but even if it involves the peculiarity of
grafting the pronunciation of Cornish as it was at the
end of the 18th century on to the lexicon of the language as it had been two and three centuries earlier,
the step was necessary if the language was to have a
future at all. And a future it seems likely to have,

because the existence of an agreed orthography has

assured it of a present, encouraging its use for the

creation of a modern literature. Already the tale of

Tristan and Yseult, believed to have originated in

Cornwall, has now at last been told again in Cornish[4];

and it is salutary to remember that a new work of

today can be the classic of tomorrow.

No-one now learns Cornish at his mother's knee,

and learning it is an intellectual pursuit; what is

more, some intellectuals (such as Dr. A.L. Rowse, who

is as proud of being Cornish as a man can be), are

sceptical about the necessity or desirability of re-

viving the language. Consequently, the awareness of a

Cornish identity finds expression also in other than

linguistic fields. The most recent is the attempt to

revive the powers of the ancient Cornish Assembly

called the Stannary, which possessed certain legisla-

tive and judicial rights, including "power in Chancery

to judge in equity, power of the Star Chamber to judge

and punish riots, perjurers, etc., power to hold a

Parliament and to make laws". In 1508 Henry VII granted

it a Charter of Pardon, which included a right of veto

over Westminster. It is evidence of Cornwall's resignation to English rule that we hear of no invocation

of this right in following centuries - until in January

1974 two Cornish patriots (Mr. F. Trull and Mr. B.

Hambley) saw in a dispute between the Pay Board and

workers of the English China Clay Company their chance

to revive the dormant powers of the Stannary. The

necessary workers' signatures to a petition for its

convening were obtained and sent to the Lord Warden of

the Stannaries - an office designed to be a link bet-

ween the Crown (represented by the Duke of Cornwall)

and the Stannary, and whose continued existence is

proof of the reality of the old Assembly's powers.

Nothing came of this; but Professor R. Pennington,

Director of Legal Studies in the University of Birming-

ham, has stated his belief that "the Stannary has a

valid constitutional foundation . . . On a strictly

legal basis they *do* possess the power to reject Parlia-

mentary Bills while they are still in passage through

the House . . . They should ask Prince Charles to issue

instructions for the convening of the Stannary . . .

The Prince, presumably, would refuse. They could then

seek a Writ of Mandamus against him"[5]. On the 28

May 1977 the Stannary received significant judicial

recognition: sitting in the Stannary Court at Newquay a Judge upheld a man's right to stake out land owned by other people in Cornwall and then to mine it for tin. The claimant's right so to "bound" areas was admitted on the ground of a custom never revoked since medieval times, but his request actually to mine on his staked-out claim was rejected on a technicality.

In view of this official recognition that Cornwall already possesses an Assembly with valid powers, and that the "miners" of whom the early Stannary was composed was a broad term covering more than workers underground, one might think that Cornish nationalists would do better to base the Assembly they demand on a body as old as Tynwald and as specifically Cornish as that is Manx, rather than set up a new *Cuntelles Kernow* ("Assembly of Cornwall"). In any case, the important thing is that the traveller who crosses the Tamar westwards should realize that he is entering what was once a different country.

Notes to Chapter Six

1. The Dumnonii are found also in the region of Glasgow and Western Ireland (*Fir Domnann*). The *Civitas Cornoviorum*, however, was in central Britain, with Viroconium (Wroxeter) as one of its chief towns and

they are mentioned as in Caithness also.

2.   Strabo 3,176.

3.   Cf. the name Dorchester, where, from Old Welsh
      Durngaeir, we should expect *Durchester*.

4.   *Trystan hag Ysolt*, by A.S.D. Smith ('Caradar'),
      posthumously published in 1951 and completed by
      D. Watkins in another posthumous publication in
      1973.   It is based on Joseph Bédier's *Le Roman de
      Tristan et Iseut* (1946), which conflated various
      ancient versions.

5.   The *Sunday Telegraph Magazine*, Summer 1975.

7. BRITTANY

Brittany presents us with the unique phenomenon of a Celtic people which returned to the Continent from the British Isles and occupied territory inhabited five hundred years before by a different Celtic stock. The territory was known to the Romans as *Armorica*[1], the stock was Gallic, and their language was Gaulish. It is not known how long it took Gaulish to disappear from Gaul after its conquest by Julius Caesar between 59 and 49 B.C., nor how far intermarriage with Romans had changed the ethnic characteristics of the Armoricans, when, some time between 446 when the Britons vainly appealed to Rome for help, and 461 when a British bishop was present at a small episcopal Council in Tours, the first immigrants, fleeing from Saxon invaders or roving Irishmen, arrived not only from Devon[2] and Cornwall[3], but also from South and North Wales and even from England[4]. Certain it is that not a single inscription in Gaulish has yet been found in Armorica, that Gaulish place-names are few there[5], and that inscriptions from elsewhere in Gaul show purely Gallic names passing through Latinized Celtic in two generations to become wholly Roman in the third[6]. Immigration, which continued until nearly the end of the

7th century, seems not to have encountered any resistance, which was just as well; for the immigrants
were not warriors like the Vikings, bent on plunder
and conquest, but fugitives seeking a peaceful settlement, rather as the Welsh established a "colony" in
Patagonia in 1865. Indeed, Brittany has been called
"our earliest colony"[7].

Once established, however, in the western extremity of Gaul, the settlers began to extend eastwards
where the land was better. As early as 520 some Gallic
bishops were complaining about the unorthodoxy of two
Breton priests; and in 576 we hear of a Gallo-Roman
Bishop of Vannes invoking the aid of the Franks
against a Breton chief. By this time Gregory of Tours
could refer to the country and its people, not as
Armorica and Armorici, but as Britannia and Britanni.
In 845 Breton ambition had swollen enough for Nomenoé,
first King of Brittany, to proceed from the defeat of
Charles the Bald and the conquest of Rennes and Nantes
to attempt to free Brittany from the spiritual authority
of the Bishop of Tours, which Charlemagne had imposed
on it. Expansion continued under Salaun (Solomon) till
874, and in 890 the Bretons under their king, Alain,

were strong enough to defeat the Normans at Questem-
bert; but this was only a temporary relief and it
took the help of Saxons from England to drive the
Normans out in 939. The successful leader, Alain II
(Barbetorte), exchanged the title of King for the more
appropriate one of Duke, and Brittany remained a Duchy
and Vassal of the French Crown till the 16th century.
For their Brythonic kinsmen the country was *Letau*
(in today's Welsh, *Llydaw*), from which the Anglo-
Saxons formed the name *Lidwiccias*; but in Latin
(which was still the language of law) it was called
Britannia Minor, a reminder that the proud name "Great
Britain" referred originally only to the greater extent
of her territory.

It is in the latter part of this period that there
appear our earliest documents containing words in Old
Breton. In any case, the language in earlier documents
would have been indistinguishable from Old Cornish;
and this close resemblance to Cornish is not such a
straightforward matter as it sounds. If the first
emigrants from Britain arrived before 461, that was
before Brythonic had dissolved into Welsh and Cornish;
and since the cause of the emigration was the approach

of the Saxons, one would expect the first wave to have
come from the nearer counties of Dorset and Devon.
The explanation given by K. Jackson is that the newcomers were later swamped by the second wave from
Cornwall. Be that as it may, our first recognizably
Breton words are, as usual, glosses on Latin texts of
the 9th and 10th centuries, such as various manuscripts
of Orosius' *Historia adversos Paganos*, the *Etymologiae*
of Isidore, some *Scholia* on Virgil, and the Latin
Grammars of Alcuin and Eutychius. The so-called
Collatio Canonum has 320 of them. Occasionally the
Breton is part of the text, as with the 70 names of
plants and trees in the Paris *Computus*, and the numerous
personal names in the Cartularies of Redon and Lander-
ennec (11th century, but copies of earlier documents).
One of the documents in the former yields our only piece
of continuous Old Breton (four lines).

Brittany now begins to be caught up in international events. One-third of William the Conqueror's
army in 1066 consisted of Bretons. In 1156 Henry II
helped Duke Conan IV maintain his rule and had his
third son, Geoffrey, marry Conan's daughter and so
succeed him as Duke. Civil war between Pretenders to

the Dukedom in the 14th century saw English and French

rivals in support of each, and in 1378 the English pro-

tégé, Duke Jean IV, ceded Brest to England, who held it

for 19 years. In 1475 there was another alliance bet-

ween the Duchy and the English throne, when Duke

Francis II joined Edward IV against the French, and

although he was defeated, his daughter and successor,

Anne, married the next two French Kings, Charles VIII

and Louis XII, one after the other. Then, when her

daughter married the French King, Francis I, Brittany

was part of her dowry, and in 1532 the *États de*

Bretagne, not without bribery, voted for union with

France. Brittany then became an autonomous province

responsible for its own taxes and exempt from military

service outside its own borders. A special clause

guaranteed that Bretons could be tried only by Bretons

for acts committed in Brittany.

These privileges were of course precarious.

Brittany was already rebelling against imposed taxes in

1675, and her Public Prosecutor, La Chalotais (1702-

85), was imprisoned for his championship of her right

to pay lower taxes than the rest of France. Four nobl

had already been executed in 1720 for seeking indepen-

dence. During the Revolution the terms of the treaty
were quietly waived, but the main quarrel was over
religion: civil war broke out in 1793, and two years
later an English squadron landed a force of emigrés
on Carnac beach. The persecutions subsequent on the
failure of this effort led to another rebellion in
1797, when Georges Cadoudal took up the cudgels for
Brittany, refused Napoleon's bribe of a large sum of
money and a general's commission, and landing in France
in 1803 was arrested as a conspirator and executed in
Paris. (If he really was being subsidized by the
British Government, it was only tit-for-tat for the use
by the French of Charles II's Breton mistress, Louise
de Keroual, as a secret agent).

While the Revolutionaries had enforced centralism
because regional champions were considered reactionaries,
the Governments of the 19th century were even more
opposed to them because they seemed to threaten the
unity of the State[9]. Yet it was in that century that
Bretons began to take steps to preserve their linguistic
and cultural heritage. In 1838 a Breton delegation
attended a meeting of a Welsh Society in Abergavenny,
and the occasion was celebrated in an ode by Lamartine,

who was present. The year 1867 saw the first Inter-
celtic Congress, and among those who signed a petition
asking for the use and teaching of Breton in schools
was another, less well-known, poet called Charles de
Gaulle, the great-uncle of the future President. In
1900 Brittany began sending representatives to Welsh
Eisteddfodau. Politically, however, the situation
remained unchanged; and the first official use of
Breton by a French Government, when peasants were
exhorted in 1914 to exchange their gold coins for
paper money, had no more long-term significance than
Austrian warning-notices in Friulan in 1918. In
World War II Brittany damaged her cause by producing
more than one collaborator though she was also strongly
represented in the *Résistance*.

The eastern limit of the old Duchy of Brittany lay
far beyond what was for centuries to be the linguistic
frontier. Thus Rennes, the present capital of the
Province, and Nantes were never Breton-speaking towns.
The language had come to a halt on a line from the
mouth of the River Couesnon, near Mont Saint-Michel,
in the North, to a point east of St. Nazaire in the
South. It is true that there are toponymical signs of

the presence of Bretons south of the Loire (e.g.

Brissac south of Angers) and as far east as the Doubs,

(e.g. Bretonvillers), but these cannot be taken as evi-

dence of a Breton-speaking population in the area. The

present linguistic frontier runs from Plouha on the

bay of St. Brieuc in the North southwards (west of

the town St. Brieuc) to a point on the southern coast

east of the Peninsula of Rhuys. The Breton-speaking

area west of this imaginary line constitutes Lower

Brittany (Breizh Izel, La Bretagne Inférieure[10])   as

opposed to Upper Brittany (Breizh Uhel). Since the

French Revolution the Province has been divided into

five *Departements* : Finistère (the whole of the western

extremity), Côtes du Nord and Morbihan in the centre,

and Ille-et-Vilaine and Loire Inférieure (or Atlan-

tique, as it had itself renamed) filling the space as

far as the old eastern boundary of the Duchy; but the

names of the four main dialects are taken from the

dioceses Léon and Tréguier in the north, *Cornouaillais*

in the centre, and Vannes[11] in the south-east (half of

which is not Breton-speaking and never has been).

Isoglosses, however, never coincide with diocesan

boundaries, because distribution of linguistic features

was affected by trade-routes and the siting of fairs.

The last Breton-speaking king died in 1084, so that from then on Breton was no longer the language of the governing class. In other words, the situation was similar both to that in Wales at a later date, when English was adopted by the aristocracy, and to that in Scotland, which, as we shall see, was at no time completely Gaelic-speaking. But the new unit is as conscious of its Celti heritage as the old.

Notes to Chapter Seven

1. Or *Aremorica* (Caesar *B.G.* 5, 53, 6); cf. Welsh *ar y mor* and *arfor (dir)* "coast". The word in fact simply means "coast-dwellers" and is applied also to the Aquitani by Pliny and to other Gauls by Eutropius (9,21).

2. An area then known as Dumnonia; whence the name of the old kingdom of Dumnonée in N. Brittany.

3. Experts would have us believe that the similarity between Cornwall and Breton Cornouaille is a coincidence, the first coming from Anglo-Saxon *Cornwealas*, the second from Latin *Cornu Galliae*, and that neither is connected with its own Celtic name *Kernyw* (W. *Kernow*, Br. Kerneo; cf. Mt. Kern in the *Carnic* Alps).

4. E.g. Léon, and Caerleon in Monmouthshire; Daoulas and Dowlais in Glamorgan; Motreff, and Mochdref in Denbighshire; and Yvias, and Ewyas in Hereford shire.

5. One is Ushant, representing, as the Breton name *Eussa* shows, Gaulish *Uxama* "the highest"; cf.

Welsh *uchel* "high" and Latin Superlatives in
-issimus. *Iuppiter Optimus Maximus* was *Juppiter
Uxellimus* in (Celtic) Noricum (*Corpus Inscr. Lat.*
111, 5145).

6.   Rushforth, *Latin Inscriptions*, No.16: Epotsori-
      vidus - Gedemon - Otvanevnus - Julius.

7.   Nora Chadwick, *Early Brittany*.

8.   Cf. the dubious linguistic parentage of the
      Commentary on Donatus, and the fact that
      missionaries from Britain could work in Brittany
      in the 8th century.

9.   This is still the official attitude. In 1974 the
      President declared himself in favour of regional
      languages provided that they did not threaten
      "national unity".

      This was an advance on President Pompidou's
      statement that "there is no room for regional
      languages in a France which is destined to mark
      Europe with its seal". However, the Breton
      Cultural Charter promulgated in February 1977 was
      considerably watered down later: cultural sub-
      sidies for Brittany's 7% of the population will
      be only 0.56% (4.5 million francs) of the total
      for France; still no degree in Celtic studies;
      little done for nursery-schools; and Loire-
      Atlantique separated from the other 4 *départements*.

10.   "Inférieure", because nearer the mouth of the
      rivers, i.e. more downstream. Cf. the Roman Pro-
      vinces of Upper and Lower Germany.

11.   The name comes from the tribe of the Veneti, who
      occupied the area in Roman times. It is well-known
      (thanks to *Paris* from the *Parisii*) that the more
      important towns of an area lost their original
      names to the names of the tribe; (otherwise Paris
      would have been called after Lutetia): thus *Nantes*
      from the Namnetes, *Rennes* from the Redones, *Corseul*
      from the Coriosolites (all mentioned by Caesar, *B.G.*
      2, 34 and 3,9).

8. SCOTLAND

That we could not consider the formation of Wales without at the same time learning something of the origins of Scotland is not without its significance. It puts in the foreground the fact that Scotland has never had a single language spoken within its borders, and that therefore Gaelic has never been spoken over the whole of her territory. The Brythons who had pushed north to the Clyde and the Forth shared the country with a people called the Picts. Who these people were, is disputed. Irish legend brought them from Scythia, a modern theory will have them Frisians, and claims that their language is the parent of Lowland Scots[1]. True it is that there was an *enclave* of Picts in Galloway, that the name *Dumfries* may owe something to Frisia[2], and that the learned Welsh for the Firth of Forth (originally *Gweryt*, which looks like a cognate of *Forth*), is *Y Mor Ffrisaidd* ("The Frisian Sea"); true too that they differed from the Celts to their south by the light colour of their hair, which led Tacitus (*Agr.* 11, 2) or his source to suspect a Germanic origin, though other ancient writers tended to call Celts all blond peoples living north of the Alps. (Their name, which Romans could not resist deriving from their own word *picti* ("painted", *sc.* with woad, or tattooed), is

first found in A.D. 297). There are, however, strong

reasons for believing them to be Celts: the Place-

Names of N.E. Scotland are Celtic without being Irish;

one of their tribes bears the Celtic (latinized) name

Verturiones[3]; and in the Celtic part of Aquitania

there lived the Pictones or Pictavi (from whom Poitou

took its name)[4]. It may also be significant that the

weems or caves (from Gaelic *uaimh*) found in the south

of their territory and probably used as larders are

also found in Cornwall (under the name *fogevyow*).

Finally, if there is any truth in the story of Avienus

(op. cit.), that Celts drove out the Ligurians (sic!)

from Frisia in the 7th century B.C., then the "Frisian"

invaders were Celts themselves!

Whether the Picts' Celtic speech was Brythonic or

Goidelic, is still disputed, though the name of their

champion against Agricola in A.D. 83, Calgācus, if it

contains the Gaelic word *colg* meaning "sword" or "rage"

would indicate Goidelic. This would explain why St.

Columba needed no interpreter when he met the Pictish

king, Brude Mac Maelchon, in Inverness in 565 (two

years after leaving Ireland). That he did need one

when speaking with someone in Skye, as Adamnan's *Life*
expressly states, accords with the belief that the Pic
were in the process of assimilating an autochthonous
people. Their capital was Scone.

Probably even before the Roman withdrawal in 410,
the Brythonic ancestors of the Welsh had penetrated
into Pictish territory in the West, leaving that
Pictish *enclave* in Galloway, and had established the
Kingdom of Strathclyde without having to do much
fighting. Next to arrive (*ca.* 550) were the Scoti[5]
from Ireland, who founded a Kingdom north of Strathclyde (in Argyll), which they called *Dalriada* from
the district *Dáil Ruighe Fhada* ("Long Arm's Portion")
in Ulster's County Antrim, from which they came. Despite unity under King Aidan brought about by St.
Columba, they were at first a little more than a clier
kingdom of the Picts under King Angus Mac Fergus; but
when about 843 their own King Kenneth Mac Alpin, who
was a Pict on his mother's side, ascended the Pictish
throne as King of the United Kingdoms of Scot-land and
Pict-land (though Irish annals still called him "Rex
Pictorum"), it was by the Celtic name *Alba*[6] or the
Latin name *Scotia* that the united kingdom was called.

Meanwhile, as we have seen, the Angles had
arrived in the south-east of the country, so that now
both in the east and in the west foreign salients
protruded into what was to be Scottish territory.
Strathclyde was first attacked by a joint army of
Angles and Picts, allied after a marriage between a
Pictish princess and the Angle King's son, Eanfrith,
and its army defeated at Dumbarton; then it was the
turn of the Danes, who sacked Dumbarton in 870, and
finally, about 945, Strathclyde was united to Alba
by Malcolm I. The Kingdom had, however, meanwhile
reoccupied middle Cumbria and in 1018 its last king,
Owen the Bald, helped Malcolm II of Scotland to defeat
the Northumbrians at Carham, to annex the Lothians,
and thus to carry the Scottish border to the Tweed.
With the creation of the present Border in 1092 Strathclyde ceased to exist as a separate Kingdom, and the
last we hear of Scotland's "Welsh" is a reference to
"Brets" in S.W. Scotland in 1296. Edinburgh (which
name may or may not commemorate the Northumbrian king,
Edwin) had been captured *ca.* 960 and the Scottish
capital moved there from Dunfermline.

While Scotland was thus taking shape in the south,

another people was invading it in the north-west. By
800 the Hebrides and many of the Western Isles and the
extreme North were in Viking hands (whence the Gaelic
name for the Hebrides, *Innse Gall*, "Islands of the
Foreigners"); but far from holding up the formation
of a united country, the common danger and damage
hastened the process of unification, being probably
responsible for the union of the Scottish and Pictish
Kingdoms in 843. At the same time the contemporary
Viking invasions of England weakened the power of
Northumbria, and the confederation of Danish communities known as Danelaw cut off Saxondom between the
Cheviots and the Forth, thus linking the future of the
area with the history of Scotland. Gaels began to
settle in the Lowland hills, as place-names attest;
but Orkney and Shetland, even after their annexation
to the country in 1472, were never to become parts of
Gaelic-speaking Scotland.

There is no inevitability about what happened in
these centuries. At one point it was possible that the
two foreign salients in the south would consolidate
their positions, and we should have had a piece of
Wales and a piece of England north of the Border; whil

north of the Clyde and Forth Scots and Picts would

have combined (with consequent fusion of the two

Celtic tongues to produce a specifically Scottish

Gaelic even further removed from Irish), and would

have formed a Kingdom of North Britain or Scotland.

This would have placed Scotland's southern border on

the line of the Antonine Wall instead of on that of

Hadrian's (which however runs a little south of the

Cheviots, the present border). A century later (the

7th), Anglian (Northumbrian) power could have extended

beyond the Lothians to incorporate Brythons, Scots and

Picts. This would have been to anticipate what

Edward I later did in Wales; and it is what the North-

umbrian King, Egfrith, tried to do in 685. Fortunately,

the country was saved to become Scotland by the Pictish

King, Brude Mac Bile (672-693), who defeated and killed

Egfrith at the Battle of Nechtansmere in Angus.

What in fact happened was that the grandson of

Malcolm II, Duncan, who rose from ruler of Strathclyde

to King of a united Scotland in 1034, was murdered by

his general, Macbeth, in 1040, which brought to the

throne in 1057 his son the "Prince of Cumberland" as

Malcolm III (Canmore, "Big head"); and it was this

dynasty which welded into one Scottish nation four
peoples separated by race, language, and customs:
Brythons, Angles, Scots and Picts. His method was
the opposite of what one would expect: instead of
trying to make the others Scottish, he and his succes-
sors forced Celtic Scotland to adopt English law and
custom and therefore prepared the way for the extension of what was to be the English language. Half-
English by birth and living at the court of Edward
the Confessor during the usurpation of Macbeth, he was
also urged in that direction by his wife, the Saxon
princess, Margaret (sister of Edgar Atheling), who
set about the anglicization of the Church.

The change from Anglo-Saxons to Anglo-Normans did
not affect this policy, but it did mean that anglicization meant something different. Above all, it
meant the feudal system; and in so far as this was
distinct from Scottish tribalism, it was a further
wedge driven between the two sections of the people.
More, the feudal barons installed in Scotland were
seen by English kings as outposts of their dominions,
on whom they could rely in times of conflict. Their
expectations were fulfilled when in 1296 the Scottish

King, Balliol, having challenged the overlordship of
Edward I and having renounced his allegiance, received
little support from the barons, who watched Edward de-
pose him, march off with the Stone of Scone, sack and
seize Berwick, and call himself King of Scotland:
and in the following year it was the common people
(burghers and peasants) who responded to the call of
William Wallace and defeated an English army at the
Battle of Stirling Bridge.

There was bound to be a Celtic reaction. Malcolm's
son was allowed to reign only on condition that he
brought no Anglo-Normans into Scotland; and rebellions
troubled the reigns of Alexander I (called "the
Fierce" from his reaction), David I (1124-53), husband
of a Norman widow, who completed the organisation of
Scotland from the Moray Firth to the Tweed on Anglo-
Norman principles, and his grandson, Malcolm IV.
Early in the 13th century, however, Celtic or anti-
Norman resistance ceased. The renunciation of Scottish
claims to Cumbria and Northumbria by Alexander II in
1236 provoked no popular reaction: Scotland's kingdom was to stop at the Solway and the Tweed. But in
the west there were to be acquisitions: in the reign

of his son, Alexander III, the Western Isles were
recovered from the Norsemen after a great victory
over Haakon of Norway at Largs (1263), and Gaelic
took root there to such good effect that today,
though having the greatest number of Norse place-
names in Scotland, the Hebrides are the strongest
bastion of the language.

Alexander III did homage to Edward I "for land
held of the English king", but the exact relationship
of the two kingdoms was never clearly defined.
Tradition has it that he added the phrase " saving my
kingdom of Scotland". In any case, that is what
corresponded to Scottish feeling; and the consequent
friction between the two countries and the ever-
present threat to Scottish independence must certainly
be considered the explanation of the paradox that the
loss of the customs and even to a large extent of the
language which the Scots had brought to the country
did not lead to any weakening of national feeling, but
on the contrary strengthened it and enabled Highlands
and Lowlands to constitute a united country. The
hammering of the Wars of Independence (1286-1371) did
but harden national sentiment. Two later kings of

Scotland, James IV in 1513 and James V in 1542, actually invaded England; and defeat at Flodden and the
Solway respectively only confirmed the Scottish sense
of being different. For years they were allies of
France against England. Even the accession of a Scottish king, James VI (1567), to the English throne in
1603 did not have the disastrous effect on national
identity that, as we shall see, followed that of the
Welshman, Henry Tudor, in 1482; and when full
political union came in 1707, and forty-five Scotsmen
sat in the English Parliament, the consequent improvement in economic conditions produced indeed a material-
ly more contended population, but it left national
sentiment beneath the surface sufficiently strong to
revive when economic wellbeing deteriorated.

Today the Act of Union is still variously judged:
whereas some see it as the culmination of a process
and point out that the Lowlanders are of the same
stock as the English, and their previous separation from
England merely an historical accident, the more nation-
ally minded see it as a distortion of history and refuse to consider Scotland as other than a "unitary
Celtic society superficially Saxonised in certain Low-

land areas"[7].

The fundamental difference between the conditions
of Wales and Scotland after the determination of their
frontiers was not so much the fact that Scotland was
an independent kingdom recognising the overlordship of
England as that whereas Wales, with the exception of
South Pembrokeshire, was almost completely Welsh-
speaking, Scotland was divided linguistically into two
parts. It was as though to the geological division of
the country into two zones separated by a fault called
the Highland Line running from the Firth of Clyde
east-north-east to Stonehaven, there was to correspond
a linguistic division: the area north of the fault,
the Highlands, was to be characterized, not only by
stone, heather, lochs, and steep-sided glens, but
also by Gaelic, while in the Southern Uplands to the
south running from Galloway to the Cheviots, and
characterized by grass and broad dales, Gaelic was to
be lost where it was spoken (e.g. in Galloway) and two
forms of English - Scots, the language of Lothian, once
known as *Inglis* and now sometimes called *Lallans* ,
and the English introduced from England - were to take
its place. In the rift-valley between these two zones

(the Central Lowlands), Gaelic and English were to
contend with one another. This double linguistic
tradition has hindered the development of a sense of
ethnic identity, and thus provides an answer to the
question[8] why Scottish nationalism was so slow in
developing; it also explains why the fate of Gaelic
is very much less of an emotive issue in Scottish
Nationalism, both ancient and modern; indeed, if
emotions were to be roused at all, there was more
likely to be friction between the two linguistic
groups, not indeed on grounds of language, but
because the Highland Gaels, by clinging to their old
clan-system and tribal customs, seemed to an earlier
age to represent a lower stage of civilisation and were
less reconciled to the fall of the house of Stuart.
Thus it was from them that the Old and Young Pretenders in 1715 and 1745 drew their chief support; and
it was the failure of these rebellions that settled the
Highland Question: the chiefs became landlords, and
their clansmen, tenants; and the warrior-qualities
of the Highlanders were given an outlet in the Highland
regiments raised by the Elder Pitt.

The fact remains that from the days of her Kingdom

Scotland has been a bilingual country, and even

without the English connection would have had to face

the problems that bilingualism brings, as Belgium and

Canada have shown. Fortunately, both linguistic groups

have always had roots going deep into the country's

history, and that country was not the artificial

creation of statesmen, but the natural result of an

historical process. A modern Scotsman does not feel

more Scottish for being able to speak Gaelic, and the

English-speakers feel just as Scotch, because they

are not interlopers, but the descendants of those who

have been Scotsmen as long as the Gaels. This is

lucky for Scotland, but unlucky for Gaelic.

Notes to Chapter Eight

1. Citing Ptolemy's *Taixeli* in N.E. Scotland, the
    Frisian island of Texel, and the Frisian word for
    "thistle", *tiksel*; and comparing in Scots the
    dropping of final D (*lan*), CH for GH (*nicht*),
    OO for OU (*hoose*), irregular plurals (*shoon*/shoes
    kye/cows), and such adverbs as *forbye* ("also").
    According to this theory the arch-villain is Bede
    the hero - Procopius, who in his *De bello Gothico*
    of *ca*. 550 has three nations, Angili, Frissones,
    and Brittones, inhabiting an island called Britti
    (8, 20, 4-7). But Procopius himself locates
    Brittia "between Britain and Thule", and it is now
    believed to be Denmark.

2. See W.J. Watson, *Celtic Place-Names of Scotland*
    (1926), pp. 421-3.

3.   Ammianus Marcellinus, the continuator of Tacitus
     and the last Latin historian of antiquity (*ca.*
     332-400), xxvii. 8, 5, where they are linked
     with the Caledonians (Dicalydones).

4.   Caesar *B.G.* 3, 11, 5 etc., and Strabo 4,190.

5.   *Scota* or *Scotta* is also a Gaulish name, of
     uncertain etymology.

6.   Celtic or not, and whether connected with Latin
     albus (white), as an old Welsh name for Britain
     (*Enys Wen* "White Island") and its obsolete cog-
     nate *elfydd* (world) suggest, or with non-Indo-
     European *alp* (mountain) or with the River-Name
     Albis (Elbe), the name *Alba* was of elastic con-
     notation. The early sources of Avienus called
     Britain "Insula Albiorum" (*Or. Mar.* 112) and
     according to Pliny (4, 16, 102), following the
     geographer Isidore of Charax, *Albion* was the
     native name for Britannia. From these writers
     it passed into Ptolemy's *Geography* and Bede's
     History. That is its sense too in early Celtic
     writings (whence its use in the famous reproach
     'Perfide Albion', first printed in 1793, though
     Bossuet had already said 'Perfide Angleterre' in
     a sermon). Later it was restricted to Scotia,
     as above, but today it has been expanded again
     in modern Celtic to be the name of the whole of
     Scotland.

7.   H. Trevor-Roper, reviewing W. Ferguson's *Scot-
     land's relations with England* in the *Times
     Literary Supplement* of 9 September 1977. In ano-
     ther review a year later we are reminded that the
     English did not think fit to ask the Scots' per-
     mission before executing Charles I, though he
     was their King too, or before abolishing the
     monarchy and the House of Lords, and that the
     Scots thought they had the right to protest about
     all these measures - so far had unification already
     gone!

8.   Asked by T. Nairn in *The break-up of Britain*, as
     quoted in *Y Ddraig Goch*, Ebrill 1978, p. 8. See

also Patricia Nichols, *Ethnic Consciousness in the British Isles* in *Language Problems and Language Planning* (LPLP), N-ro. 1, p.15.

9. IRELAND

One would have thought that an island was a natural unit, and that there would be no place here for the contraction or expansion of territory which we have seen respectively to be involved in the formation of Wales and Scotland. *Dis aliter visum*: it was not to be; what God had joined, man was allowed to put asunder. The north-eastern part of the island has been politically detached, and while it still bears the name of Ireland, it is not part of the land of Eire.

Greek and Roman historians, wiser than they knew, were always careful to distinguish Ireland from Britain[1]; and this they must have done because of Ireland's distinctive name. This is the more notice-able in that their geographers had long been using the generic terms "The Brettanike" (on the model of "The Keltike") for *Britain* or "The Brettanic Isles" for all the islands lying off Gaul[2], as Chrysostom was still doing in the 4th century (*Homiliae* viii)[3].

The first man to call Britain "Great" was Marinos (Ptolemy's immediate predecessor), but the name could go back to Pytheas via the geographer Eratosthenes; and the Little Britain from which it was distinguished was Ireland[4]!

Irish evolved through the same phases as the descendants of Brythonic, with an archaic form transitional
between Primitive and Old Irish i.e.

PRIMITIVE 4th-7th centuries OLD   8th-10th centuries

ARCHAIC   7th-8th centuries MIDDLE 10th-13th centuries

MODERN 13th century onwards

We do not speak of Common Goidelic as we do of Common
Brythonic, because the Goidelic speech of Ireland
transplanted itself to Scotland and the Isle of Man by
emigration, and the languages spoken in all three
places were, down to the 10th century, indistinguishable from one another. For our knowledge of Primitive
Irish we depend partly on inscriptions in Ogam and
Latin and partly on words borrowed from Latin. These
latter were mostly taken directly from British Latin
as pronounced by Brythons, not indirectly through
Brythonic, as is shown by such words as *scrîn* (shrine)
from *scrinium* (c f. W. *ysgrin*), and *lacht* (milk) from
Vulgar (ungrammatical) Latin *lactem*, not from the
equivalent of W. *llaeth*.

The earliest borrowings having taken place when
Goidelic had no P, that letter in Latin words was rendered by QU, which Old Irish handed down as C; e.g.

pluma became *clumh*, *purpura corcair*, *Patricius Coth-
riche*. Later, when the Goidels had learnt to pronounce
P, it could be kept; hence *pacem* "peace" yielded *pog*,
and *Patricius* now became *Padric* (today *Padraig*). The
first group probably goes back to the time of St.
Patrick's mission to Ireland between 432 and 461, and
the second will have been the result of intermonastic
contacts, when final syllables had already been lost,
i.e. after 500[5].

Deductions from inscriptions are bedevilled by the
possibility that a given letter represents an earlier
sound; e.g. the name SAGRAGNI is rendered in Latin
SAGRANI, which presumably means that by that time
Goidelic GN had become N, but that GR had not yet
become R (with compensatory lengthening of the preceding vowel); e.g. *brón* ("grief", W. *brwyn*) from Brythonic *brugno-*). Every stone permits a similar peep
into a vanished phase of the language.

The day in A.D. 81 when the Roman Governor of
Britain, Agricola, stood on the coast of Northern
Cumbria (Galloway[6]) and, looking across at Hibernia,
decided not to invade, was a fateful one for the "sacred
island", as Avienus called it in the quoted poem[7].

What might not three centuries of Roman rule have done

to forge a nation! As it was, the Irish tribes were

left to freedom and their own devices. These included

incessant warfare among themselves, as the five king-

doms subdivided into nearly a hundred smaller kingships

fought out their petty quarrels. The fighting must

have been savage; for all that ancient geographers

can tell us about these early Irish is that they were

"completely uncivilized" (Mela 3, 53) and "wilder than

the Britons" (Strabo, 201, alleging cannibalism, glut-

tony, adultery, and incest, charges which recall the

beliefs entertained about the early Christians by ig-

norant outsiders). Tacitus, who had probably not read

Strabo, states (*Agr*. 24, 2) that "in character and

culture they are not very different from the Britons",

and this accords with what linguistics have shown to be

the identity of their Celtic origin. Indirect support

is given to this by Tacitus himself, when he records

the reception by Agricola of an Irish chieftain driven

from his kingdom *domestica seditione* and hoping for

restoration with Roman help[8]. In what language was

the interview conducted? Presumably there was a Brito-

serving as interpreter on Agricola's staff, and he

could understand his fellow-Celt even though he was a
Goidel himself; or, more interestingly, perhaps a
Roman soldier had learnt enough Brythonic. Be that as
it may, here was the perfect pretext for invasion, and
Rome did not take it; and perhaps it was just as well,
for Agricola's estimate of one legion and a few auxi-
liaries (about 8000 men) as sufficient for conquest
might have proved over-optimistic, with disastrous
results for his military reputation (to the Emperor
Domitian's delight).

It was the Norwegians and Danes who eventually did
invade. By that time, the middle of the 9th century,
the Roman Empire had long since fallen in the West and
Europe was relapsing into barbarism. Ireland had been
continuously torn by the struggle of its three leading
dynasties, Tara, Leinster and Munster, and then, just
after the introduction of Christianity, of the four
Kingdoms of Tara, Oirghialla, Aileadh and Cruachan among
themselves and with the dynasties of Ulster, Leinster
and Cashel.

Nor had the Church been powerful enough to impose
order on this chaos; but the Church had done something
valuable none the less. The monastic communities that

had sprung up all over Ireland since the mission of

St. Patrick in 432 kept alight the torch of secular

learning; their missionaries carried it with them to

Britain and the Continent[9]; and when the Danish in-

vasions forced many Irishmen to flee, the learning

they carried with them brought about a little Renaissanc

akin to that greater one which Greeks fleeing from Turl

were to cause four centuries later. The other perma-

nent result of these invasions was city-life: Dublin,

Cork, Limerick, Wexford all began as Danish towns,

whose foundation integrated Ireland into European

trade.

Unity was as far away as ever. A King of Leinster

had been the ally of the Danes of Dublin, and had been

defeated with them at the Battle of Clontarf in 1014,

when Brian Bruce of Cashel in Munster for a brief mo-

ment came near to being the champion of all Ireland.

Only in the Church was a sort of unity attained, when

St. Malachy became Abbot of Bangor.

Then came 1166. What the Romans had refused to

do, England did: Henry II agreed to help an Irish

fugitive king to return to his country. He was told t

solicit the aid of a Marcher-Lord, and he succeeded in

winning the support of the Earl of Pembroke, nicknamed
Strongbow, with the promise of his daughter in marriage
and the succession to his kingdom. This was "the
accursed visit"[10] which brought the English into Ireland. But the English whom Dermot MacMurrough introduced were mostly the sons of Welsh mothers, and being
therefore half-Celtic and probably bilingual in Anglo-
Norman and Welsh, were easily assimilated by the conquered people and in one or two generations had passed
from being Anglo-Norman to being Anglo-Irish. Meanwhile, however, Henry II had been, as rulers often were,
alarmed by the success of his subordinate, and had
landed near Waterford in October 1171 to receive the
homage of the Irish kings. He gave Leinster to Strongbow, but kept Dublin, Waterford and Wexford for himself;
and he rewarded the English Pope, Adrian IV, for sanc-
tioning the invasion by making the Irish Church (whose
different origin had in 597, the year of St. Columba's
death, brought St. Augustine hurrying to Kent to enforce the supremacy of Rome) conform to the practices
of the English Church and in particular to its dating
of Easter. In 1175 Henry was accepted as Overlord by
the *Ard-ri* ("High King", the lofty title of one who was

now merely *primus inter pares*).

The Anglo-Norman feudal system did not penetrate into Ireland as it had done into Scotland; the precondition of intermarriage between the royal families on each side was lacking. The result was that the opposite happened: the feudalism of the Anglo-Norman or Anglo-Welsh barons began to resemble Celtic tribalism, and though they were still distinguishable from the old Celtic chieftains of the West, they no longer resembled the English of the Dublin "Pale", at whose expense indeed they often extended their territories. The process was facilitated by the concentration of the Plantagenet kings on their Norman and Angevin empire, and their lack of control over their representatives in Ireland. Injustices went unchecked, and therewith, the first seeds of discontent were sown.

A graver result was that Ireland became a potential danger to the reigning monarch as the place where disloyalty could begin. When the house of Lancaster came to the throne in the person of Henry VII in 1485, it was in Ireland that the Yorkists began plotting and from where Lambert Simnel and Perkin Warbeck set out on their futile impersonations. In retaliation Henry subordinated the (baronial) Irish Parliament to the Privy

Council in England (Poynings' Law). Later, when the

Earl of Kildare rebelled against Henry VIII in 1534,

he and his five uncles were hanged at Tyburn; but the

crucial factor was that the Earl had sought the aid

of a foreign power. In 1541 Henry VIII made himself

King of Ireland and set about the task of forging a

loyal English-speaking people. It was no use: the

Reformation and the abolition of the monasteries

brought the Jesuits to Ireland, and this was felt as

a constant threat to Protestant England. Under Eliza-

beth judges refused to swear allegiance and an English

standing army was imposed. As if to justify these

measures and to prove that the threat from abroad was

far from illusory, first the Pope (1578), then Philip

II (1580), then Philip III (1602) of Spain sent armies

to Ireland in support of rebellions. In the greatest

of these, led by Hugh O'Neill of Ulster from 1593 -

1607, the throne of Ireland was offered to the Spanish

royal House[11]; but when it ended in defeat, at Kinsale

in 1601, James I allowed Hugh to be Earl of Tyrone,

with free exercise of his religion. Conciliation, how-

ever, came too late: the Earl fled with his peers and

left Ulster open to the "Plantation" of English and

Scottish Lowland Protestant settlers. *Hinc illae*

lacrimae.

Thus English fear and the cruelty of its reaction

taught Ireland to hate; and this hatred was the cause

rather than the result of Ireland's devotion to Catho-

licism. The Reformation had not in itself provoked

any great resistance; but the misgovernment of Eliza-

beth's lieutenants meant that belonging to a different

creed became a part of patriotism. In 1641 the Catho-

lic Old English joined the Gaels, and that was the

real beginning of Irish Catholic nationalism. So to

other differences had been added the most irreconcilabl

of all: religion, with all that it implies of fanati-

cism and distrust. Results were soon seen: in the

next rebellion of the same year 1641 thousands of Pro-

testants perished, with the result that when the Civil

War broke out in England in 1642, one of the aims of

the Parliamentarians in their attitude to Ireland

(where the distribution of loyalties was extremely com-

plicated) was to avenge the massacre. This was done b

Cromwell at Drogheda in 1649, but it should be remem-

bered that the garrison slaughtered there consisted of

Royalists of the Earl of Ormond, a staunch Protestant.

The final settlement was harsh: 40,000 Puritans were

settled on the lands of those who had resisted, and the

dispossessed were transplanted beyond the Shannon.   But

thirty-eight Puritan M.P.s represented Ireland in

Parliament at Westminster, and the English market was

open to Irish traders, so that in effect the two

countries were united.

England, however, was not too keen on union at

this time.   Ireland was expensive to maintain: the

profits (£100,000 in 1662) were less than expected,

and there were not the resources for investment.

After the Restoration, therefore, union was sacrificed

to the jealousy of English traders: direct trade bet-

ween Ireland and the colonies was forbidden (1663) and

even the export of cattle to England was halted (1666).

Thus the one thing that can reconcile a people to

subordination, economic prosperity, was made impossible.

The "Glorious" (because bloodless) Revolution came

when it did in 1685, because James II had tried to make

the army Catholic by recruiting shiploads of Irish

peasants - a move which coincided with an upsurge of

anti-Catholic feeling in England consequent on the

French persecution of the Huguenots.   It was necessary

to move fast, and the Irish campaign of William of Orange

(1689-90), when the Protestants of N.Ireland constituted

a bridge-head for the English Army until more troops

could be landed, showed the significance of Ulster as a

permanent garrison. With the Protestant cause secure,

William imposed relatively generous terms; but the

Protestant Parliaments of both England and Ireland

frustrated his purpose by passing anti-Catholic Penal Laws

Ireland thus entered on the 18th century as a

heavily anglicized country nevertheless conscious of its

separate identity. Swift's was but one of many voices

raised in English for Ireland (1720). The Jacobite

danger disposed Walpole to conciliation; but in fact

Irish loyalty was to be shown in 1760, when Catholics

and Protestants were united in their resistance to a

French landing at Carrickfergus, and again in 1779 when

a force of 40,000 volunteers was formed to defend the

country against a possible French invasion during the

American War of Independence. England showed her grati-

tude by abolishing the laws against the free export of

Irish wool and glass, and was soon ready, thanks to

Grattan's eloquence (which had already won a reduction in

the Penal Laws) to repeal the Act of 1719 which had given

the English Parliament the right to legislate for

Ireland. The Catholics, however, now wanted complete

emancipation, and in this they had the support of the

United Irishmen, a body originating among the Pres-

byterians of Ulster and created in 1791 by Wolfe Tone

of Belfast, who saw that political liberty could be

won only by a religious alliance. Unfortunately,

there were those who saw in Catholic Emancipation the

end of Protestant rule in Ireland, and the new Lord-

Lieutenant, Lord Fitzwilliam, was prevented from

granting the complete emancipation which he saw to be

essential, if rebellion was to be avoided. Before

long, Wolf Tone was a fugitive rebel, attempting thrice

to land in Ireland with a French army and perishing in

the attempt (1798). Pitt decided that the time for

union had come, but it took a good deal of bribery and

intimidation to produce the necessary votes for the

disappearance of the Protestant Irish Parliament in 1800,

and the hoped-for emancipation of the Catholics did not

immediately follow owing to the opposition of George

III. Pitt resigned and a hundred Irishmen took their

seats in the House of Commons.

While it was a young Protestant, Robert Emmet, who

reacted to the Union with violence (1803), the Catholics found their champion once again in an orator, Daniel O'Connell. After Grattan's death in 1820, it was O'Connell's popularity in Ireland which led Peel to secure the emancipation of the Catholics, i.e. above all their eligibility to sit at Westminster (1829). Ireland, however, had taken note of the fact that the concession was made out of fear; and O'Connell's sights were now set on the repeal of the Union and the removal of the social and economic disabilities depressing the Irish countryman. The Potato Famine of 1845-6, which reduced the population from 8 1/4 to 6 1/2 million, had among its permanent results the rise of the Fenian Movement among the new emigrants in America and their later organization in Ireland itself (1858). Thus a party committed to nothing less than independence came into being not long before the movement for Home Rule was launched by a Protestant in 1870. In the same year Gladstone, having in the previous year disestablished the Protestant Church, passed his first Land Act to protect Irish tenants against their landlords, who, besides being absentee, practised through their agents all the tricks supposed to be in landlord's book.

The greatest of the Home Rulers, Parnell (another Protestant!), combined the struggle for Home Rule with agitation for more agrarian reform; and Gladstone's second Land Act of 1881 became known as "the Magna Carta of Irish Tenants". Gladstone was trying to make amends for what he saw to be England's failure to let Union redound to Ireland's advantage, but his two Home Rule Bills (1886 and 1893) were rejected. The social and economic reforms that followed were no longer enough and those for whom not even Home Rule would be enough, those who wanted Ireland to "go it alone", came together about 1906 in a party that took its name from the slogan of the Hungarian patriot, Ferencz Déak (1803-76): *Sinn Fein* ("We ourselves"). Meanwhile the Protestants of Ulster (and some Catholic businessmen) were opposing Home Rule for very different motives and with a very different alternative. The formation of an Ulster Volunteer Force had provoked that of the National Volunteers in the South, when the outbreak of war with Germany in August 1914 caused Asquith's Home Rule Bill, passed earlier that year, to be suspended. The leader of the Irish Home Rulers at Westminster, John Redmond, surprised the German Ambassador by promising the

Government the support of Ireland; but though Irish-

men volunteered in thousands, Sinn Fein saw in England's

difficulty their greatest chance. Undeterred by the

failure of Casement, they came within an ace of seizing

Dublin Castle on Easter Monday 1916, but in six days

were forced to surrender.

The subsequent execution of the ringleaders has

taught the world to be afraid of creating martyrs;

for the end of the war found Sinn Fein stronger than

ever. In the General Election of December 1918, 76

Irish constituencies returned their candidates (against

7 for the old Nationalist Party which wanted Ireland

part of the U.K.). In January 1919 Sinn Fein set up an

Assembly of Ireland (*Dáil Éireann*) and proclaimed the

Saorstát Éireann (Irish Free State), which for some time

served as a duplicate Government, raising its own Armed

Forces (the Irish Republican Army or I.R.A.) and through

its president, Eamonn De Valera (1882-1975), raising

five million dollars in the U.S.A. for an Irish National

Loan. In a few months the killings had begun[12]; and

they were continuing, when, in February 1920, Lloyd

George proposed to Parliament the partition of the

country: a Northern Irish Parliament of 52 members,
and a Southern one of 128, with 20 members from each
forming a Council of Ireland (a body to be proposed
again in 1974) with 42 representatives in Westminster.
In June 1921, the North having with some reluctance
accepted partition, the Northern Parliament was opened
by the King with Sir James Craig as Prime Minister.
The amputation of Ulster had been performed.

At the same elections in Southern Ireland Sinn
Fein won 122 of the 126 seats, but the Parliament
that assembled on 28 June consisted of only the four
Unionists of Trinity College. De Valera agreed to a
truce, but now even dominion status was not enough;
and having come to Downing Street to say so for the
first time in July 1921, he left negotiations in September to a delegation under Arthur Griffith, a former
President of Sinn Fein, on the ground that, as President
of Ireland, he himself was superior to Lloyd George.
The acceptance by the Delegation and the Dáil of the
latest concessions and their rejection by De Valera and
Sinn Fein produced a new situation: confrontation was
now between two groups of Irishmen, and the object of
Sinn Fein's hatred was now an Irish Government, which

bore the very name of Irish Free State that they them-

selves had devised a year before. To them the name

was a mockery while Ireland was not a Republic and had

lost most of her ancient *Cúig* of Ulster[13].

It was in fact over the Border that fighting

broke out in February 1922. Michael Collins, the

Irish Prime Minister, asked Britain for arms, and in

August was himself their victim, killed in an ambush;

after which it was nothing less than Civil War lasting

several months. In 1925 the boundary was fixed, with

certain Catholic areas of Tyrone and Fermanagh still

on the northern side of it. When De Valera's party,

later and still known as Fianna Fail[14], became the

largest party in 1932, the links with Britain were

progressively reduced until in 1937 a republican con-

stitution was adopted and the Free State took up the

ancient name of Eire. In April 1949 Eire ceased to

belong even to the Commonwealth.

Meanwhile Ulster too had not been evolving as

Churchill had expected. He evidently saw partition as

a temporary expedient: "one day Ulster will join with

Southern Ireland: that is our policy", he said in

1921. But events south of the Border were not calcul-

ated to inveigle Ulster Protestants; and the Northern
Ireland Parliament embarked on a series of measures
that made of Ulster something not foreseen by those
who set it up as a last resort. In June 1922 proportional representation was abolished in local government elections, to the detriment of Catholics, as
Collins pointed out; and soon afterwards constituency-
boundaries were so fixed that Protestant areas had
several constituencies, while Catholic areas constituted single ones. This kept Catholics out of local
government and, as its first fruits, enabled Tyrone
and Fermanagh to be retained by "Ulster" despite their
largely Catholic populations. The resulting political
system would have certainly called forth the word
apartheid if so much Afrikaans had been known at the
time.

So what we have arrived at is not one unit, but
two, sharing the same tortured history and the same
linguistic evolution, but identical now only in the
same lush grass that awoke the admiration of Pomponius
Mela's informant[15] and gave the Emerald Isle its name.

Notes to Chapter Nine

1.   Caesar *B.G.* 5. 13 *Hibernia dimidio minor quam*
     Britannia.
     Strabo 2, 13 "Ireland lying beyond Britain" (also
     2, 115 and 201, all of which places justify the
     proposed insertion of "and" at 2, 63).
     Mela 3, 6, 53 *Super Britanniam Iuverna est.*
     Pliny 4, 103 *inter Hiberniam ac Britanniam Mona.*
     Avienus, *Ora Mar.* 108 *insula . . . quam gens*
     Hiernorum colit.
     Cf. however Diodorus 5, 32, 3 "those of the
     Britons who inhabit Iris".

2.   e.g. Strabo, no doubt following Pytheas, 114,
     129, and 147, etc.

3.   Cf. St. Jerome *Commentary on Jeremiah; progeniem*
     Scotticae gentis de Britannorum vicinia, and
     Epistola ad Ctesiphontem 139, 9: *Britanni . . .*
     et Scotticae gentes.

4.   It must be remembered that Classical writers made
     the mistake of believing that the western point
     of Britain lay off the Pyrenees (which therefore
     were imagined to run north-south), so that Ire-
     land had to be either between Britain and Spain
     (as for Caesar and Tacitus) or north of
     Britain (as for Strabo, Mela, and Pliny).
     The mistake was first made by Polybius and re-
     peated by Caesar *B.G.* 5, 13, 3, Strabo 2, 1, 13,
     Pliny 4, 16, 102, and Tacitus, *Agr.* 24. Ptolemy
     corrected the mistake, but himself went wrong
     over "Scotland", representing it as inclined at
     right angles to "England". On the origin
     of this error see J.J. Tierney, *Ptolemy's Map of*
     Scotland in the *Journal of Hellenic Studies,* 1959,
     pp. 132-148.

5.   With this Irish conversion of Latin P to QU com-
     pare her agreement with Latin in the retention of
     Indo-European QU. There must have been some
     phonological reason for this rejection of P in
     favour of the velar.

6. J.K. St. Joseph, *Air reconnaissance in Roman
    Britain*, in the *Journal of Roman Studies*, 1977,
    p. 133.

7. Probably continuing the Greek confusion of the
    name *Iwerio* with the Greek word for "holy"
    (hieros) - an apt coincidence for the "Island of
    Saints".

8. "The domestic rebellion" could be that recorded
    of the Aitheach Tuatha against their Milesian
    overlords in the first century A.D. These may be
    the Aduatici mentioned by Caesar and Diodorus and/
    or the Attacotti mentioned by Ammianus Marcellinus
    and Jerome as being, with the Scotti and Picti,
    ravagers of Britain.

9. A Swiss Canton and the French for "cab" are unex-
    pected traces: St. Gall preserves the name of St.
    Cellach, left by St. Columba in Helvetia on his way
    to Bobbio; and the word *fiacre* derives from St.
    Fiachrach who laboured in Gaul and whose name was
    adopted by a Parisian hotel which happened to be
    the first to provide public transport. There is a
    small town called Saint Fiacre in Lower Brittany.

10. P. Mac Giolla Cheara, *Scéal na h-Eireann*, cuid a
    h-aon, p. 81.

11. This was not the last time that Ireland thought of
    a foreign king: during World War I Republicans
    seriously considered inviting a German Prince to
    be King in the event of a German victory.

12. For a blow-by-blow account of the slaughter on both
    sides in this and following years (which puts the
    situation in Ulster from 1969 to 1978 in the shade),
    see Michael Gilbert's *Churchill*, Vol. 4, pp. 445-
    471.

13. *Cúig Uladh* was one of the five Provinces of ancient
    Ireland. The new "Ulster" consists of six counties
    of the original nine.

14. "Champions of Ireland", *Fail* ("destiny") being an old term for Ireland as the Island of Destiny.

15. 3, 33: *Iuverna . . . adeo luxuriosa herbis, ut se exigua parte diei pecora impleant, et nisi pabulo prohibeantur, diutius pasta dissiliant.* ("Ireland, so luxurious in grass that flocks are full after only a few hours' grazing, and if they are not prevented from eating, will graze until they burst").

10. THE ISLE OF MAN

One might suppose that an island as diminutive as Man was from the first a natural unit, but even geographically this is not quite so. There is a watershed which divides the island into two parts, and the differences between those who live north and south of it were once sufficiently marked for each to give its allegiance to a different contender for the Manx throne after the death of Godred II, and even to fight a battle on opposite sides in 1228. It is even the reason why there are still today two Deemsters (Judges). Furthermore, as a glance at the map will show, there is a "Highland Line" running from Skyhill on Ramsey Bay in the north-east across Sulby Glen and Killabraaga to the Parish of Ballaugh in the north-west, so that at least in one small area Man had the same distinction already met in Scotland and Wales: between the Highlands or mountainous area, where life is harder but the old Celtic traditions and language flourish longer, and the Lowlands or plains, where the process of anglicization takes place more quickly.

The Romans were not tempted to invade Man, nor does there seem to have been much trade between Man and Britannia (only five Roman coins have been found on the island). Man's relations were with Ireland, and in

particular with Ulster, as several of her legends show.

This is only to be expected, since her language is

Goidelic and bears a similarity to Ulster Irish[1] which

would be more obvious than it is but for the historical

accident that led writers in Manx to adopt a spelling

based on English. The Goidels of Man must have come

from Ireland, just as some centuries later Irishmen

established themselves and Gaelic in Scotland. Since

they presumably did not find an empty island, there must

have been Brythons already inhabiting it; and this

supposition is confirmed by indications of Brythonic

pronunciation in names on one of its six Ogam inscribed

stones, where the fortunate survival of the (third)

letter B in a name that must correspond to the juxta-

posed Latin AMMECATI shows the assimilation of B to a

preceding M characteristic of Brythonic at that date

(end of 5th century). The name therefore was originally

the same as that of the Gaul, Ambigatus, whom we have

already met, and it appears in Irish as Imchadh. *Man*

may well be a general term meaning "island"; for the

Romans used the same name ("Mona") for both Anglesey

and Man, and Pliny's variant, *Monapia*, being a compound

reminiscent of the Belgic *Menapii*, suggests that the root is not pre-Celtic, as some would have it. This accords with its apparent reappearance in Scotland's Clackmannan and the Manaw Gododdin which formed the northern part of the old kingdom of Gododdin. The alternative name of the Orkney island called Mainland, Pomona, also looks as though it is related.

After three centuries (from the sixth to the ninth) under Welsh kings, Man was occupied by the Vikings, indeed became their base in the area and, with the Hebrides, gave its name to the Viking "Kingdom of Man and the Isles", when it was formed by King Godred Crovan (Orry) in 1079, thirteen years after he had fought against Harold of England on the Norwegian side at the Battle of Stamford Bridge[2]. The problem for these Norse kings was to satisfy their putative Overlord, the King of Norway, without offending their neighbouring ruler, the King of England. To one or the other they had to turn in times of crisis: Godred II, for example, was doing homage to the King of Norway at the beginning of his reign (1153), but three years later he had to put himself under the protection of Henry II; his successor, Reginald I, who had provoked

King John in 1206 by interfering in Ireland, fell foul

of him again in 1210 by wishing to do homage in Norway.

Henry III bound Harald I to him by a knighthood; King

Haakon of Norway bound him by his daughter's hand;

but then fate intervened, for Harald and Cecilia per-

ished in a shipwreck off Shetland (a strange antici-

pation of the death in 1290 of that Norwegian bride-to-

be Margaret, the five-year-old Maid of Norway, who

died in Orkney on her way to marry Edward I). In the

end, Man fell neither to Norway nor to England: by a

treaty between the Scottish King, Alexander III, and

King Haakon, whom he had defeated at Largs in 1263,

Man became part of the realm of Scotland.

A few place-names in -by and -wick, some graves,

the decoration on certain crosses, and several Runic

inscriptions, are the only tangible remains of the

Viking period; but its influence still survives in the

name of the supreme Assembly: Tynwald (i.e. Thingwald,

"Field of Assembly"); in the fact that one of its two con-

stituent elements, the House of Keys, consists of 24

members, eight of them originally representing the

Isles of Lewis and Skye; and in the title of the

bishopric: "Sodor and Man", the first element of this

being the Latin form of *Sudreyjar*, the Norse name for

the Southern Isles. The bishopric was transferred

from Trondhjem to York by Calixtus III as late as

1458.

It was in fact Reginald I who in 1219 effected the

transfer of Man's allegiance from the old Celtic Church

to that of Rome; and the deed of gift whereby "we have

given to the representative of the Roman Church . . .

our Island of Man" can be seen in a fresco in the

Vatican. The Popes did not forget Man: in 1459

Calixtus III made a rescript threatening with excommu-

nication "all those who shall dare to molest this

Island". Linguistically, juxtaposition with the

Norsemen seems to have had no effect - unless the

occasional non-Celtic word-order is to be ascribed to

it; and it may be significant as a sign of the tough-

ness of the language that some runic inscriptions bear

fathers' names in Norse and their sons' names in Manx.

If in 1285 Alexander III (also on his way to a

wedding) had not fallen over a cliff, the Scottish

connection might have lasted longer. As it was, there

was immediate bickering over Man between Edward I and

Balliol, his own choice for the Scottish throne. Ed-

ward's victory settled nothing; it took the victory
of Edward III over the Scots at Neville's Cross in
1346 to put the island definitely in English hands.
This, however, was far from meaning Direct Rule; in
fact, Edward's first delegated ruler, William de
Montecute, had not even to pay homage. Only in 1405
when the island passed to Sir John Stanley, was homage
one of the conditions.

The Stanleys (later Earls of Derby) ruled the
island as Kings and, from 1504, as Lords, till 1736,
some of them like absentee landlords. The existence
of the island seems sometimes to have slipped the
memory of its real Overlords in London. The Act of
1539 suppressing the monasteries and confiscating their
lands did not mention Man, but the property of Manx
religious houses was seized by the Crown as though
there were no distinction between the two countries.
On a second occasion, however, the failure to mention
Man was taken as excluding it, with tragic consequences:
Charles II had granted a general amnesty to all who
had supported the Parliamentarians, and on the strength
of this William Christian, nicknamed Dhone ("dark-
haired") returned to the Island. It was he, who in

hope of land-reform had championed the Parliamentary
cause in defiance of the Royalist Countess Derby, who
had been left as ruler when the "Great Earl" was captured at the Battle of Worcester and executed in 1651.
The eighth Earl of Derby was able to claim that the
pardon did not cover offences against the Lord of Man,
and the autonomy of the Island was then demonstrated
by the execution of William Christian on Hango Hill
(1663) [3].

The last two Stanleys saw the introduction of a
Manx coinage (1663) and the settlement of the Land
Question, whereby tenants, though continuing to pay a
fixed rent to the Lord, could resume the cancelled
right to bequeath their estates to their sons. The
negotiations were carried out by Bishop Wilson, better
known for his overseeing the translation of the Bible
into Manx and for his attempt to enforce ecclesiastical
discipline in defiance of the civil authorities.

The tenth Earl dying without issue, the Lordship
of Man passed to the second Duke of Atholl. The new
dynasty made a good start with the passing in 1737 of
a Manx "Bill of Rights" guaranteeing trial by jury and
establishing the right of the Keys, the Council and the

Deemsters to fix the Customs-duties. This last pri-
vilege, however, brought into the open a question
whose solution meant the end of the Lordship of Man.

Where there are Customs and Excise, there is
smuggling; and Man had been called a "nest of smug-
glers" by its first Methodist preacher in 1758 and was
still to be "the very head-quarters of smuggling" for
Burke in 1774[4]. The loss to the revenue of England
had become such that the only remedy seemed to be that
the English King should buy the island, i.e. buy the
sovereign-rights of its Lord. This was done in 1765.
Man then became the only part of the British Isles to
be acquired by purchase, as Louisiana and Alaska were
to be by the U.S.A. Though they were not represented
in the Government that was from now on going to tax
them, Manxmen accepted the transaction with such pass-
ivity that in 1774 the Government had no hesitation in
taxing a wide range of imported articles, in striking
contrast, as Burke pointed out, with her hasty repeal
of such taxes on the American colonies. The docility
of the Manx was partly due to the good administration
of their Governor-General, the fourth Duke of Atholl,
whom the British Government appointed in 1793 as a

consolation for not having the purchase-price increased.
This demand of his was finally met in 1828 and involved
the cession of his last claim on the island.

The Revestment (as the transfer of Lordship is
called) did not end the traditional apparatus of self-
government: a two-chamber legislature consisting of the
Legislative Council and the House of Keys, which two
bodies still sit together in the ancient Tynwald (somewhat as the American Senate and House of Representatives
combine to form Congress). The House of Keys finally
became a democratically elected body in 1866, at the same
time as another Act concerning Customs and Harbours allowed
the island to levy its own taxes and to spend its own
monies. Tynwald's control in fact is now almost complete
over internal affairs, and its approval is necessary even
for the Lieutenant-Governor appointed by the Crown; but
a serious curtailment of independence is the necessity of
submitting all legislation to the scrutiny of Whitehall
before it can receive the royal assent, whereas Whitehall
can apply the legislation of the United Kingdom to the
island through an Order-in-Council.

In its relations with the various elements constituting the United Kingdom and neighbouring dependencies
the British Government has displayed the same

Portrait of Ned Maddrell, the last Manx Speaker
(Photograph by courtesy of the Manx Museum)

flexibility of design and lack of insistence on uni-

formity as were characteristic of the Roman Republic

and early Empire: the Channel Islands, Man, Northern

Ireland, Scotland and Wales, each has stood (or will

stand) in a different relationship with the Crown.

Notes to Chapter 10

1.   According to *An t-Ultach* of Feb. 1966, p. 9, Manx
     resembles Gaelic in morphology, but Irish in
     phonology. Another writer, however, in the same
     magazine for Jan. 1977, p. 4, describes Gaelic as
     "in some ways like the Irish of Tyrconnel and in
     others more like that of Munster, so that Scots-
     men can understand simple sentences spoken slowly".
     What emerges from the present study is the extra-
     ordinary independence of Manx.

2.   A detailed account of the Scandinavian period is
     given in the *Chronicle of the Kings of Man and the
     Isles,* composed most probably by the monks of
     Rushen Abbey some time after 1376, unfortunately
     not in Manx but in Latin. (How many thousands of
     pages of text has "dead" Latin's refusal to lie
     down cost the young languages of Europe and their
     modern students!) Six hundred years had to pass
     before two enterprising Manxmen - Mr. G. Broderick
     and Mr. B. Stowell - provided a Manx version of
     this Chronicle.

3.   Charles upheld William's appeal, but it had arrived
     too late.

4.   Speech on American Taxation.

11. THE SIX LANGUAGES COMPARED

CONTENTS

A. INTRODUCTION

As we have seen, the family of Celtic languages consists of two branches according as they kept original Indo-European Q (Goidelic) or changed it to P (Brythonic): e.g. the word for *four*: I-E. *k^{w}etuor*, Latin *quattuor*, Irish *ceathair* (Gaelic *ceithir*, Manx *kiare*), but Welsh *pedwar* (Cornish *peswar*, Breton *peder*). The identical phenomenon in the word for *five* (I-E. *penk^{w}e*, Sanskrit *páñca*) is found in the second of the two syllables; for in the first it is Latin and Goidelic which have changed original P to K^w, this time however through the different process of assimilation to a following syllable, which happened to be K^w: hence Latin *quinque*, Irish and Gaelic *cuig*, Manx *queig*, against Welsh *pump*, Cornish *pymp*, Breton *pemp*. (A line-up of neighbouring languages reveals some unexpected alliances: Latin's neighbours, Oscan (the language of Pompeii) and Umbrian, belong, with *petora* and *pump(erias)* to the P-group, as do the Greek dialects of Boeotia and Lesbos with *pettares, pesures* for *four*, and Aeolic with *pempe* for *five*, whereas Attic and Doric Greek substituted T for Q in both (*tessares, pente*) but Latin's other neighbour, Faliscan, belongs with it to the Q-group. Thus Goidelic-Latin-Faliscan confront Brythonic-Greek dialect-Osco-umbrian[1]. It is not possible, however, to deduce a prehistoric juxtaposition of Brythons and

Oscans, because the loss of original I-E. initial

P is common to both Brythonic and Goidelic (cf. Irish

ean, Welsh *edn* "bird" with Latin *penna* "wing" and Greek

petomai "I fly")[2]; thus the Brythonic change from Q

to P must have taken place later, when Brythons and

Oscans could not have been neighbours. The only other

member of the I-E. family to forsake Q is the Germanic

branch, which must have passed through a P-phase to

arrive at F, e.g. Gothic *fidwor* "four" and *fimf* "five"

where the first F of the one and the last F of the oth

represent original I-E. Q, whereas the first F of *fimf*

represents secondary P and was changed either by the

same process of spirantization or by assimilation (as

Latin P was to Q)[3].

These coincidences between Celtic and Latin are

only a part of the agreement between them. Both, for

example, have the Genitive of O-stems in -*i*, Superla-

tives in (*iss*)*imus* (cf. Old Irish *nessam*, W. *nesaf*

"next"; and Gaulish *Uxama*), the lack of a special for

for the 2nd Person Plural of the Pres. Ind., the Medic

Passive Termination -*r* found also in Tocharian and

Hittite, and a Subjunctive in -*a*. Evidently, despite

heir totally different appearance, Latin and Celtic

are more closely related than Latin and Greek, though

he student, having to wrestle with the same syntac-

ical constructions in both (e.g. the Absolute Partici-

ial Clause and the Accusative and Infinitive) receives

he opposite impression.   In other words, within Indo-

uropean there was an Italo-Celtic group.

If Gaulish had not succumbed soon after A.D. 500,

e might have had a seventh Celtic language to cómpare

are.   As it is, what we can know of it is almost en-

irely lexical.   Its phonology can be deduced only

rom its orthography (in the Greek and Latin alphabets),

hich includes a few attempts at innovation, such as

he Ð and ÐÐ apparently representing the sound *ts*.   An

llusion in the second poem of Virgil's juvenile *Cata-*

epton (if it is by him) indicates that the Gauls had

 peculiar way of pronouncing T.   (Certainly their

neta sometimes stands for a T).   Probably too the

onsular official whom Augustus dismissed because he

rote *ixi* for *ipsi*[4] was of Gallic origin.   Its surviv-

ng vocabulary is enough to show that Gaulish belonged

o the P-group;   e.g. *petorritum* "a four-wheeled car-

iage", mentioned by Horace (*Epist.* 2, 1, 192) and the

name-element *epo* "horse" (Latin *equus*) as in *Epore-dorix* (Caesar *B.G.* 7, 38, 2) and *Eporedia* (Tacitus, *Hist.* 1, 70), the modern Ivrea. (As this links Gaulish with Oscan rather than with Latin, it is strange to find initial S preserved as in the names *Segomarus* ("Great strength") and *Senicius*[5]). The occasional loss of intervocalic G after aspiration reminds one of silent Irish *gh* (e.g. *Camulori* for *Camulorigi*) and of the fate fo such a G in Old Welsh, as seen in the name *Urien* out of *Urfien* out of *Urbgen*. No less than 180 Gaulish words, mostly agricultural, were absorbed into Latin and thence into French or its dialects; e.g. *carruca* (charrue) "cart", *soc* "ploughshare" (Ir. *soc*, W. *swch*), *leuga* (lieue) "league"[6].

Of its morphology we know hardly more for certain than that it had at least four Declensions correspond-ing to Noun-stems in *-a* and *-ia*, in *-o* and *-io* (includ-ing a Dative Plural in *-obo* corresponding to Irish *-aibh*), in *-i*, *-n*, and *g* (*-rix*), and in *-u*; that it had both a Strong and a Weak Preterite, with 3rd Person Plural in *-s* (as in Osco-Umbrian): *dede* and *iouru* "set up", and *karnitu* "statuit et locavit" (according to the Latin version *below* it), where the T represents the D of Germanic Weak Verbs. One of the rare complete

sentences must suffice as an example: ARE SEQUANI

AREOS IOURUS LUCEO NERTECOMA(RI or RIGI), which has

been translated:"On the Seine[7] (cf. *Aremorica*), the

neighbours set up Lucius to Nertecomar(ix)". It seems

also to have had a Past Participle; e.g. the name

Contextus (Latin *contectus* "covered" or possibly *cog-

natus*). As for what we would most like to know, the

mechanism of the language, its syntax, beyond the fact

that the sentence apparently did not begin with the

Verb - perhaps the result of Latin influence - there

is nothing.

Thanks, however, to the 58 Personal Names in

Caesar's *Commentaries on the Gallic War*[8], to the 112

Proper Names in Gallic inscriptions on stone or (from

the various potteries) on terra-cotta, to the 20 or so

words in the Vienna Gaulish-Latin Glossary (including

avallo "apple"), to a few others recorded in ancient

writers both Latin and Greek, and to such loan-words

as we have just seen in Gallo-Latin, Gaulish deserves

a place in our present study and will be called on

whenever it has something to contribute[9].

B. ANALYSIS

Having divided the Celtic family of six into two equal parts according to their treatment of I-G. K^w, we have now to see how these six members are related to each other in respect of their specifically Celtic phenomena, incidentally noticing any points of contact that these have with other members of the family.

1. The expression of the genitive of relation by juxtaposition and the ellipse of the first Definite Article:

Irish:	doras an tighe	)	
Gaelic:	dorus an tighe	)	
Manx:	dorrys y thie	)	the door of
Welsh:	drws y tŷ	)	the house
Cornish:	darras an chy	)	
Breton:	dor an ti	)	

Observation   (i) Goedelic, however, puts the second noun in the genitive case, because it has preserved its inflections (less so in Manx). Cf. p.262, n.4⁵

(ii) Cf. the "Construct State" in Hebrew and Arabic.

2. The invariable Relative Pronoun, with the case shown (a) by the appropriate Possessive Adjective before the relevant Noun or (b) by the appropriate pronominal Preposition (§ 13):

(a) "This is the boy whose father is ill" (lit.

"that his father is ill").

I.   Seo an gasur a bhfuil a athair tinn

G.   Seo an gille a bheil a athair tinn

W.   Dyma'r bachgen y mae ei dad yn sâl

C.   Otta an map yu[10] a das claf

B.   Setu ar paotr a zo klanv e dad

Obs. Manx uses the prepositional pronoun from *ec*
("at") in its emphatic form: *Shoh yn guilley
ta yn ayr echey ching.*

(b) "The country from which he came" (lit. "that

he came from it")

I.   An tir a dtainig se asti

W.   Y wlad y daeth ef ohoni

B.   Ar vro a zeueas anezi

Obs. (i) Gaelic prefers to put the Preposition
         before the Rel. Pron., as in English:
         An dùthcha as an tàinig e.

   (ii) Manx again uses the appropriate emphatic
        prepositional pronoun, putting it in the
        place of the Relative: *Yn cheer voishyn*
        ("from it") *haink eh.*

  (iii) Cornish uses *may* (*mayth* before vowels in
        all senses, or omits the Rel. Pron. and
        uses the pronominal Preposition: *An pow
        may teth ef* or *An pow deth ef anodho.*

   (iv) Some parts of Brittany use *ma* instead of
        a, but still have the pronominal Preposi-
        tion after it.

    (v) In both (a) and (b) Irish and Gaelic use
        the dependent form of the Verb.

   (vi) Irish "a" with the dependent form of the
        Verb can also mean "all that":

Ar dhiol tú a rabh de chapaill agat?
Did you sell (all that you had of i.e.)
all your horses?

Gach duine da rabh i lathair
Everyone (of all who were) present.

The Gaelic equivalent is *na: Roinn iad na
fhuair iad de iasg* "They divided what they
had of fish" (i.e. "all their fish")

The Manx equivalent *ny* is also the ordinary Rel. Pron. (§ 10.) (But cf. the
phrase for "Once upon a time": *Keayrt dy
row* "A time of those that were").

(vii) An invariable Rel. Pron. is used in the
same way in Slovene and Arabic.

3. Plural Nouns take a singular Verb:

I. Tá na fir sa tigh   )
) The men are in the house.
W. Y mae'r dynion yn y tŷ)

Obs. (i) This does not show in Goidelic, because
the 3rd Person Plural is the same as the
singular.

(ii) Plural Personal Pronouns however take the
Plural.

(iii) The Rel. Pron. "a" takes a singular Person
after a plural antecedent.

4. The sentence normally starts with the Verb:- "The
woman came"

I. Thainig an bhean

G. Tàinig a' bhoirannach

M. Haink yn ven

W. Daeth y wraig

C. Deth an venen

B. Devas ar wreg

Obs. Gaelic *bean* and Cornish *gwrek* are used in the
sense of "wife"; Welsh *benyw* in the sense of
"female".

This order is frequently disturbed by another

characteristic, viz.

5. An aptitude and fondness for emphatic expression:

A. The subject can be emphasized by being put first;

but then it is felt as dependent on an understood

"It is", and so must be followed by a Relative

Clause:-

"(It is) the woman (who) came"

I. (Is é) an bhean a thainig

G. Is a'boirannach a thàinig

C. An venen a dheth

B. Ar wreg a zeuas

Obs. (i) Welsh uses its unique *sydd* "who (which)
is": *Y wraig sydd wedi dod.* But when the
Complement is a Demonstrative Pronoun or
includes the Def. Art., the Present Tense
of the Verb To Be is *yw* (cf. Cornish
below) (and the negative of *sydd* is *nyd yw*
"who is not"): *Melltigedig yw pob un nid
yw yn aros* ("Cursed is everyone that con-
tinueth not").

(ii) Cornish and Breton use this word-order
without any idea of emphasis (the so-
called "impersonal" construction, the verb
after "a" being always 3rd Person singular):

C. My a red)
) it is I who reads
B. Me a lenn)

instead of

C. redyaf)
)   I read
B. lennan)

So with the verb *To be*:-

C. My yu[11]   instead of   Yth of)
) I am
B. Me a zo   "   "   Oun)

(iii) So too when the Object is emphasized (but
      then the Person of the verb in the Rela-
      tive Clause varies with that clause's
      subject):

      C. Ger a redyaf   ) It is a word which I
)
      B. Eur ger a lennan) am reading

(iv) Other parts of the sentence may also be
     emphasized by being put first, the Welsh
     Relative Particle then varying according
     as the Relative Pronoun is subject/object
     or in some other case (as after an adverb
     phrase).

B. When the Verb is emphasized, it is also put first

   in the Infinitive (Verbal Noun) and picked up by

   the Verb *To do* in the Relative Clause:

I. Leigheamh a ghniodh sé)
)
W. Darllen a wnai ef   )
) He was reading (lit.
C. Redya a wre   ) "Reading is what he was
) doing").
B. Lenn a ree   )

Obs. (i) Irish, Welsh and , less often, Cornish use
       the Verb *To be* in the Rel. Cl., treating
       the Verbal Noun as a Participle (though
       Welsh omits "yn" before it); so:

       I. (Is) ag leigheamh atá se)
) lit. "Reading
       W. Darllen y mae ef   ) he is "
)
       C. Ow redya yma ef   )

(ii) Breton uses these two "emphatic forms of
expression with little difference of meaning; i.e. *me a skriv* = skriva a ran = "I
am writing".

(iii) Cornish usually combines them, and then emphasis is achieved, e.g.

Redya my a wra I shall write (lit. "(It is)
writing (that it is) I who shall do").

(iv) Different is the use of the Verb *To do* as
an Auxiliary Verb (§ 11c).

C. Welsh has a Particle *mai* (*taw* in the south) to em-

phasize part of an Indirect Statement ("that it is

. . . that"):

Dywedir mai torri ei galon a wnaeth It is said that
it is break his heart that he did (i.e. that what he
did was to break his heart).

Gwn mai gwr Duw ydwyt ti I know 'tis a man of God
you are (i.e. that you *are*, as you claim, a man of
God).

Obs. This Particle is now used even after *gan* ("since")
and *pam* ("why"): *Gan mai eu methiant hwy sydd
wedi achosi'r syfyllfa* ("since it is their failure that has caused the situation"); *deall pam
mai Cymry brwd yw gwrthwynebwyr* ("to understand
why it is fervent Welshmen who are opponents").

6. The Mutations (phonetic changes in some initial consonants under certain conditions; viz. by Aspiration
Eclipse, Softening, and Nasalization)[12].

There is, however, considerable variation among the

six (and even among the four main dialects of Irish);

and comparison is complicated by the different termino-

logy employed for each of the languages. Irish, for

example, speaks of Aspiration and Eclipse; Welsh of

Aspirated, Soft and Nasal Mutations; while Cornish

and Breton have also Hard (B. Reinforced) and Mixed

Mutations, but lack the nasal one. These terms over-

lap in varying degrees: thus Irish Aspirates are so-

called only because an H is introduced after the affec

ed letter; but while this equates PTC with the Welsh

Aspirates (though Irish TH is pronounced H), the other

aspirated letters have nothing to do with aspiration

as a sound, being variously Fricatives and Spirants (*Bh*

and *Mh*, pronounced V or W according as the following

vowel is "broad" (a, o, u) or "narrow"). They may

lose their sound altogether (as do medial *dh*, *gh*, and

initial *fh* and *sh*[13], or take on a sound peculiar to

Irish (as does initial *gh*).

Nor are its "eclipsed" letters any more phonetical

homogeneous, comprising as they do the sonant Occlusive

(b, d, g), the Nasals (m, n, ng), and the labio-velar

(*bhf*). Similarly, the Welsh "Soft" letters include th

sonant (voiced) Occlusives B, D, G, the Fricatives F

(pronounced V) and DD (voiced *th*), the Liquids L and R,

and silent (unwritten) G; and its Aspirates have a

corresponding nasal form (*mh*, *nh*, *ngh*). Thus Irish

Aspiration covers two of the three Welsh classes of
Mutation, and Nasals are grouped under the Eclipsed,
so-called because G is "eclipsed" by the prefixed N.
(In fact the two letters coalesce to produce a Nasal,
as in the Genitive Plural after the Def. Art., e.g.
Dun na nGall "Castle of the foreigners", known to us
as Donegal, whereas, when B eclipses P etc., the voiced
sound *replaces* the unvoiced).

Moreover, while Cornish Aspirate and Soft Mutations
are similar to Welsh under the same names, and its Hard
and Mixed are similar to Breton's, Breton itself describes its "Soft" mutations as "accommodated to their
vowels" and calls its Aspirates "Spirants".

It is clear, therefore, that however useful this
nomenclature may be for teaching these languages, it
must be abandoned in any comparative study such as the
present. Like must be compared with like, and the
likeness is phonetic.

Let us see Mutation at work on two occasions:

A. After the Possessive Adjective

  (i) "my": Irish, Gaelic, Manx, Cornish and Breton
     aspirate; Welsh nasalizes ; e.g. "my country":

I. mo thir	*C.* ow thyr	(Gaelic would use
G. mo thir	*B.* va zir	*dùchtha*, Welsh
M. my heer	*W.* fy nhir[14]	*Gwlad* in the sense
		of "motherland")

(ii) "thy": Irish, Gaelic, Manx aspirate; Welsh, Cornish, Breton "soften"; e.g. "thy house":

I. do theach   *W.* dy dy

G. do thaigh   *C.* dha jy

M. dty hie   *B.* da di

(iii) "his": as for "thy": e.g. "his dog":

I. a chủ[15]   *W.* ei gi

G. a chù   *C.* y gy

M. e choo   *B.* e gi

(iv) "her": Goidelic leaves consonants unchanged; Brythonic aspirates; e.g. "her dog":

I. a cú   *W.* ei chi

G. a cù   *C.* y hi

M. e coo   *B.* he c'hi

Obs. Before a vowel, however, *a* ("her") requires the insertion of H, except in Cornish. In Breton it is added to the pronoun: e.g. "her soul".

I. and *G.* a h-anam; *M.* a h-annym;
W. ei henaid; *B.* heh ene;   but *C.* hy enef.

(v) "our" "your" "their": In Irish all eclipse; in Gaelic, "our" and "your", though the same words as the Irish (*ar*, *bhur*) and "their" (*an*, which becomes, as always, *am* before *b*, *p*, *f*, *m*) do not mutate; in Manx the word *nyn* used for all three eclipses, but the phonetic spelling changes the initial letter according to the sound; in Welsh and Cornish "our" and "your" do not mutate, but Welsh "their" does, while Cornish "their" aspirates C, K, P, T, thus agreeing with Breton as far as K, P, T are concerned. Breton, however, conforms in not mutating after "our" (*hon*) though it changes the pronoun itself to *hor* before consonants other than N, D, T, L, H, and to *hol* before L, but goes its own way in mutating by "reinforcement" (i.e. changing sonants to surds after "your" (*ho*).

Before a vowel Eclipsing means the insertion
of N in Irish and Gaelic, except after the latter's *an (am)* "their", which, ending itself in
a nasal, does not require another. So too
Manx *nyn* requires no further N (e.g. G. *an
athair*, M. *nyn ayr*, but I. *a n-athair*). In
Brythonic the inserted sound is H; but Welsh
and Cornish agree again in not inserting it
after "your" but in inserting it after "their",
though it is with Breton that Cornish agrees
in not inserting it after "our" e.g.:-

(a) "our cow"

	our	*your*	*their*	*cow*
I.	ár	bhur	a	mbó
G.	ar	bhur	am	bó
M.	nyn	nyn	nyn	mooa
W.	ein	eich	eu	bo
C.	agan	agas	aga	bugh
B.	hor buoc'h	ho puoc'h	o	buoc'h

(b) "our soul":

I.	ár	bhur	a	n-anam
G.	ar	bhur n-anam	an	anam
M.	nyn	nyn	nyn	annym
W.	ein henaid	eich enaid	eu	henaid
C.	agan enef	agas enef	aga	h-enef
B.	on ene	hoc'h ene	o	ene

Obs. (i) Only Irish justifies the term "Eclipse"
by actually writing down both initial consonants. Manx reproduces the sound, which
is not always that of the first of the two
consonants of the Irish, so that the appearance of the same word is often completely
changed; e.g. beside *nyn mooa* above, *nyn
badjer (ár bpaidir)* "our prayer" *nyn gharey
(ár ngardha)* "our garden" *nyn volt (ár
bhfolt)* "our hair", and *nyn dhalloo (ár*

dtalamh) "our ground", we have *nyn
ghooinney* (*ár nduine*) "our man" (from
dooinney), *nyn jeer* (*ár dtir*) "our land"
(from *cheer* (*tir*) with T palatalized by
following I in contrast to *thalloo* above),
and *nyn Yee* (*ár nDia*) "our God" (from *Jee*
(*Dia*) similarly palatalized; cf. *dooinney*
above).

(ii) Brythonic has special forms for the Possessive Adjective after certain words, with
varying mutation; e.g.

W.: after *and, with, to, from*: e.g. "and my"
is *a'm*, which does not nasalise, but
aspirates a vowel, whereas the others
(*a'th* "and thy" etc.) mutate as before:
a'm tir "and my country".

C.: after *and, to, of*: e.g. "and my" is *h'am*;
but only *'th* ("thy") mutates, and now by
"mixed mutation" (softening or surdizing
or aspirating according to the consonant):

		(torn "hand" (but *dha dhorn*)
·ha'th	"and thy")	(hallos "power"(" " *allos*)
dhe'th	"to thy")	(clogh "bell" (" " *glogh*)
a'th	"of thy")	(wely "bed"(as before)(from *gwely*)
		(wolok "sight"(" ")(from *golok*)

(Note: "of our (your, their)" are written
a'gan, a'gas, a'ga)

B.: after *to, in*: e.g. "to my is *d'am*, which
continues to aspirate K and T but not P:
d'am c'hi "to my dog", but d'am pabell
"to my tent" (against *va fabell* "my tent")
But *d'az* "to thy", *ez* "in thy" surdize

("reinforce") sonants instead of conversely; e.g. *d'az preur* "to thy brother"
(*breur*), *ez kodell* "in thy pocket" (*godell*)
(against *da vreur, da c'hodell*)

B. After the Definite Article

All agree in mutating the initial consonant of
feminine Nouns in the singular Nom. and Acc., but the
mutation varies: unlike the others, which "soften",
Irish aspirates C and P and does not change D and
T; Breton (which adapts the final consonant of the
Article to the following initial; v. below § 7) also
does not change D, and changes G to C'H (but drops G
before W); and Cornish changes GO to W. E.g.

	the	*chair*	*cow*	*goat*	*goose*	*leaf*
I.	an	chathaoir	bhó	ghabhar[17]	gé[17]	duilleog
G.	a'	chathair	bho	ghabhar	ghéad	duilleag
M.	yn	chaair	vooa	ghoayr	ghuiy	duillag
W.	y[16]	gadair	fuwch	afr	wydd	ddeilen
C.	an	gadar	vugh	avar	woth	dhelen
B.	ar	gador	vuoc'h	c'havr	waz	delienn

Obs. (i) Manx has also some idiosyncrasies of its own:-
B before W is dropped in a few words: *bwoailey*
"striking", but *yn woailley* "the blow".
B before OO may become W (corresponding to
Irish BH before a "broad" vowel): *yn wooa*
instead of *yn vooa* "the cow".
QU becomes WH: *Quaiyl* "court", but *yn whaiyl*.

(ii) Breton also mutates masc. sg. Nouns beginning
with K (but to C'H, not to G): *ar c'haier*
"the exercise book".

(iii) Both Cornish and Breton mutate masc. plur.
Nouns denoting persons: "the boys" - *an
vebyon, ar baotred.*

(iv) Breton also mutates fem. plur. Nouns denoting
persons and masc. plur. of nouns denoting
animals and things when they begin with K
(which becomes C'H as in ii): *ar c'heginerezed*
"the cooks", *ar c'hezeg* "the horses", *ar
c'hirri* "the carts".

(v) Cornish mutates a few miscellaneous masculine
Nouns after the Def. Art. (e.g. *deth* "day",
but *an jeth*), and even has its one and only
nasal change in *an nor* (masc.) "the earth",
in the sense of "world", thus distinguishing
from *an dor* "the earth" in the sense of
"ground". Similarly in Breton *dor* "door",
but *an nor*.

(vi) The Goidelic Article also mutates in the Gen.
sg. masc. and the "Dative" (Prepositional)
case of both genders, and before a vowel requires the insertion of H in the Gen. sg.
fem. and in all cases of the Plural, both
genders, except the Genitive, which prefixes
N and eclipses a consonant:-

fear "man": an fhir "of the man" (G. a' fhir;
        M. yn fir)

bád (m) "boat": ins an bhad "in the boat" (G.
        anns a' bhata; M. sy bhaatey)

guala (f) "shoulder": ar an ghualainn "on the
        shoulder" (G. air a' ghuaillinn; M. er y
        gheaylin)

obair (f) "work": na h-oibre "of the work" (G.
        ditto; M. ny h-obbyr)

Albanach "Scotsman": na h-Albanaigh "the Scots-
        men" (G. na h-Albannaich; M. ny Albanee)

ubh (f) "egg": leis na h-uibheacha "with the
        eggs" (G. leis na h-uighean; M. lesh ny
        oohyn)
                : na n-uibheach "of the eggs" (G.
        nan ugh; M. ny oohyn)

cailin "girl": scoil na gcailiní "the
girls' school" (G. sgoil nan caileag;
M. schoill ny 'neen)

Obs. The table reveals some disagreement
within the Goidelic family: Gaelic Gen.
plur. Def. Art. is always *nan* (*nam* before the letters b, f, m, p: *mìos nam pòg*
"the month of kisses" (honeymoon)); the
Gen. plur. of many masc. Nouns (and *ugh*
is masc.'.) is the same as the Nom. sg.
(as is also that of some feminines);
nan (*nam*) does not mutate; Manx *ny* does
not take H and is also Gen. plur. without
taking N. but otherwise "eclipsing".

(vii) Goidelic also prefixes T (a relic of an old
Def. Art.) to masc. Nouns beginning with a
vowel in Nom. and Acc. sg. (e.g. *an t-Ultach*
"the Ulsterman"), and to all nouns beginning
with S followed by a vowel or by *n, l, r* on
the following occasions; e.g. (confining
ourselves to Irish):

masc. Gen. sg. teach an tsagairt "the priest's
house"

fem. Nom. and Acc. sg. an tsuil "the eye"

m. and f. Dat. sg. ar an tsraid "on the street"

Obs. In Manx the presence of the T is indicated
by orthographic changes; e.g. "the eye"
y tooil; "the street" *y traid*; "the bee"
(shellan[18]) *yn çhellan*; "the rod" (slat)
yn clat (through *tlat*)

7. The lack of an Indefinite Article:

Here of course they agree with Latin and Slavonic;

but Breton, perhaps under French influence, has devel-

oped one, which, like the Def. Art., mutates and adapts

its last letter to the following initial; e.g. *eur gador*

"a chair", *eun daol* "a table", *eul loc'h* "a lake".

8. <u>An interrogative Particle introducing a question</u>
(followed by Mutation and, where it exists, the dependent form of the Verb). Here again there is one
exception: Manx omits the Particle. (Cornish omits
it only before vowels of *bos* "to be" and *mos* "to go"):

	Is he?	*Did you hear?*
I.	An bhfuil sé?	Ar chuala sibh?
G.	A bheil e?	An do chuala sibh?
M.	Vel eh?	Cheayll shiu?
W.	A ydyw ef?	A glywsoch chwi?
C.	Yu ef?	A glewsough-why?
B.	Hag hen a zo?	Ha te a glevas?
	(lit. Is it he who is?)	

Obs. (i) Before the Past Tense of Regular Verbs Irish
changes *An* (with Eclipse) to *Ar* with *Aspiratio*
(that being the feature of Active Past Tense
initial letters in all Goidelic), whereas
Gaelic combines *An* with the preterite Particle
do.

(ii) For negative questions, instead of the *nach*
(G. *nach*(do), M. *nagh*) of Goidelic, Cornish
and Breton simply put the interrogative Particle before the negative, and Welsh uses its
unique *Oni* (aspirating C, P, T). Hence:

I.   Nach gcuala sibh?

G.   Nach do chuala sibh?

M.   Nagh geayll shiu?

W.   Oni chlywsoch chwi?

C.   A ny welsough-whi?

B.   Ha ne glevjoc'h ket?

Obs. Gaelic, as usual, does not eclipse
(because it keeps the Particle *do*; but

even the Future would be *Nach cluinn tu?*
(with termination *idh* dropped, as also
after *An*) against Irish *Nach gcluinfidh
tú?*

9. The Impersonal Verb and the Passive

The characteristic letter, R, is found also in
Latin, Hittite, and Tocharian; but because the Impersonal Form ("There is a -ing") is similar to the Passive in the absence of reference to an agent, Latin
took the bold step of extending it from the 3rd
Person sing., to which it naturally belongs, to all the
other Persons except the 2nd plur. (e.g. *amoR, amabaR,
amaboR, reguntuR, auditoR*). Celtic, however, with the
exception of Manx, which has lost it, uses the form
in its original sense, so much so that it appears even
in the verb *To be*. E.g.: "The book is being read"
(Latin: *liber legitur*) is expressed as "There is a
reading (of) the book":-

I. Léightear an leabhar
W. Darllenir y llyfr
C. Redyer an lyver
B. Lenner al levr

Obs. (i) So with other tenses: e.g. "was read":
       léighadh, darllenwyd, redyas, lennyod.

   (ii) Brythonic inflected Present Tense is strictly
        a Future; and in Gaelic these "Present" end-

ings form the Future Passive, i.e. *Leughear
an leabhar* means only "The book will be read";
for which Irish uses its special Future Tense
consonant F: *léighfear*. Gaelic in fact has
lost even the form of the Present Active, and
Manx uses it as a Future.

The Impersonal Forms of the Verb *To Be* are:-

I. tathar   )
)
G. thathar   )
)
W. yr ydys   )   "One is"
)
C. eder   )
)
B. oar   )

Obs. (i) So with the other tenses; e.g. the Past "One
           was": I. *bithear* G. *bhatar* W. *buwyd* C. *bes*
           B. *boed.*

      (ii) For the use of Impersonal *tathar* etc. with the
           Present Participle to form Passive Continuous
           Tenses see § 11.

When it comes to expressing the Passive in other

ways, there is considerable divergence. Welsh, not

having a Past Participle, uses the verb *cael* ("get")

with the Verbal Noun and a Possessive Adjective, so

that the above sentence can also be expressed by *y mae'r

y llyfr yn cael ei ddarllen* (lit. "the book is getting

its reading"). This idiom is particularly used when

the time is continuous ("is being"). Irish too uses

the Verbal Noun qualified by a Possessive Adjective,

but these are then dependent on the Verb *To Be* and the

preposition *do*, and used mostly for the 3rd Person:
Tá litir d'a scríóbhadh ("A letter is being written"),
Béidh na preataí da gcur ("The potatoes will be being
sown"). To the phrase *Ta mé do mo (ta tú do do)*
bhualadh the Impersonal Passive is preferred.

The Past Participle is used, where it exists,
i.e. outside Welsh, mostly to form the Perfect Passive,
the emphasis being on the completion of the act;
Goidelic, not having a Perfect Active Tense, is often
obliged to have recourse to this form; e.g. the
Irish *Ta se déanta agam* (lit. "It is done by me", i.e.
"I have done it"). All the other Celtic languages can
(as I-E. usually does) use their Past Participle with
the Verb *To Be* as one of the alternative ways of expressing the Passive; e.g. in the Preterite, for
"he was killed": G.*Bha e marbhte,* M. *Va eh marrit,* C.
Ef a ve ledhys, B. *Hen a voe lazhet.* Cornish and
Breton can then distinguish state from action by using
the Imperfect instead of the auxiliary *(Ef o*[10] -, *hen*
a oa -).

Welsh, however, overcame the lack of a Past Participle by the use of the Preposition *wedi* ("after")
with the Verbal Noun; i.e. "after seeing" = "seen";

and whether this is Active or Passive depends on whether or not there is a Possessive Adjective before the Verbal Noun referring back to the subject of the sentence. Thus *y maent wedi fy ngweled* "they are after my seeing" is Active i.e. "they have seen me"; but *y maent wedi eu gweled* "they are after their seeing my" is Passive, i.e. "they have been seen"[19].

Obs. The change from the Present of the Verb *To be* to the Imperfect (*yr oeddent wedi fy ngweled*) provides a Pluperfect ('they had seen me"), which is useful to Welsh, because its normal form in *-aswn*, except in dependent clauses, is used mostly in the sense of "could (would) have".

Goidelic also uses a Preposition with the Verbal Noun to form a Past Participle, but here the Preposition is that for "on".

G.   Tha mi air teachd)
) I have come (lit. "am on coming")
M.   Ta mee er jeet   )

The Irish *ar* in this idiom is found only when a Possessive Adjective makes the Verbal Noun equivalent to a Passive Participle as shown above.

Eagran nua ar n-a chur in eagar ag . . . A new edition arranged by . . .

Tá an cuid is mó diobh ar na n-eadartheangadh o'n Bhearla. Most of them have been translated from the English.

G. *Bha treubhan nan Cruithneach air an ("their")*

tional fo Chalgach.

M. *Va cleinyn ny Gruithneeyn er nyn jaglym fo Chalgach.*

("The tribes of the Picts were assembled (lit. "on

their assembling") under Calgacus).

Strictly this Past of state is equivalent to a

Pluperfect of action: "had been assembled" (cf. Latin

collecti erant).

For the real Perfect Passive, however, Manx uses

the Preposition *er* with the Infinitive *To be* and the

grammatical Past Participle, i.e. says "is on (after)

being -", i.e. "has been"; e.g.

Ta'n thie er ve lhieggit   The house has been demolished

for which the Gaelic equivalent would be   *Tha an taigh*
                                              iar a leagadh[20]

Obs. (i) The existence of the Past Participle of some
intransitive Verbs allows Irish to form a
Perfect Active with the Verb *To be* as auxiliary
(cf. Verbs of Rest and Motion in French and
Italian); e.g. from *imeacht* to go away, and
from *teacht* to come:

Bheidis imithe abhaile/they would have gone home
Tá Tomás tagtha abhaile/Thomas has come home

A Welsh Continuous Perfect can be formed with
the Perfect of *Bod* and the Verbal Noun; e.g.

Bûm yn canu/I have been singing

Cornish has Perfects only for MOS ("go") and
DOS ("come"), but like Old Irish (Goidelic!)
converts the Preterite of other Verbs to the
Perfect by prefixing the Particle RE (cf.

Goidelic AR above,) e.g. *re-dhyskys* "I have
learnt". Breton, perhaps under French influence, uses the locution *am eus* (lit.
"there is to me" and so "I have") as an
Auxiliary Verb with the Past Participle and
an object; but if this object is a Personal
Pronoun, the Possessive Adjective is used instead in accordance with Celtic usage (and
the neutrality of the Verbal Noun);e.g. *Me
am eus o galvet* "I have called them" (lit.
"there is to me their called").

(ii) The use of "after" with the Verbal Noun is
found also in Irish, but then the implication
is that the action has "just" been performed:
Ta mé indiaidh (or tareis) teacht "I have
just come".

(iii) Gaelic also devised a Preterite Passive formed
from the Verbal Noun and the Possessive Adjective, but made them dependent on the Past
Tense of the Verb *To Go (chaidh)*; e.g. *Chaidh
mo bhualadh* (lit. "my striking went", i.e.)
"I was struck". Manx can also, at least with
some verbs, use the verb for "go" for the Preterite Passive, but it then has a personal
subject: *Hie eh er coayl* (lit. "He went upon
losing" i.e.) "He was lost" (cf. Italian *andò
perduto*). Gaelic uses this same phrase *air
chall* with the Verb *To be*.

The link between the Passive and the Verbal
Noun plus Possessive Adjective is shown by
such usages as that in the Irish proverb: *Ma's
maith leat do mholadh, fagh bás; ma's maith
leat do chaineadh, pós.* "If you want to be
praised, die; if you want to be abused,
marry").

10. Tenses of the Verb To Be

(a)   Every one of the six languages except Manx has a

Present and Past of Habit, and Welsh has also a second

Past Tense for continuous action (*oeddwn*). A peculiarit

is the use of the Habitual Present as a Future also

(except in Breton), though in Irish this sense is

confined to dependent clauses; e.g. after *mă* ("if"):

I. *bim, bionn*; W. *byddaf*; C. *bydhaf*; and even Manx

has a special form for the Future after *my* ("if"): *my*

vees ee ("if she will be"). But the Celtic verb has

no simple Present Tense (v.§ 9, *Obs*. ii): in Irish,

except for verbs concerned with the senses, the basic

reference is to habit; in Welsh, to the future, of

which a trace is to be seen in the Irish rule that this

tense must be used after *nî shilim* ("I do not think"),

nî doigh ("it is improbable") etc., in order to express

the Future: e.g. *nî doigh (doiche) go dtig sê* (" . . .

that he will come", instead of *dtiocfadh*).

(b) Cornish has a variety of forms for the Present

Tense of BOS. There are five equivalents of "he is"

and three of "they are", the choice depending on the

type of sentence. In Goidelic there are special forms

for the Present and Future in all (except a few) verbs

in the Relative Clause: *a* ("which") *bhîos, bhêas,*

bhuaileas ("which is, will be, strikes"), which is se-

mantically useful in Manx, where the Relative Pronoun

ny is usually omitted, especially in the Nominative:

e.g. *She mish loayrys* (not *ny loayree*) *rish* ("It is I
who will speak to him"); cf. G. *Is mi a labhaireas
rish*). Goidelic has a special form of the Verb *To Be*
in Negative and Interrogative sentences: *bhfuil, raibh*
(Manx: *vel, row*) for Present and Imperfect respectively,
and this form is used also after the negative Relative
Pronoun *nach* (Manx: *nagh*). In Brythonic, Welsh has a
special form of the Verb *To Be* in such cases only in
the 3rd Persons of the Present, *y mae* and *y maent.*
becoming *nid* (*nad*) *ydyw*, *nid* (*nad*) *ydynt*. (*Nid* may
still be used with *ydyw*, *ydynt*, in Relative Clauses
instead of *na*(*d*)). In Cornish *yma* ("is", of place)
cannot be negatived (the equivalent negative being
nyns us), but in Breton the corresponding *eman* has the
normal negative *n'eman ket*. It is interesting that
Breton has a Past Participle for its Verb *To Be* (*Bezan*),
namely *bet*. Did the others lose it or did Breton in-
vent it?

11. Special features of Verbs:

(a) The lack of an Indo-European Present Participle:

Its place is taken by the Verbal Noun dependent
on a Preposition; viz. I. *ag* (G. *a'* before a consonant),
W. *yn*, C. *ow*, (which unvoices sonants , thereby being

distinguished from *ow* "my", which aspirates surds),

B. *O* (which "mixes" its mutations, thereby being dist-

inguished from *O* "their", which aspirates surds). In

Manx *ec* is seen only when the Verbal Noun begins with

a vowel, for it is then prefixed as the letter G: *Ta*

mee screeu ("I am writing"), but *Ta mee geeck* ("I am

paying"). Thus not all words beginning with G are

found under this letter in the dictionary.

As this substitute for a Present Participle is in

fact composed of a Preposition and a Noun, the Object

must be in the Genitive, though this is visible only

in those languages which have preserved their Declen-

sions, viz. Irish, Gaelic and, to a lesser extent,

Manx, e.g.

I. Bhí sé ag baint an fheir   ) He was cutting the
G. Bha e a' gearradh an fheðir) grass (lit. he was at
) the cutting of the
M. Va eh giarey yn faiyr (nom)) grass)

(The Brythonic of this is : *W.* Yr oedd ef yn torri'r
gwellt; *C.* Yth esa ow treghy an wels; *B.* En a oa
troc'han ar c'hlazenn).

When the Object is a Pronoun, we are back again with

the Possessive Adjective (i.e."at (in) his striking"

for "striking him"), except in Manx, which, omitting

the Preposition, can put the Pronoun after the Verbal

Noun   (even when it has prefixed G); e.g.

I. Tá sé (ag) mo bhualadh)

G. Tha e gam bhualadh   )

W. Mae'n fy nharo i   )   He is striking me (lit. He

C. Yma orth[21] ow hnoukya)   is at my striking)

B. Eman ouz va c'hwistan)

but *M.* T'eh bwoailley mee

Obs. For the same phenomenon in the Past see § 9.
Hence the Continuous Tense in the Passive can be
rendered by the Impersonal Form:-

> *G.* Thatar ag mo (or 'gam) bhualadh - I am being
>
> hit (lit. There is a being at my hitting)

Obs. Gaelic uses *Thatar* with *air* and the Verbal Noun
(cf. above § 9, to form a Perfect Passive; e.g.
Thatar air mo bhualadh "I have been struck",
which is an alternative to *Tha mi air mo bhualadh*

(b)   A Particle before the Past Tense:

In Goidelic *do* before a vowel or F (*d'iarr sé* "he

asked", *d'fhregair sé* "he answered", cf. Manx *dreggyr*)

but it is optional in Manx affirmative statements, e.g

daink mee or *haink mee* ("I came"). In Irish, negative

Adverbs as well as other Adverbs, interrogative Part-

icles, and the Conjunctions "that" and "unless" have a

characteristic final consonant, R (relic of the old

Preterite Particle *ro*): *Ar, nar, car* ("Where?"), *gur,*

munar ("unless"). Gaelic, however, keeps *An* with *do*,

and also *gu'n* (Irish *go*). In Brythonic, the Cornish *R*

besides changing a Preterite into a Perfect, e.g.

re-dhyskys "I have learnt", also changes a Present Sub-

junctive into an Optative: *Dew re-dhanvonno* ("God send"),

as it does also in Breton (*Doue ra danvono*); for which

the Goidelic Particle is *go* (Manx *dy*). Welsh and

Cornish *A* and Breton *Ha*(*g*) do not suffer change with a

Past Tense (§ 8).

c. The Verb To Do as an Auxiliary Verb:

In Gaelic, Manx and Cornish it is used with the

Infinitive (Verbal Noun) as in English, but without any

idea of emphasis:-

G. Rinn mi bualadh an dorus   ) I struck the door
M. Ren mee bwoailley yn dorrys) (lit. "I did strike
C. My a wruk knoukya an dorras) the door")

When the Object is a Personal Pronoun, Gaelic and

Cornish use the Possessive Adjective with the Verbal

Noun in the manner already seen; e.g.

G. Rinn mi a bhualadh) I struck him
C. My a wruk y gnoukya) (lit. "I did his striking")

But Manx treats the Verbal Noun as an Infinitive

and makes it take an accusative Pronoun *after* it. Hence

Ren mee bwoailley eh for the above ("I did strike him").

Obs. (i) Particularly when several words intervene, Manx
        can put the Pronoun before the Verbal Noun
        preceded by the particle Y, but its case is
        still accusative: hence the above could be:
        Ren mee eh y bwoailley.

(ii) In Negative and Interrogative sentences, the use of the Verb *To do* in Manx is little more than a literal translation of the English:

Ren shiu rieau goll? Did you ever go?

Cha ren ee toiggal   She did not understand

(iii) Even in Irish the verb is used as an Auxiliary to stress the Infinitive, but as in Manx the preceding Pronoun is personal and accusative:

Rinne sé i a fhorbairt He did improve it

Rinneadh an leabhar seo a ullmú ag an Cholaist This book was prepared by the College

(iv) Auxiliary "do" frequently expresses the Future except in Irish and Breton; e.g.

G. *Ni* ("You will do") *thu mo bhualadh*) You
M. *Nee*[22] *oo bwoailley mee*   ) will
) strike
C. *Y-whreth ty ow hnoukya*   ) me

In Welsh it is mostly interrogative:-

A wnewch chwi fynd? Shall you go?
(M. Jean shiu goll?   C. A wreugh-why mos?)

(v) So in Manx the Conditional of *jannoo* ("to do") can serve as auxiliary "would":-

Yinnagh ee loayrt rish y moddey   "She would speak to the dog"

(vi) Cornish also uses *mynnaf* ("I wish"; W. *mynnu* B. *mennoud*) as a Future auxiliary: *A vynnough-why mos?* "Will you go?"

12. Infixed Pronouns

This is found in Old Irish (e.g. *ro-s-gab* "had seized them"; but is now a Brythonic feature.

(i)   With the Relative Pronoun (cf. § 5 A):

W. *Hi a'm gwelodd*)
C. *Hy a-m-gwelas*) She saw me (alternative to
)   *Gwelodd hi fi* etc.
B. *Hi am gwelas*)

(ii) With Negative Adverb:

 W. Ni'th welais)
 C. Ny-th-welys) I did not see you (alternative
 B. N'ez kwelis ket) to *Ni welais di* or *mohonot*)

(iii) With Negative Relative Pronoun: only Welsh and

 Breton:

 W. Dwy gerdd nas clywswn
  Two songs which I had not heard

 B. Daou gan n'az plijont
  Two songs which do not please you

(iv) With Particle RE in the Optative: only Cornish

 and Breton:

 C. Lowena re'm bo! May there be joy for me!

 B. Sant Ildud r'am diwalo! May St. Ildud protect me!

(v) After the meaningless Particle *fe* (Welsh):

 Fe'm gwelodd She saw me (Cf. (i) above)

 Fe'ú ysgrifennwyd They were written

(vii) With Relative Particle *y* (Welsh):

 lle y'm ganed where I was born·

 Pan y'i sefydlwyd When it was founded[23]

(viii) After *Pa* (when), *Ma* (if), *Ra* (Optative "that")

 (Breton):

 P'az kwelan When I see you

 M'am gwel If he sees me

 R'am kwelan O that I may see you!

(ix) In Negative Command after *na* (Breton):

 N'am selaouit ket Do not listen to me

Obs. Breton's Infixed Pronouns are only of the 1st and
2nd Persons.

13. Pronominal Prepositions:

Goidelic and Brythonic agree in forming these

with all the more frequent Prepositions; e.g. with "on"

I. orm   *G.* orm   *M.* orrym)

W. arnaf *C.* warnaf *B.* warnon)   on me

with "between":

I. eadrainn *G.* eadarainn *M.* mastain[24])

W. rhyngom   *C.* yntredhon   *B.* enetrezom) between us

Obs. Breton has also the Impersonal: warnor "on one",
ganeor "with one".

Some of these are used with the Verb *To be* to form

Periphrases for Verbs, especially of certain emotions

and physical feelings such as fear, hunger, etc. e.g.

I. Tá eagla (ocras) orm   )   I am afraid (hungry)

M. Ta aggle (accyrys) orrym)   (lit. There is fear

W. Y mae arnaf ofn (newyn))   (hunger) on me)

Obs. (i) For these Cornish and Breton use the Verb *To
have* (Cornish also *To bear* (*perthy*) and *To
take* (*kemeres*):

   C. Perthaf own *B.* Aon am eus (§ 14) I am afraid

   (ii) Cornish does sometimes use the Verb *To be*, but
the Preposition is then *dhe* ("to"), not *gans*:

   Yma nown dhym or ewl dybry a-m-bus (§   14)
   I am hungry (lit. There is hunger to me or I
   have a desire to eat)

   Breton: naon am eus   I have hunger (as above)

   (iii) A preceding Prepositional Pronoun in Welsh
mutates the Noun.

So too "I prefer", taking "with" in Goidelic (le^{25})

and Brythonic (*gan*):

I.	Is fearr liom	)	
M.	Share lhiam	)	
		)	I prefer
W.	Y mae'n well gennyf	)	(lit. "It is better with
C.	Gwell yu genef	)	me")
		)	
B.	Gwell eo gan in	)	

So with the Infinitive (as Subject):

(Goidelic) *I.* Is maith liom bheith sa bhaile) "I like
            M. S' mie lhiam ve ec y thie   )) being
            W. Mae'n dda gennyf fod gartref)) (I am
                                                )) glad to
            C. Da yu genef bos yn-chy   )) be) at
                                                )) home"
            B. Da eo ganin beza er ger   ))

Obs. Cornish and Breton agree in extending the range
of such compounds: e.g.

    C. avello   *B. eveldan*   like him

    C. agesof   *B. egedoun*   than I

    C. a-*ughon*   *B.* a-*ziohon*   above us

To these Breton adds: *hervezoun* "according to me",
emezoun "I say" (parenthetic), *ac'hanoun*[26] "of me",
evidoun "for me", *davedoun* "towards me", *nemedoun*
"except me", *estregedoun* "other than I", *parvedoun*
"but for me".

Pronouns infixed in compound Prepositions are

found in all six; e.g. "after me":

I. in mo dhiadh (*M. my yei* or *my lurgh*)

W. ar fy ol C. war ow lergh B. war va lerc'h

14. Lack of a Verb *To have*:

All resort to the Verb *To be* with the preposition

"with" (Goidelic strictly "at") e.g. "I have butter"

is literally "There is butter with me":

I. Tá im agam

M. Ta eem aym

W. Y mae ymenyn gennyf

C. Yma genef amanyn

B. Amanenn a zo ganen

Cornish and Breton reveal their close relation-

ship in the possession of another way of saying "I

have" etc., viz.:

	Cornish		*Breton*
(my)	a-m-bus	(me)	am-eus
(ty)	a-th-us	(te)	az-peus[27]
(ef)	a-n-jeves	(en)	e-neus
(hy)	a-s-teves	(hi)	he-deus
(ny)	a-gan-bus	(ni)	on-eus
(why)	a-gas-bus	(c'hwi)	ho-peus[27]
(y)	a-s-teves	(i)	o-deus

In § 9, we saw that Breton goes so far as to use

this verbal periphrasis as an Auxiliary Verb with the

Past Participle. Even stranger is its use of the Past

Participle *bet* ("been") after *am eus* etc. to mean "had"

e.g. *naon am eus bet* "I have had hunger (i.e. been

hungry)". Hence for the Perfect Tenses of *To be* it has

to resemble German and Italian in using *To be* as the

Auxiliary: *me a zo bet* or *oun bet* "I am been" for "I

have been", *bezin bet* "I shall have been", etc. Moreover, since *beza* is used with the Past Participle to

form the Perfect Infinitive of all verbs (e.g. *beza*

graet "to have done"), the Perfect Infinitive *beza*

bet has the two meanings: "to have been" and "to have

had"!

For other missing verbs see pp.229 and 238.

15. The relationship between Subject and Complement:

In Welsh the indefinite Complement of the Verb

To be and some other Intransitive Verbs must be pre-

ceded by the Preposition *yn* (also used for making

Adverbs out of Adjectives, and "softening", except

Ll and *Rh*): e.g.

A ydych chwi'n barod?   Are you ready?

Y mae fy nhad yn feddyg   My father is a doctor

Obs. The only approach to this elsewhere in Brythonic
is the Cornish use of its adverbial *yn* before
predicative Adjectives of state e.g. *mos yn claf*
(no mutation!) "to go sick", especially a Past
Participle, e.g. *Whelas an nef yn ygerys* "He saw
heaven opened". (Cf. Irish: *Tá mé go maith* "I am
well").

This is the Brythonic indication of what is clearer

in Goidelic, that for Celts there was something special

about the substantive relationship. Here *Tá* requires

the Complement-Noun to be preceded by the Preposition

i in the sense of "in his state (capacity) of",

followed by the appropriate Possessive Adjective: e.g.

Irish:

Bhí sé i n-a rígh ar Eirinn   He was King of Ireland

Tá siad i n-a bpaistí go foill They are still children

Obs. In the emphatic form (§ 5): *Rígh a bhí ann;*
Paistí atá ionnta

So Gaelic: *Tha i 'na caileag mhath*
She is a good girl

Feumaidh gun robh so 'na shealladh
uamhasach
This must have been a terrifying sight

and in emphasis: *An e rathad math a tha ann?*
Is it a good road?

and Manx: *T'eh ny ree* He is a king
V'ee ny ben vie She was a good woman

The reason for this peculiar view of reality may

have something to do with the fact that the verb *Tá*

(as its Latin cognate *Stat* shows) did not originally

denote existence, and even now is strictly confined

to impermanent states and conditions[28]. Thus it has

to be used in the same way before Participles refer-

ring to the position of the body; e.g.

I. *Tamuid 'nar seasamh* We are (in our) standing up

G. *Tha sibh 'nur laighe* You are (in your) lying down

M. *T'eh ny hoie*   He is (in his) sitting down

I. *Bi do thost!*   Be (your) silent!   )with "in"

M. *Ta mee my chadley*   I am (in my) sleeping) understoo

Obs. (i) Cf. the Cornish use of the Preposition *a* ("of")
with the Possessive Adjective before *Stand,*
Sit, Lie:

My a wel an dheu dhen a'ga saf
I see the two men standing

So: *a'y eseth* (him) sitting;
a'y wroweth (him) lying down

There are two ways round this difficulty with *Tá*:

(a) to put the Preposition *ar* before the Complement:

Tá na "Chieftains" ar an ghrupa ceóil is fearr sa tir
The "Chieftains" are the best song-group in the country

Bhí sé ar bhuachaill comh breágh agus a casfair ort
He was as fine a boy as you would meet

Obs. This is especially frequent with the superlative
in the plural in the sense "one of the most ...":

Tá sé ar na fir is saidhbhe sa tir
He is one of the richest men in the country

(b)   to insert *mar* ("as") before the Complement:

Bhí an Club Leabhar mar lathair scaipiuchain
The Book Club was a distribution-point.

When the condition is a permanent one, however,

a different verb is used, namely IS (cognate with

Latin EST) (Past Tense BA), which requires no preposi-

tional link with the Complement, but is itself hedged

about with various requirements according as the

Complement is definite or indefinite, the Subject a

Demonstrative Pronoun or a Proper Name etc.; e.g.:

Is Éireannach mise   I am an Irishman
Is é seo mo pheann   This is my pen
Is i Nora an mhaighistreas Nora is the mistress
Is sibhse na paistí   You are the children

So in Gaelic: *Is iad na Romanaigh a thug duinn* "It was

the Romans who gave us". (There is no need to say

B'iad as the English has it, because it is always true

that the Romans gave). In Manx *Is* and *Ba* hardly

survive except (a) as a prefix to certain Adjectives

in such verbal phrases as we have already seen (§ 13),

e.g. *Shegin dou* "there is compulsion to me", i.e. "I

must" (v. § 20); (b) to emphasise the Subject of a

sentence, e.g. *She Yernaghyn t'aynin* (Irish: *Is*

Éireannaigh atá ionainn "They are *Irishmen*", lit.

"It is Irish men they are").

Obs. Introductory "It is" is always *Is* , and can even
     be omitted so long as the Relative Clause follows
     (v. § 5):

     (Is) ó Shéamus a fuair sé an t-airgead
     It is from James that he got the money

     In Negations and Questions IS disappears, the res-

pective particles being enough; e.g. (from Irish):

An Éireannach tusa?   Are you an Irishman?

Ní hé seo mo pheann   This is not my pen

Ní hí Nora an mhaighistreas Nora is not the mistress

Nach sibhse na paistí?   Aren't you the children?

In the Past the characteristic letter R (§   8) re-

appears:

Nior dhuine bocht é   He was not a poor man

Ar (Nar) dhuine saidhbhir é? Was he (not) a rich person

Obs. (i) But *gur* introduces the *Present* Tense in Indi-
         rect Statement: *Deirim gur duine saidhbhir é*
         "I say that he is a rich man". The Negative
         however, is *nach,* because *nar* is needed for

the Past, ("that he was not"). Similarly,
gurab é is the Indirect form of *Is é* and
becomes *gurbh'* (neg. *narbh'*) *é* in the Past.

(ii) The Manx Interrogative is *Nee*: *Nee Manninagh
eh*?   "Is he a Manxman? (*She*, "Yes"); and the
corresponding Negative is sometimes *Nagh*,
sometimes *Nagh nee*. Its equivalent to *gur*
is *dy nee*.

(iii) Manx is less strict about the substantive
relationship, especially in Indirect Statement, e.g.

*Cha nel mee smooinaghtyn dy vel mish yn
chied phersoon* . . .
I don't think that I am the first person . . .

(where Irish would have: *gur mise*).

This distinction between the two senses of *Being*

seems to have vanished from Brythonic. Traces of it

may perhaps be seen in (a) the use by Cornish and

Breton of a special form of the Verb *To be* for refer-

ence to Place (as in Spanish);   (b) the Welsh defective

verb OES ("There is") used as in the Druidic question

A oes heddwch? ("Is there peace?") (cf. Cornish *üs* and

Breton *eus*);   and (c) the ellipse of the *Verb To be* in

Welsh also before *sydd* (*sy'n*) ("who is"): *Pwy sy'n

dyfod*? ("Who is coming?"); *Fy nhad sy'n dyfod* ("It is

my father who is coming").

Obs. Thus Irish has six ways of expressing such a simple
idea as "She is a good girl":-

Is cailín maith í   She is a good girl

Is cailín maith atá inntí It is a good girl she is

Tá sí 'na cailín mhaith   She is a good girl (now

Is maith an cailín í   It's good the girl is

Is maith an cailín atá innti   There's a good girl

Cailín maith is eadh í[29]   A good girl she is

16. Lexicon

Many words in the six languages are derived from one and the same root:-

	Irish	*Manx*	*Welsh*	*Cornish*	*Breton*
bad	droch[30]	drogh	drwg	drok	drouk
bird	ean	eean	edn	edhen	evn[31]
brother	-bráthair[32]	braar	brawd	broder	breur
dog	cu	co	ci	ky	c'hi
dogs	coin[33]	coin	cwn	cun	kon
I hear	cluinim	cluinym	clywaf	clewaf	klevan
land	tir	cheer	tir	tyr	tir
sea	muir	muir	môr	mor	mor
black	dubh	doo	du	du	du
house	teach	thie	ty	chy	ti
pure	glan	glen	glan	glan	glan
rider	marcach	markiagh	marchog	marghak	marc'heg

Obs. (i) The Gaelic of these has not distanced itself from Irish except in the spelling *eun* ("bird") and in losing the Present Tense of *cluintinn*.

(ii) Sometimes the resemblance conceals a difference of usage; e.g. Goidelic *cu* means "hound", with which word it is cognate, K having become H in Germanic. (The word for "dog" is *madadh* (M. *moddey*), and a fox is a *madadh ruadh* ("red dog"), cf. rare Welsh *madyn*), as well as a *sionnach*. Similarly, the more common word for "sea", at least in Ulster, is *fairrge*. Note that Goidelic *muir* is feminine, Brythonic *mor* is masculine, while Latin *mare* is neuter!

Celtic *mor* survives in Morecambe Bay; cf.
the old name of Seatown: Moridunum.

(iii) The first eight of these words have cognates
in Latin: *trux* "grim", *penna* "wing"; *frater*;
canis; *inclitus* "famous"; *terra* ; *mare*.
Four of these are found also in Greek:
petomai; *phrater*[33a];*kyon* ; *klyo* (cf. the
Gaulish name-element *clouto*, etc. ("famous")
and Latin *inclitus* above: Verucloetius
(Caes. *B.G.*1,7,3), Clutorix). The genuinely
Celtic word for "horse", *marka* (mentioned by
Pausanias 10, 19, 11) has yielded in frequency
in Goidelic and Welsh, just as *equus* did in
Romance, to the Vulgar Latin *caballus* ("nag");
whence Irish *capall* (Manx *cabbyl*), Welsh
ceffyl; but not before giving to Germanic
the word *mare* (German *Mähre*, English *mare*;
cf. Anglo-Saxon *mearh* "horse", masculine).
Goidelic has also the Q-group cognate of
equus: *ech* (Gaelic *each*) corresponding to
P-group *hippos*, whence Cornish and Welsh *ebol*,
Breton *ebeul* ("foal"), and Gaulish names such
as *Eposognatus* (Livy 38,18,1) alongside
Equonius, Equirus.

Other words conceal this Goidelic-Brythonic

identity under the different guise that phonetic

evolution has conferred on them; e.g.:

		Irish	*Manx*	*Welsh*	*Cornish*	*Breton*
1.	eight	ocht	hoght	wyth	eth	eiz
2.	fish	iasc	eeast	pysg	pysk	pesk
3.	human being	duine	dooinney	dyn	den	den
4.	man	fear	fer	gwr	gour	gour
5.	old	sean	shenn	hen	hen	hen
6.	sister	-shiur	shuyr	chwaer	whor	c'hoar
7.	I take	beirim	goym	cymeraf	kemeraf	kemeran
8.	water	uisce	ushtey	dwr	dour	dour
9.	who? which?	cia?	quoi?	pwy?	pyu?	piou?
10.	young	óg	aeg	ieuanc	yowynk	yaouank

Obs. (i) Gaelic differs only in *piuthar* for "sister"
and some minor points of spelling.

   (ii) The Latin cognates of these are:

   1. *octo*.

   2. *piscis*: So while Goidelic *iasc* is a true
      cognate, i.e. an independent development
      of an Indo-European root, with loss of
      initial P as already mentioned, Brythonic
      lost its own word (unless it survives in
      the name of the River Usk (*Wysg*), as Sir
      Ivor Williams argues in his *Enwau Lleoedd*),
      and had later to borrow the Latin word.

   3. *homo*: Cf. Old High German *gomo*, surviving
      in *Bräutigam* ("bridegroom")·

   4. *vir*: The Germanic cognate is Anglo-Saxon
      wer, as in English *werewolf*. Cf. the same
      parallel in *fîr/gwyr/verus/Wahr/wary* "true",
      with shift of sense in English.

   5. *senex*: Another example of the line-up
      illustrated, i.e. S--- in Latin and Irish,
      H--- in Greek and Welsh (and we may add
      Armenian with *hin*). (Cf. Welsh *hester* "a
      two-bushel measure" (Spurrell) and Old
      Irish *sesrae* "a gallon" (Pokorny), both
      from Latin *sextarius* (the sixth part of a
      measure)"less than a pint" (Kennedy). For
      "old" Cornish and Breton prefer respectively
      coth and *kozh*, reserving *hen* for use in
      stock phrases. In all six Celtic languages
      this Adjective precedes its noun and there-
      fore mutates it.

   6. *soror*: See note 23.

   7. *fero*: The Manx is a different root, the
      Future Tense of *goaill*; Brythonic represents
      the compound *confero* , whence the 'softening'
      to M after *cy-*; cf. *adferaf* "I restore".

   8. *unda*: "wave": The River-name *Usk* (v.No.2)
      used to be as cognate with Irish *uisce* ,
      but, as Sir Ivor Williams asks, Why call a
      river 'Water'? (unless a Genitive is under-
      stood, as in 'Whiskey' sc. *beatha* "water of
      life").

9. *quis* : Another example of the line-up illustrated earlier (v. No. 5).

10. *iuvencus* "bullock" (a castrated, therefore
young, ox).

Pursuing them into Greek, we find: 1. *okto*;
5. *henos* (only of the last day of the month,
when the moon is old); 6. *heor* (the Vocative of
an obsolete word dredged up by the lexicologist
Hesychius); 7. *phero*; 8. *hydor* ; 9. *tis* .

With other words there is a cleavage between

Goidelic and Brythonic; and neither may be homogeneous

e.g.:-

	Irish	*Manx*	*Welsh*	*Cornish*	*Breton*
1. bread	aran	arraɲ	bara	bara	bara
2. to eat	ithe	ee	bwyta	dybry	debrin
3. electri- city	leictr- eachas[34]	electragh	trydan	tredan	tredan
4. every	gach	gagh	pob	pup	pen
5. to go	dhul	goll	mynd	mones	mont
6. language	teanga	chengey	iaith	yeth	yezh
7. parish	parroiste	skeerey	plwyf	plu	plou
8. peace	siothchain	shee	heddwch	cres	peoc'h
9. people	daoine	deiney	pobl	tus	tud
10. region	duthaigh	ard	bro	bro	bro
11. sky	spéir	speyr	nef	nef	nenv
12. war	cogadh	caggey	rhyfel	bresel	brezel
13. white	ban	bane	gwyn	gwyn	gwenn
14. with	le	lesh	gan	gans	gant
15. without	gan	gyn[35]	heb	hep	hep

Obs. (i) Gaelic differs only in *sith* "peace" (Irish
sioth "agreement") and a few details such as
gun ("without"). With *sgire* "parish", however,
it agrees with Manx.

(ii) It may happen that a Goidelic or Brythonic cognate is obsolete or rarely used; e.g. Irish *bairgean* "loaf" and *nem* "sky", *find* "white", and Welsh *tud* "a people". Goidelic *pobal* (and B. *pobl*) is "a people", though Manx *pobble* may be used as in Welsh.

(iii) Latin cognates are: 1. (of *bara*) *far* ("spelt") The Germanic cognate is Anglo-Saxon *bere* ("barley"). 2. (of *ithe*) *edere*, which has a cognate in Welsh *ysu* ("to consume"), as its Past Participle *esus* shows. The root for "to drink" is common to both groups: *ibhe* (less frequent than *ól*, however,) *iu, yfed, eva, evan*; so to the noun "drink": *deoch, jough, diod, dewas, died*. 5. (of *mynd*) *meare*. Cornish *mones* is often contracted to *Mos*, as *bones* ("to be") to *Bos*. 6. (of *teanga*) *lingua*, from *dingua* contaminated by "Sabine" L and *lingere* ("to lick" cf. Germanic cognate *Zunge* and *tongue*; (of *iaith*) *iocus* ("joke"), because jokes depend on speech. Cf. OHG cognate *jehan* ("to speak") and Polish *język* "language". 7. (of *parroiste* *parochia*,a mistransliteration of the Greek ecclesiastical term (v. below); (of *plwyf*) *plebs*("common people"); cf. Italian *pieve*, Friulan *plev* "parish (-church)", Cornish Place-Names such as *Pelynt* ("Parish of St. Nent"), and the many places in Brittany beginning with *Plou* (e.g. *Plougasnou*). 8. (of *siothchāin*) *situs* ("inactivity"); (of *heddwch*) *sedere* ("to sit"): for S becoming H see above *senex*. *Pax* for *peo'ch* is ruled out by *pax* for *pōg* . 9. (of *daoine*, the plural of *duine* above) cf W.*dynion, homines*; (of *tud*) *tu*(*mere*) ("to swell"): the Irish and Gaelic cognate *tuath* means respectively "countryside" and "country folk"; the Gaulish cognate appears in the Place-Name *Teutoburg*. The Germanic cognates are Gothic *thiuda*, OHG *diot* (German *deutsch*), A-S *theod*,all meaning *.Volk*. So did Old Welsh *tud*, now replaced by *pobl* from *populus* in the new sense, and the Oscan cognate *touto* ("state" 10. (of *bro*) *margo* ("border"): cf. the German cognate *Mark*, used of regions on the border, e.g. *Ostmark* ("Austria"), and the Old Irish

cognates *bruig* and *mruig*. In both Cornish and
Breton *bro* is used to designate foreign
countries; e.g. C. *Bro Sawson* "England" ("Land
of the Saxons"), B. *Bro C'hall* "France" ("Land
of the French"; cf. the Irish town Donegal from
Dun na nGall "Fort of the foreigners", and
Gaelic *Gall* "A Lowland Scot"). 11. (of *nef*)
nebula ("cloud"). 13. (of *gwyn*) *video* ("I
see"): the more obvious Old Irish cognate *find*
was displaced by *ban*, which some link with
fanum "shrine"). 14. (of *le*) *planta* ("sole of
foot", cf. *planus* "flat"), with normal loss of
initial P (v. Nos. 2 above in Lists 1 and 2,)
giving *leth* "side" and "half" (W. *lled*), and
eventually *le*; (of *gan*) *cum* ("with"). 15.
(of *heb*) *sine* ("without") with addition of
suffix k^{we}, as shown by Irish cognate *seach*
("beyond", "apart from").

There are Greek cognates for only: 2. *pino*; 7.

paroikia ("district"; cf. *dioikesis*"diocese"); 8.

hesychos; 11. *vephos* ; 14. *platys*.

It is therefore surprising sometimes to find a

Goidelic root used in one of the Brythonic languages

instead of the Brythonic root; e.g. Goidelic for "kiss"

is *pog*(M. *paag*) from Latin *pacem*, as being the kiss of

peace;   and up comes Breton with *pok* instead of the root

cus borrowed by Welsh and Old Cornish from Anglo-Saxon

cyssan. (Modern, i.e. Middle,Cornish uses the Verbs *am*

and *bey* (M. *baa*), the latter being perhaps related to

Latin *basiare*). Oddly, Breton's verb *pokad* is intran-

sitive (i.e. takes *da* "to", as Cornish *am* takes *dhe*).

Similarly, Breton's *ober* "to do" is linked with Irish *obair* "work", and its *mat* "good" with Irish *maith*, while Old Welsh *mad* and Cornish *mas* have been mostly replaced by *da*. With *boghosek* "poor" and *pystry* "witchcraft", it is Cornish which is un-Brythonic through the link with Irish *bocht* and *piseog*. Sometimes Cornish and Breton will disagree with Welsh without agreeing with Irish: e.g. both have *ker* for "town" (cf. *Keresk* "Exeter" and Breton place-names such as Kerjean) against Welsh *tref*, though *tre* is frequent in Cornish village-names (e.g. *Tredinnick*), as indeed in Welsh itself (e.g. *Tredegar*), and occurs as *trev* in Breton in the name for a division of a parish; but the Irish for "town" is *baile* and for "village" *sráidbhaile* (lit. "street-town").

17.   Indirect Negative Command ("not to"):

Goidelic and Brythonic go their separate ways, each peculiar, and in Brythonic without uniformity. Thus Goidelic uses the Preposition for "without" (*gan*) *Duirt mé leis gan filleadh* ("I told him not to come back") (Manx: *Dooyrt mee rish gyn cheet er ash*). Note that the idiom can be extended to other uses of the Infinitive; e.g. *Má's aidhm an Rialtais gan ionad láidir iarbhunoideachais a bheith i lar na Gaeltachta*

("If it is the Government's aim that there should not

be a strong further-education centre in the heart of

the Gaeltacht").

Obs. Cf. the use of *gan* with the Verbal Noun to form a
Past Participle Passive (like Spanish *sin*):
Fagfar an obair gan deanamh ("The work will be
left undone"); *D'fhan an trunc gan fholmú* ("The
trunk remained unemptied"). So Manx: *gyn castey*
"unconquered".

In Brythonic, Welsh goes its own way with the use of

an idiom used illogically in Direct Prohibitions ("Don't"):

Peidiwch â (lit. "Cease with . . ."):*Peidiwch â thalu*

("Don't pay"). Hence in Indirect Speech: *Erfyniaf*

arnoch beidio â mynd yno ("I beg you not to go there");

and so with all negated Infinitives: *Penderfynasant*

beidio â chychwyn ("They determined not to set out");

and after *am* ("for not -ing"):*wedi ei alw ei hun yn*

ffŵl am beidio â chadw brandi yn y tŷ ("having called

himself a fool for not keeping brandy in the house").

Obs. (i). The absorption of the negative idea into
peidio is so thorough that it can be used in
the second part of an alternative ("or not"):
pr'n bynnag a oedd hynny wrth ei fodd ai peidio
("whether this was to his liking or not"), and
even after *ni allaf* ("cannot but"): *ni allwn*
ni . . . beidio â chydymdeimlo â'r nofelwr
("we cannot but sympathise with the novelist").

(ii) Welsh, however, can come close to Irish when
it uses its Preposition for "without" (*heb*)
with the Verbal Noun after the Verb *To be*;
e.g. *Gwell i ti fod heb addunedu* ("It is better for you not to vow"; lit. "to be without vowing") instead of *beidio a addunedu*.
Thus arises a new negative Perfect Tense; e.g.
Yr wyf heb ei weld ("I have not seen him";
lit. "I am without his seeing"), and *Dyma
rywun sydd heb ganu eto* ("Here is someone
who has not sung yet"), which is the colloquial equivalent of *nid yw wedi*.

Cornish agrees with Welsh so far as "to be with-

out" is concerned (*bos hep*) e.g. *Meth yu genef ow bos*

scryfa ("I am ashamed not to have written": lit. ". . .

my being without writing"); but even here a Subjunc-

tive Clause with *na* or *mana* may be used (cf. Latin

ne); e.g. *Gwell yu dhen na wrellen-ny mos* ("It is

better for us not to go"; lit. "that we should not

(do) go"). Such a Subjunctive Clause is always used

with Indirect Command: e.g. *Orden dhe'th tus na wrello*

hy knoukya ("Order thy men not to strike her"; lit.

"that they may not (do) strike her"), and *Arghaf* (or *My*

a ergh) *dheugh na wrelleugh henna* ("I ask you not to

do that").

Breton uses *chom heb* ("to rest without") in this

way, but like Cornish uses (and prefers) a dependent

clause with *na*: *Gwello'ch eo deom na afem* ("It is better

for us not to go"; lit. "that we should not go"), and

Arch'han (or *Me a arc'h*) *na c'hri kement-se* ("I ask

you not to do that"; lit. "that you shall not do"),

though having no Subjunctive, it uses the Conditional

(*afem*, from *mont*) or the Future (*c'hri*, from *ober*).

For "cannot but" Breton uses *hep* with *tremen* ("to

pass"); e.g. *N'hell ket tremen hep hen ober*"He cannot

but do it" (lit. "dispense with doing it"; cf. French

se passer de), while Cornish uses *omwytha rak* ("refrain

from").

18. Indirect Statement

Once again there is a division of method, but

this time not cleanly between Goidelic and Brythonic:

(a) by a conjunction (English "that") introducing a

Subordinate Clause, as in Indo-European generally;

namely I. *go* G.*gu* M. *dy* Breton *e* :

I. Créidim go bhfuil sí tinn   )
)
G. Tha mi a' creidsinn gum beil si tinn) I believe
) that she
M. Ta mee credjal dy vel ee ching   ) is ill
)
B. Me a cred e klañv eo hi   )

(b) by the Infinitive of the Verb *To be* followed by a

Noun-subject of the Dependent Clause, or preceded

by a Pronoun-subject in the form of its Possessive

Adjective. Hence the above sentence in Welsh and

Cornish:

w. *Credaf ei bod yn glaf*   (lit. "I believe her
c. *My a grys hy bos claf*   being ill").

Here the Infinitive represents a Present or an

Imperfect. When the dependent Verb is in the Future

or the Conditional, however, both languages use their

conjunction for "that" (*y*):

W. *Dywed y bydd ef yn gweithio*) He says that he
C. *Ef a lever y fyth ow queithio*) will be working

When the dependent verb is in the Past, Welsh resorts

to the verb *darfod* ("to happen"), expressed or, more

often, understood, with the Preposition *i* ("to"), and

the Subject; e.g. *dywed (ddarfod) iddo weithio* ("He

says that he worked"; lit. "that it happened to him to

work"). (Less usual is the use of the Infinitive with

a dependent Genitive expressed by the preposition *o*

("of"): *Dywed weithio ohono* (lit. "the working of him")

So *o'i frawd* ("that his brother"). This is also used

in prayers as an alternative to the Subjunctive: e.g.

. . . *fyw ohonom.* . . "that we may live").

Cornish goes its own way with the Past Dependent,

either simply using the conjunctive *y* ("that"); e.g.

Certan yu y scryfas dhedhy ("It is certain that he wro⁺

to her") or by something reminiscent of the Latin

Accusative and Infinitive, with *dhe* ("to") placed

between the Object and the Pres. Inf.; e.g. *Ny glewys*

ef dhe wül drok ("I have not heard that he did evil";

lit. "him to do"); *Ellas my dhe nagha ow Arluth!*

("Alas that I denied my Lord!"); *Scryf ynno an bylen*

dhe leverel y vos ef myghtern Edhewin ("Write on it

that the villain said that he was king of the Jews").

(The same construction is used when a Preposition is

used instead of a Conjunction; e.g. *Wosa y dhe derry*

dredho ("After they had broken through it"; lit.

"them to break"), *drefen hy dhe vos* ("because she is";

lit. "because of her to be")).

When the Dependent Clause is negative, the six

coalesce again, using the negative conjunction (*nach*

etc. Breton *ne*) with a finite tense:-

I .	Créideann sé nach bhfuil sí tinn	)
G.	Tha e a' creidsinn nach bheil i tinn	)
		) He believes
M.	Ta eh credjal nagh vel ee ching	) that she is
W.	Cred ef nad yw hi'n glaf	) not ill
		)
C.	Ef a grys nag yu hy claf	)
B.	Hén a gred n'eo hi ket klanv	)

19. The distinction between Real and Unreal Conditional
    Clauses

In both groups this distinction is also shown not

only, as elsewhere, by the Mood and Tense, but also by

the Conjunction ("If"):

	Real	Unreal		Real	Unreal
I.	má	dá	*W.*	os	pe
G.	ma	na'n	*C.*	mara	mar(s), a
M.	my	dy	*B.*	mar, ma	ma, mar

(a) <u>Real</u> (e.g. Near Future: Future Tense in both clauses):

"If he comes, I shall tell him"

I. Má thiocfad sé, innseochad[36] mé dom é.

G. Ma thigeas[37] e, innsidh mi dà e.

M. My hig eh, inshym da.

W. Os daw ef, dywedaf iddo.

C. Mara te eh, leveraf dhodho.

B. Mar deuy (or, Ma teuy) hen, me a lavaro dezan.

(b) <u>Unreal</u> (e.g. Remote Future: Imperfect Subjunctive after "if" . . . Conditional):

"If he were to come (came, should come), I would tell him"

I. Dá dtigeadh sé, inniseochainn do é.

G. Na'n tigeadh e, innsinn dà e.

M. Dy harragh eh, inshin da.

W. Pe delai ef, dywedwn iddo.

C. Mars teffa eh, my a vynsa leverel dhodho.

B. Ma teufe (or, Mar deufe) hen, me a lavarfe dezan.

Obs. (i) *Ma* (*my*) aspirates; *da* (*dy*) voices (eclipses or softens), but *na'n* does not mutate at all; *os* and Breton *mar* do not mutate (but *mar* prefixes D to vocalic parts of *Bezan* (To be) and *Mont* (To go)); *pe* does not mutate; Cornish *mara mar*(*s*) and *a* and Breton *ma* unvoice (surdize).

(ii) The Verb of the Unreal Protasis is Impf. Subj. except in Breton, where it is Condi-

tional. Welsh Impf. Subj. = Impf Ind.,
except in the Verbs *To be*, *go*, and *come*; in
Irish the only difference between these
tenses is the absence of Aspiration in the
Subjunctive. The Apodosis of all six has the
Conditional.

(iii) Except in Welsh, the Imperfect Subjunctive
serves also for the Past Unreal ("If he had
come, I would have told him"). Welsh uses
its Pluperfect in *-aswn* (the same in Indi-
cative and Subjunctive): *Pe deuthai, buaswn
yn dweud wrtho.*

(iv) With the Verb *To be* Welsh *pe* combines with
the Imperfect *bawn*("If I were") and the
Pluperfect *buaswn* ("If I had been"), the *b*
being often pronounced and written *t*: e.g.

. . . *y gallasai hi fod wedi priodi gan –
waith, pe buasai hi'n ddigon gwirion.*
"that she could have been married a hundred
times, if she had been silly enough").

*Petasech chwi wedi gofyn y cwestiwn yma i
mi y pryd hwnnw, mi faswn wedi ateb yn
wahanol* ("If you had asked me that question
then, I would have answered differently").

In Goidelic a negative Protasis ("If . . . not")

requires the word for "unless" (I. *mura*, G. *mur*, M.

mannagh or *ny slooid ny*) in both Real and Unreal

Conditions; e.g.

"If he does not come soon, it will be too late"

I. Mura dtige sé (Present Subjunctive) ar ball,
béidh sé ro-mhall.

G. Mur thig e a dh'aithgearr, bithidh e ro-anmoch.

M. Mannagh hig eh (Future) dy-gerrid,bee eh ro-
anmagh.

Obs. Gaelic *mur* does not mutate but becomes *mura h-*
before vowels.

In Brythonic the Protasis may be negatived by
the negative adverb after "if"; but each member has
also its word for "unless", viz. W. *oni*, C. *marnas*,
B. *nemet ha*. Hence the above sentence runs in
Brythonic:

W. Oni ddaw ef yn fuan, bydd ef yn rhy hwyr.

C. Marnas ef a dhe yn scon, byth ef re-dhewedhes.

B. Nemet ha dont a raio, re ziwezhat a vezo.

Obs. (i) The more colloquial alternatives are respectively:
W. *Os na ddaw*, C. *Mar ny dhe*, B. *Ma ne
zeuy ket.*

(ii) In Welsh negative Unreal Conditions *pe na(d)*
is the norm: *Pe ne ddeuthai ef, byddai'n
ddrwg gennyf* ("If he should not come, I
should be sorry"); and *mar ny* is more usual
in Cornish (perhaps because *marnas* requires
to be followed directly by the subject and
the so-called "impersonal" construction,
as above: *Mar ny dheffa ef, drok bya
genef* (or, *cüth a-m-bya*)).

The notion "unless" is sometimes expressed in
English by "but for (the fact that)", "were it not
that". The equivalent expression is useful where
there is no Pluperfect Subjunctive, because it enables a Past Unreal to be expressed unequivocably;
e.g.

"Were it not that he came" ("Had he not come")

I. Murab é go dtainig sé , . .

M. Er-be dy row eh er jeet , . .

W. Onibai ei fod wedi dod . . .

C. Na-ve y vos devedhys . . .

B. Panevet ma oa deut . . .

Obs. (i) Hence *murach* can be used with a Disjunctive
Pronoun in the sense "but for":

Thabharfadh sé dom roimhe seo iad murach
tusa. He would have given them to me before
this but for you.

(ii) Welsh *onibai*, being a compound of *oni* and a
form of the Verb *To be*, requires a Subject
after it ("Unless there were . . . "); e.g.

Oni bai hynny "But for this". Hence it can
be followed by a Noun-Clause equivalent to
the Irish *go*-Clause above (viz. the BOD-
Construction shown in § 18); e.g. *onibai
ein bod yn ymladd dros waith* "were we not
fighting for work". Alternatively· it may be
followed by an Infinitive and the Preposition *o*: *Onibai dod ohono* "But for his
coming", i.e. "Had he not come".

The influence of English has led to the in-
trusion of *am* ("for") after it; e.g.*Onibai
am ei glefyd* "But for his illness".

(iii) If Cornish had not, like Breton, a Past
Participle for "come", it could not have
expressed the idea as does the Welsh, because it does not form a Perfect Tense by
the use of the Preposition "after" before
the Verbal Noun. *Na-ve* is also the Relative
"that was not" (or "but what it") (Latin
quin). *Na* itself may be used with infixed
pronoun to mean "unless" . . ., *na-s-gwytha
an Spyrys Sans* "had not the Holy Ghost
preserved her".

(iv) For Breton *panavet* in a pronominal Preposition, see § 13.

20. Methods of expressing "I must" and "I ought":

(a) MUST: Once again both Goidelic and Brythonic

(except Breton) lack a specific verb and prefer a

periphrasis with the noun "necessity" ("There is

necessity for me to"); e.g. "I must go":-

I. Is éigin damh dhul   W. Mae'n rhaid i mi fynd
G. Is eiginn domh a' dol   C. Res yu dhym mos
M. Shegin dou goll   B. Dlean mont (v. (b) below)

For the Past '("I had to") Is becomes B' (for

Ba): B'éigin (M. Beign) and Y mae etc. are put in

an appropriate Past Tense. Breton dleout "to have to"

becomes dleas or dleout a ris (§ 5B).

Obs. Each member (except Manx) has its own alterna-
     tives: e.g.
     Irish: (a) Caithidh mé "I must" and (as the
                tense shows) "I shall have to" (After
                ma ("if"): caithim).
            (b) Ní mór damh
            (c) Ní folair
            (d) Tá sé d'fhiachaibh orm ("It is obli-
                gatory on me")
            (e) Tá orm ("It is on me")"
            (f) Is dual damh ("It is my duty")
     Gaelic: (a) Feumaidh me "I must"
             (b) Tha agam ri "I have to"
     Welsh: gorfod "to oblige" or "to be obliged",
            used either
            (a) personally in the analytic tenses
                of bod:
                Y mae'r plant yn gorfod gweithio
                The children have to work
         or (b) impersonally, in the Past with i
                ("to"):
                Gorfu i'r plant weithio
                The children had to work.

Cornish: *Bysy yu dhym* ("It is important, urgent,
for me to").
Breton: *D'in eo da* ("For me is it to"; cf.
Irish (e) above).
(Breton possesses the root *red* ("necessity"), but does not use it in this
way).

(b) OUGHT: Goidelic resorts again to a periphrasis

with a noun ("right") and the verb *To be* and a

dative:-

I. Is cóir damh cuidiú leis)
)
G. Is còir domh cuidich rish) I ought to help him
)
M. S'cair dou cooney leis   )

Obs. (i) Just as "ought" is a Past Tense, so *Ba*
(Gaelic *Bu*) (with Aspiration) is frequent
instead of *Is*, without the sense necessarily
becoming "ought to have"): *Ba choir (cheart)
damh.*

(ii) Manx has also *Lhisagh mee* ("I ought"): *Lhisagh
shiu freggyrt* "You ought to answer". Then
"ought to have" is expressed by a following
Perfect Infinitive, as in English: *Lhisagh
shiu ve er vreggyrt.*

In Brythonic, Welsh has a verb with a fully in-

flected Imperfect and Pluperfect: *Dylwn (Dylaswn)*

ei gynorthwyo "I ought (ought to have) help(ed) him".

So in Impersonal Passive (§ 9): *Dylid* "One ought"

Dylasid "One ought to have".

Cognate with this is Breton's *dleout* "to have

to" (Section (a) above), which, like French *devoir*,

is used in the Conditional for "ought" and in the

Perfect Conditional for "ought to have"; e.g.

(using the emphatic construction of § 5 B)

Dleout a rafen en ober   I ought to do it

Dleet em bije en ober (§ 14) I ought to have done it

Its Impersonal Passive Present is: *dleer* "One must"

Cornish uses (a) *Y coth* (degoth) (a defective

verb used only in the 3rd pers. sing.) "It is right

for me" (cf. Goidelic above), or (b) the verb *tylly*

("to owe", "to pay", "to be worth") (Present Tense

tal), either impersonally: *Y tal dhym*, or personally:

me a dal.   Its Pluperfect *talvya* is used for "ought

to have".

Obs. (i) It is noteworthy that all Brythonic expresses
this idea of moral obligation by a word
whose basic meaning is *owe* (*debt*), and that
in this they agree not only with English
(*ought* being an old Preterite of owe), but
also with Latin (*debeo*) and Greek, whose
chreon and *chre* are used for both "must"
and "ought", naturally enough, since their
basic meaning is both "necessity" and "debt".

(ii) The Irish cognate *dlighim* "I owe" is rare in
the sense "I ought" and in the Impersonal
Passive *dlightear damh* means "I have a right
to".

21. The position of the dependent Infinitive

In Irish and Gaelic the Object of an Infinitive[38]

dependent on a preceding Verb or Preposition precedes

that Infinitive; e.g.

(a) <u>Verb</u>:

I. Cad cuige ar shocraigh sibh eadraibh feachail a chur ar Spiorad an Tiarna? "Why did you decide among yourselves to test (lit. "put a test on"; v. § 25,) the Spirit of the Lord?

G. (the same sentence) C'ar son a cho-aontaich sibh Spiorad an Tighearna a dhearbhadh?

I. *Ba mhaith liom sideog a fheiceáil* "I should like to see a fairy"

G. *Feumaidh mi am t-each dubh a reic* "I must sell the black horse".

(b) <u>Preposition</u>:

I. *Dubhairt sé liom gan an doras a dhunadh* (§ 17) "He told me not to close the door".

G. *Rinn Agricola oidhirp shonraichte air na Cruithnich a chur fo smacht* "Agricola made a special effort to conquer (lit. "to put under power; v. § 25) the Picts.

Cf. Manx: Ta'n aigney as y chooish jeh'n Slattys shoh dy chur er-ash (v. § 22) ny ooryn-doonee jeh'n thieyn-oast. "The object and purpose of this Act is to restore the closing hours of public-houses".

Obs. (i) With the Preposition *a* expressing Purpose, however, the Object follows the Infinitive and is therefore in the Genitive; e.g. *Chuaidh an cat a dh'ól an bainne.*

(ii) But as Irish uses this Preposition for Purpose only after Verbs such as "go" and "begin", and otherwise uses *le, chun,* or *fa choinne* ("for"), it may part company with Gaelic; e.g.

"Him hath God exalted . . . to give repentance to Israel"

I. Is é seo a d'ardaigh Dia . . . le h-aithrí a thabhairt do Iosrael.

G. Esan dh'ardaich Dia . . . a thoirt
aithreachais (Genitive) do Israel.

(iii) The Welsh (for Brythonic) of these quota-
tions from *Acts* 5/9 and 31 is;

Paham y cytunasoch i demtio Yspryd yr
Arglwydd?

Hwn a ddyrchafodd Duw . . . i roddi
edifeirwch i Israel.

22. Numerals

Common Celtic is (i) the use of 'twenty" (*fiche,*

ugain[39]), as a basic numeral; e.g. *forty* is "twice

twenty" (I. *Daichead,* for *dafhichid,* W. *deugain*);

the formation of interdecimal numbers by mentioning

the smaller number before the larger, not only after

twenty, as in German, etc., but also in the -teens;

e.g. *11 boats*: I. *aon bád déag* (1 boat 10), W. *un*

bad ar ddeg (1 boat on 10); and Welsh, having

pymtheg for *fifteen,* makes this its starting point

for 16, 17 and 19;   e.g. 16 *un ar bymtheg,* 19 boats

pedwar bad ar bymtheg (4 boats on 15) or *pedwar ar*

bymtheg o fadau (4 on 15 of boats).   (Here it dis-

agrees with Cornish and Breton, which have the normal

endings for -*teens,* C. -*tek,* -*dhek,* B. -*teg,* -*zeg;*

and the same disagreement occurs with 11, 13 and 14,

though 12 is unanimously rendered as a -*teen:*

deuddeg, deudhek, daouzeg). *Eighteen* is odd man out

in Welsh and Breton, being expressed as a multiple

respectively of 9 and 6: *deunaw* (2 nines) and *triweh*

(3 sixes); cf. Cornish *etek*. (Welsh, however, says

tri (fem. *tair*) *ar bymtheg* in counting). So after

twenty : 30 *deic is fiche* (10 and 20), *deg ar hugain*

(10 on 20); 75 *cúig déag is tri fichid, pymtheg a*

thrigain (15 and 3 twenties; note the switch in

Welsh to "and" from "on", which started at 41).

Irish has developed easier alternatives after twenty

for its multiples; e.g. 30 *triocha*, 40 *ceathraca*,

50 *caoga* etc., and attempts have been made to simplify

Welsh. Both Goidelic and Brythonic can call 50

"half-a-hundred" (*leath-chéad, hanner-cant*).

Nouns are in the singular after all Brythonic

numerals (v. *19 boats* above), but in Goidelic only

after 2, 20 and its multiples, 100, and 1000.

As regards mutations, the lack of uniformity

reflects the general situation. Only 2, 3 and 5

agree right across the board, the first in softening

where it can, the second in aspirating CPT, the last

in not mutating at all; but Welsh aspirates also

after 6, Breton also after 4 and 9 (but not 6, which

does not mutate in Cornish and Irish either). 7
softens CPT in Welsh, "eclipses" in Irish, and does
not mutate in Cornish and Breton. The same applies
to 8, except that it softens also in Breton. 9
does not mutate in Welsh and Cornish, but "eclipses"
in Irish and aspirates KPT in Breton. 10 (with its
compounds) agrees in softening in Irish, Welsh, and
Breton (with nasalization in Irish as for 7 etc.), but
does not mutate in Cornish, and in Welsh exempts M
and nasalizes D (i.e. makes N), itself being nasalized before those letters, before N, and before
softened (i.e. omitted) G: *Deg punt* (10 pounds),
deng mis (10 months), *deng nafad* (10 sheep, *dafad*),
deuddeng ŵr (12 men). Case, however, plays a part:
thus in Irish 3, 4, 5 and 6 "eclipse" in the Genitive
Plural[40]. Finally, in Welsh the numbers 1, 5, 7, 8,
9, 10, 20, 100 and their compounds nasalize the word
blynedd (year) and *blwydd* (year of age); e.g. *deng*
mlynedd ar hugain (30 years), *pedwar hugain mlwydd*
(80 years old), the word *deg* itself being nasalized.

The Irish for 2 (*dá*) preserves the old Dual,
requiring its noun in that Number (which fortunately
is the same as the Dative Singular). The Definite

Article remains in the sing. and does not mutate:

An dá chluais bheaga ("The two little ears"); but

the Possessive Adjective *a* aspirates *dá* for "his",

"her", and "their" (§ 6), thus leaving the distinc-

tion to the Noun: *a dhá bhroig* (*broig, mbroig*) "his

(her, their) two boots".

Obs. Brythonic (especially Cornish and Breton) preserves the Dual in compounds of *two* used instead
of the Plural with Nouns denoting parts of the
body existing in duplicate; e.g. W. *dwylaw*
(-lo), C. *dywlüf*, B. *daouarn* (cf. Irish *dorn*
"fist") for "hands"; W. *dwyael*, C. *deuabrans*,
B. *divabrant* "eyebrows"; and so on in Cornish
and Breton:-

	Cornish	*Breton*
eyes	deulagas	daoul
arms	dywvregh	divrec'h
hips	dywglun	divglun
buttocks	dywbedren	dibedren
knees	deulyn	daoulin
legs	dywver	divesker
feet	deudros	daoud

Cornish also has *dywaskel* for "wings" (alongside *eskelly*), and Breton has the useful *daouzen*
"a human pair", "a couple" (from *den* "person",
§ 16).

23. Names of the Months and Days

(a) Months

There is little uniformity. Irish and Brythonic

agree in taking over the familiar Latin names more or

less orthographically disguised for January to April;

e.g. February: W. *Chwefror*, C. *Whevrer*, Breton

C'hwevrer. Irish adds *Iul* (July) and Brythonic *Mai*

(C. *Me*, B. *Mae*) and *Awst* (C. *Est*, B. *Eos*); but

Brythonic July is *Gorffennaf* (C. *Gortheren*, B.

Gouhere), and Irish *August* is *Lughnasa* (now *Lunasa*)

from the god Lug, whose name is a frequent prefix in

Gallic names, e.g. in the town Lugdunum (Lyon and

Leiden)[41], and *May Bealtaine*, from the Carnic god

Belenus and the root *teine* ("fire"); in both of

which Manx agrees with it (*Luanistyn* and *Boaldyn*).

Irish and Brythonic agree again on the non-Latin name

for *June* (*Meitheamh*; W. *Mehefin*, C. *Metheven*, B.

Mezeven); but they part company with *September*,

October, *November*, and *December*, where Brythonic

presents a united front for *October* (W. *Hydref*, C.

Hedra, B. *Here*), but has Welsh going its own way for

September (*Medi*; C. *Gwyngala*, B. *Gwengolo*), *November*

(*Tachwedd*; C. and B. *Du*), and *December* (*Rhagfyr*; C.

Kevardhu, B. *Kerdu*), for which months Irish agrees

again with Manx in *Meadhon-Foghmair* (M. *Mean-Fouyir*)

"Middle of the harvest", *Deireadh-Foghmair* (M.

Jerrey-Fouyir "End of the harvest", *Samhain* (M. *Souney*) from the name of the festival of 1st November, which

originally came between the old and the new year,

Nodhlaig (M. *Yn Ollick*) from Latin *natalicia* "birth-

day".

Foghmair also means "autumn"; and it is to the

seasons that Manx resorts for the remaining months:

thus *January* is the "end of the winter" (*Jerrey-*

Cheuree), *February* "the beginning of spring"

(*Toshiaght-arree*), *March* "the middle of spring"

(*Mean-arree*), *June* "the middle of summer" (*Mean-*

souree), July "the end of summer" (*Jerrey-sourey*),

and December can be "the middle of winter" (*Mean-*

gheuree).

This is the system employed by Gaelic through-

out, except that instead of "beginning" etc., it uses

"First, Second, Third Month" of the season: thus

January is "the third month of winter" (*Treas mois a'*

gheamreadh), May "the first month of summer" (*Ceud mios*

an t-samhraidh), and so on. "The words "middle" and

"last" are also used, so that *October* could conform to

the rest of Goidelic with *Mios deirean nach an fhoghair*.

Manx and Breton usually prefix the word for

"month" (M. *mee*, B. *miz*) to the name and in Manx

this mutates it.   Irish and Gaelic sometimes do so.

(b) Days of the week

     Both Goidelic and Brythonic are homogeneous,
but agreement between them occurs only with *Monday*
(I. *Luan* G. *Luain*, M. *Luain* or *Lhein*, W. *Llun*, C.
and B. *Lun*), *Tuesday* (*Mairt*, *Mayrt*, *Mawrth*, *Merth*,
Meurz), and *Saturday* (I. *Sathairn*, W. *Sadwrn*).   For
the other days Brythonic sticks to the names familiar
from French (even if orthographically disguised):
Mercher (C. *Mergher*, B. *Merc'her*) "Wednesday";
Iau (C. *Yow*, B. *Ziou*) "Thursday";   and *Gwener* (W, C,
and B) "Friday". The Goidelic equivalents are :
Ceadaoin (G. *Ceudain*, M. *Crean*), *Diordaoin* (M.
Jerdein), and *Dia hAoine* ("Day of Fasting";   M.
Jeheiney). On the other hand, with *Sunday*   Goidelic
is alone in the Christian word: *Domhnach* (G. *Domhaich*,
M. *Doonee*), while Brythonic preserves the pagan name
Sul.

     The days, especially in dating, are usually referred
to with the word for "day" either before them (when
they are in the Genitive in Goidelic): *Dia Luain*,
Dydd Llun "Monday"; or prefixed: G. *Di-luain*, C. *De-
Lün*);   or joined: B. *Dilun*, M. *Jyluain*, *Jeluain* (where

J represents the sound of "slender" D, as in *Jysarn*

or *Jesarn* "Saturday")[42]. The prefix is always present

in Goidelic "Thursday" and of course has to be present

with the dependent Genitive in "Friday".

Some days in the ecclesiastical calendar have

picturesque names in Irish:

Mart na Smut ("Sulky Tuesday", from *smut* "snout",
        "pout") Shrove Tuesday[43].

Domhnach na Smut ("Sulky Sunday") the first Sunday in
        Lent.

Domhnach na Cogarnaighe ("Whispering Sunday")
                Quinquagesima, the Sunday
                before Lent.

Domhnach na Diugaireachta ("Drinking Sunday")
                Quinquagesima.

An interesting survival in Brythonic is the use

of the Latin word *Kalendae* for the first day of the

month; e.g. W. *Calan Mai*, C. *De-Hala Me* (or *Cala'*

Me), B. *Kala Mae* "May Day"[44]. (So *Kala goanv* 1 Nov-

ember).

24. Declensions and internal vocalic change (Ablaut,
    Gradation); Plurals and Gender:

Goidelic is marked off from Brythonic by its

retention of the declensional system of Nouns and

Adjectives. Irish distinguishes five declensions

according to the formation of the Genitive Singular;

Gaelic claims three, distinguishing them according
as the Noun ends in a vowel (1st), or as its internal
vowel is broad (2nd) or slender (3rd); Manx Grammars
do not allude to Declensions, but Manx Nouns could
be classified according to the presence or absence of
vocalic change in the Genitive Singular, or to the
formation of the Plural.

Of the Indo-European Cases Irish and Gaelic have
four: Nominative, Vocative, Genitive and Dative
(sometimes, and better, called the Prepositional
Case, because it is used after most Prepositions, and
in fact is not used after the verb *To give*, from which
the Dative received its name); while Manx has preserved only the Genitive, and then only for a few
Nouns[45]. The Vocative Singular undergoes Gradation
in only a few declensions, but has its initial letter
aspirated by the prefixed Exclamation *A* (M. *O*); e.g.
A mhic! (M. *O vic!*) "Son!". Gradation occurs
mostly in the Genitive Singular and may be combined
with an inflectional ending; e.g.

(a) <u>Gradation alone</u> (except sometimes Manx):-

	Nom.	Gen.	
God	Dia	De	(M. Jee, Yee)
man	fear	fir	(M. fer, fir)
father	athair	athar	(M. ayr, ayrey)
hill	cnoc	cnuic	(M. cronk, cruink)
death	bas	bais	(M. baase, baaish)

(b) <u>Inflectional ending alone:-</u>

fox	sionnach	sionnaigh	(M. shynnagh, shynnee)
horse	gearran	gearrain	(M. [46])
sheep	caora	caorach	(M. keyrey, keyragh)
friend	cara	carad	(M. carrey, -)
lake	loch	locha	(M. logh, -)

(c) <u>Gradation and Inflection combined:-</u>

belt	crios	creasa	(M. cryss, -)
foot(leg)	cos	coise	(M. cass, coshey)(G. cas)
pig	muc	muice	(M. much, muickey)
peat	moin	mona	(M. moain, moaney)
sea	muir	mara	(M. muir, marrey)

Of the above Nouns, *caora*, *cos*, *muc*, *moin* are

feminine, and *loch* can be; for *muir* v. §   16. The

typical fem. Genitive sg. has Gradation and ends in

-*e*(Irish 2nd decl.), but fem. Genitives of the 5th

decl. end in *ann* or *eadh*.

The singular Prepositional Case is the same as

the Nominative in the masculine, and as the Genitive

less final *e* in the fem., but introduces an *i* into the

Genitive of the 5th decl. (e.g. *guala* "shoulder",

gualainn; *teine*, "fire", *teineadh*, G. *teinidh*).

Manx has lost this case, though the Def. Art. after

a Preposition mutates its noun as in Irish and

Gaelic; e.g. "on the table": I. *ar an bhord*, G. *air*

a' bhord, M. *er yn voayrd*.

Irregular in all three is *bean* (M. *ben*) "woman":

Genitive *mná* (G. *mnatha*, M. *mrieh*), Dative *mnaoi*.

Adjectives behave in the same way, having four

Declensions according as they have Gradation and/or

Inflection in both genders (broad consonants) or

only in the fem., (slender), or not at all (as all

Adjectives ending in a vowel). The fem. Gen. sg.

adds *e* (except 3rd decl. in *-amhail*, which becomes

-amhla), with Gradation (1st decl.) or without (2nd

decl.). Hence:-

of a big (*mór*) man   fir móir
of Wales   na Breatain Bige ("The Little
                        (*beag*) Britain")
of a good friend   carad maith.

PLURALS:

The Nominative Plural of Nouns presents consid-

erable variety of formation. Apart from those which

repeat the Genitive Singular (as do "man", "hill",

"fox", "horse", "sea" (but G. *marannan*, M. *mooiraghyn*),

and "woman" illustrated above), there are the endings

-(*e*)*acha* (G. -*aichean*, M. -*aghyn*) as in "fathers";

- (*e*)*anna* (G. -*an*), as in "lakes"; -*annaí*, as in

"belt"; -*a* as in "feet"; -*ta* or -*taí* (e.g. *scéalta*

"stories", G. *sgeulan*); -*i* (e.g. *buachaillí* "boys",

but G. *buachaillean* "herdsmen"); -*te* (e.g. *bailte*

"towns", but G. *bailtean*, M. *baljyn*); -*igh*, as in

"sheep".

The Vocative Plural is the same as the Nominative

Plural, except in the 1st decl., when the Nominative

Singular root returns with added *a*.

The Genitive Plural either equals the Nominative

Singular or drops the final syllable of the Nom.

Plur. (3rd, 4th, and 5th decl.) (except Plurals in

-*taí* and Gaelic Nom. Plur. in -(*r*)*aichean* , which

remain unchanged).

The Plural Prepositional Case is the same as the

Nominative Plural, except for a few survivals in - *ibh*

(e.g. Irish *ar na mallaibh* "recently", *ar uairibh*

"sometimes"), interesting for the echo of Homeric

-*iphi* (Ablative, Instrumental, and Locative), Latin

-*ibus* (Dative and Ablative), and Sanskrit -*bhih* (Instrumental) and *-bhyah* (Dative and Ablative).

Adjective Plurals agree with Nouns, the Genitive reverting to the form of the Nominative Singular and the Dative to that of the Nom. Plur., both genders.

Brythonic is spared most of this, having jettisoned the ballast of Case at an early stage. It did not, however, give up the multiplicity of Nominative Plural endings: Welsh has 13 substantival Plural terminations: *(i)au*, *(i)on*, *-en*, *-i*, *-ydd*, *-edd*, *-oedd*, *-ed*, *-od*, *-iaid*, *-aint*, *-er*, *-yr*; which may or may not be combined with the 8 varieties of Gradation. Cornish has 6 terminations: *-ow*, *-on*, *-yon*, *-as*, *-es*, *-yjy*(or-*ysy*), and several types of Gradation. Breton has 9 terminations: *-ou*, *-i*, *-iou*, *-ier*, *-eier*, *-ien*, *-ed*, *-iz*, *-idi*, and much Gradation. Many of these endings are the same in all three languages, but they do not necessarily coincide in use; e.g.

	apples	W. afalau	C. avallou	B. avalou
but	cooks	W. cogydd	C. kegynoryon	B. keginerien
and	animals	W. milod	C. mylas	B. miled

Similarly the Gradation may not be the same in

all three:

chickens	W. iar,ieir	C. yar,yer	B. yar,yer
but saints	W. sant, saint	C. sans, syns	B. sant,sent
and feet	W. troed,traed	C. tros,treys	B. troad,treid

And Gradation may occur with only one or two:

| cats | W. cath,cathod | C. cath,cathas | B. kaz,kizier |
| lambs | W. cen,wyn | C. on, en[47] | B. oen,oaned |

Nor is there agreement as to when Gradation shall

be combined with a termination:-

bells	W. cloch, clych(au)	C. clogh, clegh	B. kloc'h, kleier
words	W. gair, geiriau	C. ger,geryow	B. ger, geiriou
crows	W. bran,brain	C. bran,bryny	B. bran,briny

(Welsh "bells" is an example of the several

double Plurals which it possesses, some of which

correspond to different meanings of the singular;

e.g. *llwyth* "tribe" and "load", with respective

Plurals *llwythau* and *llwythi*).

With Irregular Plurals each often goes its own

way. Thus while "dogs", as we saw in § 16, illustrates

uniformity (even including Goidelic), Breton has a

frequent alternative *chas*; and while "ox" is uniform

in both Singular (W. *ych*, C. *ojyon*, B. *ejen*) and

Plural (*ychen*, *oghen*, *oc'hen*), when it comes to *cows*

Breton prefers to its regular *buoc'henned* (from

buo'ch), which matches C. *bughas* (from *bugh*) and W.

buchod (from *buwch*), the different root *saout*. The

same thing happens with "horses": to *mirc'had* or

mirc'hien (cognate with C. *mergh* from *margh* and to

W. *meirch* from *march*), it prefers the word *kezeg*,

which must once have been the plural of *kazeg* "mare",

as it still is in Welsh (*caseg/cesig*; cf. C. *casek/

casygy*).

An unusual group of Collective Nouns forms its

Singular by adding a termination; e.g.

W. *hesg* "rushes"; *hesgen* "a rush".
   blodau "flowers"; *blodeuyn* "a flower".

W. *gwybed* "flies"; *gwybedyn* "a fly".
   moch "pigs"; *mochyn* "a pig".

W. *plu* "feathers"; *pluen* "a feather".
   blew "hairs"; *blewyn* "a hair".

W. *llygod* "mice"; *llygoden* "a mouse".
   derw "oaks"; *derwen* "an oak".

C. *logas* "mice"; *logosen* "a mouse".
   hern "pilchards"; *hernen* "a pilchard"

B. *logod* "mice"; *logodenn* "a mouse".
   gliz "dew"; *glizenn* "dew-drop".

B. *merien* "ants"; *merienem*"ant".

Obs. Breton has a large group of Collective Nouns for
   flowers forming their Singular by the addition
   of *-enn*; e.g. *linad* "nettles", *linadenn*; *askol*
   "thistles", *askolenn*; *raden* "ferns", *radenenn*.
   Cf. *gwez* "trees", *gwezenn* "a tree" and C.
   equivalent *gwyth* , *gwedhen*.

GENDER: The Neuter has been lost. A trace of it may

be seen in the uncertainty surrounding the gender of

a few words (§ 16); e.g. W. *braich* "arm" settled

for feminine only in Modern Welsh[48]. The "hopeless

muddle" which "Manx genders have got into" has been

put down to English influence[49].

25. Some Celtic indiosyncrasies

A. Common Celtic

(i) The use of the Conjunction for "and" with a Noun
    instead of (a) a Temporal Clause or (b) a
    Relative Clause

    (a)*I*. Chuala mé iad agus mé ag teacht chun a'
          bhaile
          I heard them and I (as I was) coming home

          Casadh orm é agus é ag imheacht go hAlbain
          I met him and him (as he was) leaving for
          Scotland

      M. Ren yn bock tayrn yn dooinney, as eshyn
         geamagh (§11)dy . . .
         The pony pulled the man, and him (while he
         was) shouting that . . .

         Laa dy row, as eshyn er a raad gys thie . . .
         One day, and he (when he was) on the road
         to the house . . .

    (b) . . . agus é de bhua aige chuile duine a chur
        ar shuaimheas
        . . . who has the virtue of putting everyone
        at his ease

When it comes to the more literary way of ex-

pressing the temporal relationship by a Participial

Clause ("While coming"), Irish and Gaelic use their

"Participle" (the Verbal Noun with *ag*;), but add the

pronominal Preposition *damh* etc.   E.g. the second

Welsh example on this page   is rendered in Gaelic:

Ag smuaineachadh nan nithe sin dha, feuch, dh'fhoilsich
aingeal . . .
Thinking these things (to him), behold, an angel re-
vealed . . .

(where the Irish happens to have a when-clause with
Nuair).

Ag dul síos dó, casadh a sheirbhisigh air
As he was going down, his servants met him

(where G. has: *am feadh a bha e*, and M. *tra v'eh* :
"while")

        When the Participial Clause is absolute, i.e.

unrelated by subject to the Principal   Clause (cf.

Latin Ablative Absolute), Goidelic has "And" followed

by the subject of the Participle (usually a Pronoun)

and the "Present Participle"; e.g.

Agus mé ag tagairt do'n focal seo
And while (or, since) I am referring to this word . . .

So in the Past:

Agus sin ráite agam
And this said (by me), or Having said this, I . . .

So in Brythonic:

  W. Yn y bymthegfed flwyddyn o ymerodraeth Tiberius
     Caesar a Phontius Pilat yn rhaglaw Jwdea . . .
     "In the 15th year of the rule of Tib. Caesar and
     Pontius Pilate governor (when P. was governor)
     of Judea"

     Ac efe yn meddwl y pethau hyn, wele, angel
     And he thinking (while he thought) on these things,
     behold . . .

Ni wel ond y rhaff fain, a hithau'n mynd yn edau
All he sees is the slender rope, which becomes a
thread . . .

Obs. "who has" is regularly rendered "and with (him)":

Yr oedd dyn a chanddo law wedi gwywo
"There was a man and with him (i.e. who had) a
withered hand"

Os gweli di ddyn a chas ganddo at gŵn . . .
If you see a man (and hate with him for) who
hates dogs . . .

C. Pür avar, ha'n howl noweth drehevys
"Quite early, and (when) the sun(was) just risen"

Hag ef ow covyn nebes bara, y vergh a armas
"And he (when he) asked for some bread, his
daughter cried out"

My a aswon Albanek ha'y vam ny vynnas cows Gaelek
dhodho
"I know a Scotsman and his mother (whose mother)
did not want to speak Gaelic to him"

Obs. Cornish also renders "who had" in this way, but
with the Preposition for "to":

Benen ha dhedhy dew flogh
A woman (and to her) who had two children

In Breton this construction is less frequent

(e.g. "when Pontius Pilate" is rendered simply *pa*

oa Pons-Pilat gouarnour, as it is indeed in Irish

also, doubtless because the other expression is less

dignified: *nuair a bhí Point Piolait i-na uachtarán),*

and the equivalent of Breton "and to (him)" usually

bears a concessive notion; e.g.

Al levr-man a vezo lennet, ha dezan besa dioes
This book will be read, and for it to be (though it is)
difficult.

This concessive idea appears also in the combination

of *hag* ("and") with the Relative Pronoun:

Ar skoliad-ze, hag a labour mat, ne vezo ket gopret
This pupil, who (though he) has worked well, will
not be rewarded

But a change to the Indefinite article gives it a

causal sense:

Eur skoliad hag a labour mat a vezo gopret
A pupil who works well will be rewarded

Brythonic, however, has developed its own methods

of expressing simultaneity in Participial Clauses

("While -ing"):-

Welsh and *Cornish* make a subtle distinction

between

(a) actions of the Participle which involve or explain

those of the Main Verb;   and

(b) those which are different or additional.

Thus (a) with GAN (W) and YN-ÜN (C):

efe a ddaeth atynt, gan rodio ar y mor
ef a dheth dhedha yn-ün gerdhes war an mor
He came to them, walking on the sea

and (b) with DAN (W) and YN-DAN (C):

Aeth ymaith yn y modur, dan chwifio'i het
He went away in the car, waving his hat

scolkyeugh dhy yn-dan dava
slink thither keeping in touch

Breton does not make this distinction, but uses

its equivalent *en eur* in a strictly temporal sense.

Hence the same sentence from St. Mark 6/48 runs:

e teuas daveto en eur gerzout war ar mor

Obs. Goidelic here has simple *ag* with the Verbal Noun
(I. *ag siubhal*, G. *ag imeachd*)

Welsh uses also other Prepositions with the In-

finitive, with a slightly different temporal meaning:-

(i)   YN (hardly different from *gan*, but merely
      descriptive):

      eisteddai wrth y tan yn darllen
      He was sitting by the fire, reading

(ii) WRTH (with a causal element: "On -ing"):

      gwenodd wrth weld y mab
      He smiled on seeing the son . . .

Obs. (i) When the Participle has its own Subject, this
       is put in the Dative between the Preposition
       and the Infinitive, in accordance with the
       norm:

       Wrth i landlordiaid hawlio daliadau . . .

       On landlords'claiming payments . . .

     (ii) The Goidelic equivalent is the Preposition
       ar, with the subject of the Participle depen-
       dent on *do* ("to"):

       Ar eirghe dom ar maidin
       On (my) getting up in the morning

       Ar fhagáil na haite do Sheán
       On John's leaving the place

(ii) <u>Accusative of Respect:</u>

I. (mostly after superlatives):

   Bean is finne blá   A woman most fair in bloom
   An fear is mó cail   The greatest man in fame

W. Dyn trwm ei glyw   A man heavy as to his
                            hearing (hard of . . .)
   Cymru rhugl eu Cymraeg Welshmen fluent in Welsh
   Gŵyl Gymraeg ei hiaith A Welsh-language festival

C. glas hy lagas   blue as to her eyes (blue-eyed)
   du aga lyw   black as to their colour (black-hued)
   mur aga fyenasow   great their anxiety (very anxious)

(iii) <u>Defective verbs for parenthetic "he said"</u> :

I. and G. *arsa*   W. *medd,* pl. *meddannhw; ebr*[50]
C. *yn meth'ef)*   B. *emezan* etc. (v. §   13).

(iv) <u>The expression of debt:</u>

I. Ta sgilling (G. tasdan[51]) agam air
    I have a shilling on him i.e. He owes me a shilling

W. Y mae arno swllt i mi
    There is on him a shilling to me i.e. He owes me a
    shilling

    But Manx, while keeping "on" for the debtor says:

    Ta skillin er dy eeck dou
    There is a shilling on him to pay me

    Cornish uses the verb *tylly* (§   20b)

(v)   <u>Yes and No:</u>

    All that some know about Welsh is that "it has no

word for *Yes* and *No*" (and they may have picked up this

information from the Prince of Wales, who commented

on it after his crash-course in 1967);   and in so far

as Welsh indicates affirmation and negation by

repeating in the correct form the verb of the question,

this may be accepted. The phenomeon, however, is not

a Welsh one, but includes the whole Celtic family.

Thus, to confine ourselves to the Verb "To be", the

question, "Is she at home?" and its answer appear

as follows:-

I. An bhfuil sí sa bhaile?   Tá   Níl

G. A bheil si ag an tigh?   Thà   Chan 'eil

M. Vel ee sy thie?   Ta   Cha nel

W. A ydyw hi gartref?   Ydyw   Nac ydyw

C. Yma-hy yn-tre?   Yma   Nyns-üsy[52]

B. Hag hi a zo er ger[53]   Eo   N'eo ket

Obs. (i) If the substantive verb in Goidelic is IS,
the answers are respectively *Is ea* and *Nî
h-ea* .

(ii) Breton usage varies with locality: whereas
in Tréguier the repetition of the verb (or
the use of the corresponding part of *ober*
"to do") is the norm, especially with *Eo*
and *Eus* ("there is"), in Léon *Eo* is used
throughout.

Welsh has some refinements which are unknown to

the others. Thus, if the verb of the question is in

the Perfect Tense, "Yes" becomes *Do* and "No" - *Na ddo* .

Hence:

A fu hi gartref ddoe?
("Was she at home yesterday?")
Do "Yes".   *Na ddo* "No" .

Then, if the question involves emphasis on an Adverb,

so that the interrogative particle becomes *Ai*, then

"Yes" and "No" become *Ie* and *Nage*. E.g.

Ai gartref y mae hi?
("Is it at home she is?")
Ie "Yes".   *Nage*   "No" .

Obs. So too for "Isn't it" and "Is it" etc. after a
statement.

Thus it appears that, after all, Welsh does have a word for *Yes* and *No*, and indeed sounding very much like *Yea* and *Nay*, but they are limited to a certain type of question. What is more, the other two Brythonic tongues also possess the equivalents, viz. C. *Ya* and *Na* (pron. *nay*), B. *Ya* and *Nann*, though these tend to be used otherwise than in direct replies and are less frequent than the repeated verb.

(vi) "Please" and "Thank you"

The following table shows the degree of unanimity among the six. Goidelic is united for *Thank you*, and Cornish and Breton for *Please*, while Manx agrees, at least in form; but Welsh stands alone for both

(a) *Please:*

I. Má's do thoil é   "If it is your will"

G. Ma's e do thoil e "If it is your will"

M. My sailliu[54]   "If it pleases you"

W. Os gwelwch yn dda "If you see well"

C. Mara plek dheugh "If it pleases you"

B. Mar plich   "If it pleases you"

Obs. (i) "You" is plural here except in the Irish.

   (ii) Irish uses also: *le do thoil* "with your will"

(b) *Thank you:*

I. Go raibh maith agat)

G. Gu robh math agad) "May there be good at you!"

M. Gura mie ayd   )

W. Diolch   "Thanks"

C. Durdala[55] dhys   "God repay you!"

B. Bennoz deoc'h or Trugarez "Blessing to you" or
                                  "Merci"[56]

Obs. (i) "You" here is singular.

    (ii) Gaelic also uses: *Tapadh leat*! ("Success
    with you!").

    (iii) Cornish uses also: *Grassyes* ("Thanks") and
    Gon gras dhys ("I know thanks to you").

B. Goidelic only

(i) The use of *cuid* ("share") with a Possessive

Adjective instead of the simple Possessive Adjective

on certain occasions; e.g.

mo chuid ama   "my (share of) time"

This allows the formation of a Possessive Pronoun e.g.

cara de mo chuid   "a friend of mine"

(ii) The use of the plural emphatic forms of *agam*

("at me")with IS in the sense of the Possessive Adjec-

tive; e.g. *an teach s'againne* "our house", *an bho*

s'agaibh -se "your cow". The idiom is useful to Manx

(which however drops the *is*), because it enables the

three Persons, all rendered by *nyn*, to be

distinguished; e.g. *yn thie ain* "our house", *yn thie*

oc "their house" (instead of *nyn dhie* for both).

(iii) <u>The careful distinction between movement to and</u>
      <u>from</u>

   I.e. the words for "down" and "up" vary according

as the movement is towards or away from the speaker.

Hence a different Adverb for each is required according

as the verb is "go" or "come": thus *dul suas* "to go up"

teacht anios "to come up" (with respectively *sios* and

anuas for "down"). The same distinction affects points

of the compass: the question is not, In what direc-

tion?, but is it going or coming? Thus movement from

East (*soir*) to West (*siar*) is described as *anoir* or

siar according as the verb is respectively "come"

or "go". (Similarly with North (*tuaidh*) and South

(*teas*): *dul ó thuaidh* "to go north", *teacht a ndeas*

"to come north").

(iv) <u>The 3rd Person Singular Ending -eas</u>

      It is used in the Present and Future Tenses after

the Relative Pronoun *a* in the Nominative, in

Positive sentences, except the Present Tense of eight

frequent irregular verbs, e.g.

An tusa a bheas ag obair liom?
"Is it you who will be working with me?"

Is mise an gasur a bhuaileas an chnag
"I am the boy who hits the ball"

Nuair a chaithfheas siad dhul
"When they will have to go" (§ 20)

(v) <u>Defective Verbs</u>

(a) *theip orm*   "it was too much for me"
                                i.e. "I failed".

(b) *d'fhobair damh* (or *gur*) "It lacked little to me to
                                (or, but that)", i.e. I
                                nearly . . .

(M. *dobbyr dou*). *D'fhobair gur thuit mé* "I nearly fell"

Obs. (i) Gaelic oddly uses the first one in the sense
           of the second: *Theab mi tuiteam* "I nearly
           fell"; and personally too!

     (ii) Irish also uses *sarú* "to surpass" in the 3rd
          Singular Preterite in the sense of (a):
          sharuigh orm "It was beyond me", "I failed".

(vi) <u>The placing of the Direct Object Pronoun at the
     end of its clause</u>

Má chuirtear i gló é   "If it is printed" (lit. "If
                        there is a putting in print it").

Thug sé leis chun an "He took him home".
bhaile é
(vii) <u>The use of the Verb *casain* "I twist" in the
      Impersonal Passive with the Preposition *ar* ("on")
      and the Subject to mean "I meet"</u>

     E.g. *Casadh feirmeoir orm* "I met a farmer ".

Fortunately there is *bualadh le* ("bump into"), but one

can hardly blame Manx for preferring *meeteil rish*.

Gaelic uses the verb *coinnich*. For arranged meetings

other verbs are used; e.g. Manx *quaail*, most often

found with a preceding Possessive Adjective to mean

"to meet (me etc.)": (*haink* "he came") *my whaail* "to

meet me" (cf. G. *'na choinneamh*, "to meet him");

I. *i ndáil leó* "to meet (or, to a meeting with) them".

(viii) <u>Comparative and Superlative</u>

They are expressed through the verb IS and the

Comparative form of the Adjective (usually the same

as the fem. Gen. sing.). In Present contexts, there-

fore, the Comparative "whiter" is: *níos* (G. *nas*) *baine,*

and the Superlative "whitest" is: *is* (G. *a's*) *baine.*

In the Past these have to become respectively

ni ba (G. *na bu*) and *ba* (G. *as*).

Manx has *by* (e.g. *by verchee* "richest"), but is

not so strict about using *ny's* and *s'* only with the

Present or Future.

Obs. (i) If the sentence begins with *Is e*, Gaelic
changes to *as*; if with *B'e*, to *a bu* .

(ii) Adjectives having no Comparative form (such
as Past Participles) use the Comparative of
much (*níos mó* "more"), and so for the Superlative *is mó* "most"; e.g. in Manx: *Yn
dooinney smoo ynsit* "The most learned man".

For "The more . . ., the more (less)" Gaelic and

Manx introduce the sentence with the word for "**As**"

followed by *is* and the Comparative. Then Gaelic's

second clause begins with *'s ann as* before the Compa-

rative, whereas Manx starts at once with the Compara-

tive; e.g.

G. Mar is luaite, 's ann as fearr
     "The sooner, the better"

M. Myr smo, share
     "The more, the better"

Irish, however, introduces the sentence with *Dá*

followed by the appropriate noun, and continuing

with *is amhlaidh* ("it is so"):

Dá n-oige é, is amhlaidh is fearr é
"The younger he is, the better"

Dá luathas sin deanta, is amhlaidh is fearr é
"The sooner that is done, the better"

Obs. *Dá* with a noun also expresses "However" with an
      Adjective or Adverb; e.g.
      Dá fheabhas iad   "However good they are"

It follows that the Goidelic Comparative and

Superlative can never be qualified by a Possessive

Adjective. "My eldest son", for example, can be only:

An mac is sine agam ("The oldest son I have").

(ix) The maid-of-all-work Verb *cur*

To put, send, bury, plant, rain; with as many

idiomatic uses as the English "get": e.g.

cur i n-iúl   *cur i gric*
to inform   to perform, carry out

Equally frequent in Manx is *goaill* to take; e.g.

goaill aggle   to be afraid
(cf. Gaelic *ghabh iad eagal*   "they were afraid").

goaill arrane   *goaill padjer*
to sing   to pray

(x) An abundance of Prefixes

Prefix	Meaning	The base word	The compound word
an-	(intensive)	buidheach "grateful"	anbhuidheach "very grateful"
ath-[57]	(repetition)	beo "life"	athbheochain "to revive"
comh-	(equality)	focal "word"	comhfocal[58] "synonym"
deagh-	(goodness)	faitheas "dread"	deaghfhaitheas "reverence"
droch-	(badness)	bail "success"	drochbhail "sorry state"
do-	(hard to)	sarú "surpass"	dosharuighthe "unsurpassed"
so-	(easy to)	tuigbheáil "understand"	sothuigseach "comprehensible"
ea-)) *mi-*))) *neamh-*)	(negations)	dochas "hope" beasach "polite" spleách "independent"	éadochas "despair" mibheasach "impolite" neamhspleách "independent"
fo-[59]	(under)	baile "town"	fo-bhaile "suburb"
for-[60]	(super-)	obair "work"	for-obair "superfluous work"
fior-[61]	(real)	uachter "surface"	fior-uachter "the very top"
fri(o)th[62]	(anti-)	Iudachas "Jewry" beart "act"	frith-Iudachas "anit-Semitism" frith-beart "opposition"
iar-	(after)	scolaire "pupil"	iarscolaire "former pupil"
il-	(multi-)	treatheach "talented"	ilthreatheach "versatile"

ion-	(fitness)	posadh "marry"	ionphosta ".nubile"
leas-	(step-)	athair · "father"	leas-athair "stepfather"[63]
leath-	(semi-)	marbh "dead"	leath-mharbh "half-dead"
leith-	"	eolach "knowing"	leith-eolach "smatterer"
leath-[64]	(inequality)	fabhar "favour"	leath-bhfabhar "bias"
leith-	"	iseal "low"	leith-iseal "lame"
moth-[65]	(male)	cat "cat"	moth-chat "tom-cat"
toth-	(female)	searsach "foal"	toth-shearsach "filly"
pat-	(moderate)	fuar "cold"	pat-fhuar "luke-warm"
	"	uasal "noble"	pat-uasal "shabby-genteel"
sar-	(intensive)	maith "good"	sarmhaith "excellent"

Obs. Most of these are found also in Gaelic and Manx,
the Manx spelling being respectively: *aa-*
(*aaloayrt* repeat), *co-* (*coloayrt* converse),
jeih- (*jeih-yantagh* benefactor), *mee-* (*mee-
hreishteil* despair), *neu-* (*neuhastagh* incautious),
lhiass- (*lhiass-ayr* stepfather).

Manx also uses its adverb *eer* ("even", "merely"
as a Prefix to nouns; e.g. *eer-ghuilley* "a mere
boy".

(xi) <u>The lack of some common verbs and their replace-
ment by periphrases</u>

Goidelic lacks a verb for "To know" (something).

Whereas Brythonic has W. *gwybod*, C. *godhvos*, B.

gouzout, Goidelic uses the noun *fios* "knowledge" with

the verb *To be* and the Preposition *ag* ("at"); e.g.

I. and G. *Ta fhios agam* (M. *Ta fys aym*) "there is knowledge at me", i.e. "I know"; and Irish at least
prefers this form when the object of the knowing is
a person, using *Ta aithne agam air* (M. *Ta enney aym
er*) instead of *Aithnighim é* for "I know him". There
are in fact several periphrastic alternatives; e.g.
Is eol damh, Ta sé ar eolas ag, Is feasach damh.

Similarly with "to be able": against Brythonic
W. *gallu,* C. *gally,* B. *gallout,* Irish tends to neglect
its regular verb *féadadh* and to use either the periphrasis *Is féidir liom* ("It is possible with me"),
which creates a difficulty when the Infinitive is
needed, or, in Ulster, the idiom *Thig liom* ("It comes
with me"), or even the adjective *abalta* (*Ta mé abalta*).
So too Gaelic, though possessing the verb *faotainn,*
usually expresses personal ability by *Is urraim domh.*
Manx, therefore, stands out with its normal use of the
regular verb *foddym* ("I can").

Obs. The mutation in *fios* above is due to the under-
     stood presence of the Possessive Adjective *a*
     ("its").

C. Brythonic

The peculiarities mentioned here are not shared

by all three members:

(i) The way of expressing ownership (Welsh and Cornish):

W. *piau*: originally interrogative ("To whom is it?"),

it then began to be used in a *statement* of ownership:

Myfi biau dial ("It is I to whom is vengeance", i.e.

"Vengeance is mine"). In such sentences no Object is

possible, because the presence of the Verb *To be* is

still felt. Then, following a Relative (expressed

or understood) which is felt as a Subject, it begins

to take an Object: *Myfi a biau ynys Brydain* ("I own

the island Britain"). Hence:*Pwy biau'r tŷ hwn* ? ("Who

owns this house?"); and since this equals "Whose is

this house?", *Piau* comes to be used for this Inter-

rogative Genitive Pronoun and also as the equivalent

of a Possessive Pronoun (especially after "this",

"that"); e.g. *Chwi biau hwn* "This is yours", *Hi*

oedd biau'r bwthyn "The cottage was hers" (note the

presence of the Imperfect Tense), and *Cymry biau'r dŵr*

"The water is Wales's (belongs to Wales)".

Obs. Cf. the use of *eiddo* "property", which has not
stopped at evolving into an equivalent to a
Possessive Pronoun (*Eiddo pwy*? "Whose"?, *Eiddo*
fy nhad "My father's, and *i bob cais o'n heiddo*
"to every request of ours"), but has gone on to
become a Pronominal Preposition (§ 13): *Yr*
eiddoch yn gywir "Yours sincerely".

The Cornish cognate *pew* ("owns") is similarly
used: *Pyw a bew an ky-na?* "Who owns that dog?" i.e.
"Whose is that dog?", and *My a-n-pew* (§ 12) "I
own it", "It is mine".

Obs. "Whose?" in Goidelic is expressed by combining
the Nominative of the Interrogative Pronoun
("Who?") with the Prepositional Compound "with
him"; e.g. *Cé leis an leabhar? Is liom é*   lit.
"With whom is the book?" "It is with me" i.e.
"Whose?" and "mine"(*Le*, not *ag*, is "with" of
possession). G.*Co leis an leabhar? Is leamsa.*
M. *Quoi s'lesh yn lioar? S'lhiams.*

(ii) Historic Infinitive

A Verb joined to a preceding clause containing a
Verb with the same Subject is put in the Infinitive
instead of a Finite Tense (the Past) in Welsh and Breton:

W. *Euthum i mewn i'r tŷ a gwneud cwpanaid o de·*
I went into the house and made a cup of tea.

Obs. This occurs especially when the first proposition
uses *gwneuthur* ("to do") for emphasis (§ 5);

Rhyfeddu a wnaethant a'i adael ef a mynd ymaith·
Marvel they did and left him and went away.

C. *An lader a-gemeras an on ha'y ladha ha'y dhybry·*
The thief took the lamb and killed it and ate it·

B. *Artur a zavas a mont·*
Arthur arose and went.

As in Welsh, so too especially when the first verb
is emphatic *ober* ("to do"):

Sevel a eure ha mont·   He arose and went·

Obs. (i) Sometimes an otiose *da* ("to") is put before
the Infinitive, perhaps under French influence
e.g. the last Welsh example appears in St.

Matthew (*Mazhev*):

. . . *e voent souezhet-bras. Hag i (they) da lezel anezhan* (§ 12) *ha da vont.*

(ii) The nearest to this in Goidelic is the Irish use of the Infinitive in the second of two Unreal Protases (§ 19).

Dá n-imthigheadh sí agus an gasur a tabhairt leithe

If she went away and (the boy to take)   took the boy with her.

(iii) <u>Prefixes</u>

Tables of prefixes are set out on pages 234-237.

			Welsh
ad-)[66] *at-*)	(re-)	alive revival	byw adfywiad
an-	(un-)	remember forget	cofio anghofio
cam-	(mis-)	take mistake	cymryd camgymeriad
cyd-	(co-)	to work co-operate	gweithio cydweithio
cym-) *cyf-)*	(equality)	as well	cystal
cyn-	(pre-)	native aboriginals	brodor cynfrodorion
dad-	(dis-,un-)	illusion disillusion	rhith dadrithio
	(re-)	to buy to ransom	prynu prynu
		life revival	(v.*ad*-)
dar-	(pre-)	ready prepare	parod darparu
di-	(-less)	work unemployed	gwaith diwaith
drwg-	(badness)	to opine suspect	tybio drwgdybio
		desire lust	chwant chwant
gor-	(over)	weigh outweigh island peninsula	pwyso gorbwyso ynys gorynys
gwrth-	(anti-)	war rebellion	rhyfel gwrthryfel
hy-[68]	(-able)	to bend flexible	plygu hyblyg

Cornish	Breton
tylly to pay	bevan to live
attylly repay	advevan revive
cofhe	kounan
ankevy	ankounac'haat
kemeres	kemerout
camgemeres	kammgemerout
obery	ober (to do)
kesobery	kenober
kefrys likewise	ken also
scryf screed	skrid screed
kenscryf MS	kentskrid preface
tull	touelladeg
(dyðulla)	(didouellegezh)
prena	prenan
dasprena	dasprenan
bewnans	(v. ad-)
dasvewnans	
parys	
darbary	darbar(in)
gwyth	ober
dywyth	dioberiant
tyby	
drokdyby[67]	
whans	c'hoant
drokwhans	droukc'hoant
enys	tog capital (arch.)
gorenys	gorre-tog abacus
bresel	brezel
omsevel	emsavadeg
plegya	plegan
heblek	hebleg

<u>Welsh</u>

		to love	caru
		lovable	hygar
llys -	(step[69])	father	tad
		stepfather	llysdad
rhag -	(fore-)	judgment	barn
		prejudice	rhagfarn
		to buy	prynu
		subscription	(tanysgrifiad)
tra -	(over)	sea	mor
		overseas	tramor
traws -	(trans-)	convey	cludo
		transport	trawsgludo
tros -	(trans-)	to put	gosod
		substitution	trosodod
ym -	(reflexive[70])	to bear	dwyn
		to behave	ymddwyn
	(reciprocal)	to see	gweld
		to visit	ymweld â
	(intran-	spread	lledu
	sitive)	" (intr.)	ymledu
	('middle')	to kill	lladd
		to fight	ymladd

Obs. (a) Cornish, by stressing *om* (and sometimes drop-
        ping also the Infinitive-ending) can give the
        compound a different sense; e.g. *ðmdhon* means
        "conceive", and *omladha* means "to kill one-
        self" or "each other" (for which B. uses
        emlazh without distinction, and W. uses
        ymlâdd metaphorically).

    (b) The word *gwall* (W. and C. "error", B. "crime"
        is used as a prefix in B. equivalent to *mal-*:
        gwallgas "to maltreat". In W. it appears as
        a prefix in *gwallgof* "mad".

Cornish	Breton
cara	karout
hegar	hegar
tas	tad
lestas	lezdad
brüs	barn
ragvrüs	rakvarn
prena	prenan
rakpren	rakpren
mor	mor
tramor	tramor
gorra	kas
don	dezougen
gorra	lakaat
gorra yn le	lakaat e lec'h
don	dougen
omdhon	(kas)
gweles	gwelout
omweles	emwelout (interview)
lesa	ledan
omlesa	emledan
ladha	lazhan
òmlath	emlazhan

(c) Welsh makes great use of *prif*("chief"), as in
prifysgol "university", *prifathro* "headmaster",
though *pen* "head" was available as in *pensaer*
"master-builder", *pencerdd* "chief musician". This
is the prefix preferred by Cornish (e.g.
pendyscajor "professor" against competition from
borrowed *chyf* "chief", and used in several Breton
words (e.g. *penn-arme* "army-commander", *penn-ober*
"chef-d'oeuvre"), though suffixed *meur* (fem. *veur*)
"great" is used for "university" (*skol-veur*) and
"cathedral" (*ilis-veur*) (W.*prifeglwys*[71]). Interesting is W. *carn* "arch-": *carn-fradwr* "arch-
traitor".

There is no agreement either over the word for "very".
W. *iawn* ("right") follows the Adjective; but to
its similarly placed *ewn* C. prefers *pür* ("purely"),
also used in Welsh (less emphatically) or *fest*
("firmly) placed before the Adjective. B. can
choose between *meurbed* and *kenan*, or between
suffixed *tre* and *bras* (e.g. *plijum-tre* "very
pleasant", *spontet-bras* "very frightened"), or
can double the Adjective, as Semitic sometimes
does (e.g. *tomm-tomm* "very hot")[72].

(iv) <u>Welsh PO</u>

(Originally the Subjunctive *bo*; cf. *pe*, § 19)

with the Superlative to express: "The more ...,

the more (less)"; e.g.

*Po fwyaf a ddarllenwch, mwyaf y cerwch ei
llenyddiaeth*
"The more you read, the more you will love its
literature")

Gorau po gyntaf
("The sooner the better").

Cf. *Cornish*: *Dhe* (or *sül*) *voy...*, *dhe....*; e.g.

Dhe voy y-n-gwelaf, dhe le y-n-caraf ("The more I

see him, the less I like him").

Cf. *Breton*: *Seul* ("As much") *vui...*, *seul* (with

mutation); e.g. *Seul vui a gafe a zo, seul welloc'h

eo* ("The more coffee there is, the better)[73].

(v)   <u>Welsh lack of verbs for *To bring* and (in one
       sense) *To take*</u>

The two ideas are expressed respectively by "To

come with" and "To go with" (a useful distinction

for foreigners who confuse the two verbs in English);

e.g. *Aethpwyd ag ef i'r ysbyty* "He was taken to hos-

pital" (lit. "there was a going with him"), *Mae nhw 'n*

mynd â'ch dŵr chi "They are taking *your* water".

So *dyfod yn* and *mynd yn* are used for *To become*

(something good or bad respectively): *Nid o'i bodd*

yr aeth Elin yn hen ferch "Eileen was becoming an old

maid reluctantly".

Obs. (a) Cornish and Breton also use the verb *To go*
for "become" in reference to age: C. *Galsof*
coth, B. *Me am eus eet da goz*: "I have
grown old".

(b) Irish uses the Passive of *To do* (cf. Latin),
but impersonally: *Rinneadh sagart de* "He became a priest" (lit. "There was made a priest
of him"). Manx would say: *Haink eh dy ve ny*
haggyrt   (§ 15) "He came to be a priest".

(vi)   Cornish Defective Verbs (used only in the 3rd
Person Singular)

bern "it matters"; *ny vern*   "it does not matter"

(Breton: *ne vern*)

Obs. This supplies the lack of an adjective for "important": *a vern* (noun) "of concern"; *mûr a*
vern "very important". Alternatives are: *a*
vry "of account", *a brys* "of value", *dûr* "it
matters, *ny-m-dûr* "It is no concern of mine".

Obs. Welsh also has some defective verbs, including
the cognate of the last (*dawr*): *Ni'm dawr* "I do
not care". So too: *bod o bwys* "to matter".

(vii) <u>Certain Prepositions: in Breton</u>

ouz "against", as in: *Trouc'het e benn outan*

"decapitated" (lit. "his head cut against him").

pourveziou a bado ouzin "provisions that will last

me".

diouz "detached from", "according to", and

some idiomatic uses such as: *hep kredenn diouz*

kredenn "without precise belief".

diwar "from off", also in reference to source:

beva diwar e leve "to live off one's unearned income".

Also as an equivalent to the French *dès* of time:

diwar hizio "from today".

digant "from" after verbs of taking, receiving,

stealing (cf. French *à*): *laerez digant unan bennak*

"steal from someone".

Obs. A Verb may be combined with a variety of Prepositions (as in English): *Ober* "to do"

ober evit	to replace (do for)
ober gant	to utilize, frequent, treat as, get on with one
ober ouz	to busy·oneself with, master
ober diouz	to imitate, adapt oneself to

(viii) <u>Breton *paouez* "to cease" with the Infinitive
tor "to have just"</u>

Eman o paouez sevel "He has just got up".

Obs. The Welsh idiom is to put the word *newydd* ("new")
either between *wedi* and the Verbal Noun (which
together form the Welsh Past Participle) or
instead of *wedi*,(the Possessive Adjective, if
present, respectively following *wedi* or *newydd*):
so the above sentence:-

Y mae ef (wedi) newydd codi

Similarly Cornish *noweth*:

ha'n howl noweth drehevys   and the sun just risen

(For the Irish idiom see § 9, second *Obs.*ii)

(ix) <u>The use of the Infinitive with *da* ("to") instead
of a subordinate clause (cf. English)</u>

Gortozit ar glao da devel
Wait for the rain to stop

Sonit ar c'hloch d'ar porzier da zont aman
Ring the bell for the porter to come out

Reit d'in eur bluenn d'in da skriva
Give me a pen for me to write

So after a Preposition:

Daoust d'ezan da veza klanv
"In spite of his being (lit. to him to be) ill"

Obs. (a) Just as this is a substitute for a Concessive
Clause, so other Prepositions may be followed
by the dative of the person and the Infinitive without *da*:

Kent (Goude) dezan ober se
Before (After) he had done it

Ken dezan dont
Until he comes (lit. "... to him to come")

Cf. Welsh:*Wedi i Rufain goncro darn o wlad*
"After Rome had conquered part of the
country"

Ar ol imi gael fy swper
"After I had had my supper"

(b) Goidelic agrees:

I. *Tar eis damh mo shuipear a chaitheamh*
"After having my supper"

G. *An deidh dhaibh an t-eilean fhagail*
"After they had left the island"

26. Phonology and Orthography

Despite its diffusion from a common origin

(Ireland), Goidelic pronunciation is less homogeneous

than one might have expected. Thus an Irishman can

understand a Manxman better than he can a Scotsman,

because the Danes and the Welsh both left their mark

on the Gaelic of Scotland[74]. Characteristic of all

three is the position of the stress on the first

syllable, unless a long syllable follows (indicated

by the *síneadh* or oblique accent (/) unless the

following consonant means that the syllable cannot but

be long)[75]. Fundamental is the distinction between

"broad" (before *a o,u*) and "slender" (before *e* and *i*)

vowels, and the rule that a consonant must stand

either between two broad or between two slender

vowels. The consequent necessity of inserting an *i*

to keep a syllable slender or of omitting it to keep

it broad affects both pronunciation and orthography:

that is why the genitive of *muc* is *muice*, and why

badóir ("boatman") becomes *badora*. The books warn that

broad *L*, *N*, *Gh,Dh* and slender *N* are not in English;

but the fact is that, as every consonant tends to be

affected by the vowels on each side of it and these

vowels themselves have their own peculiarities,

hardly a sound corresponds to its apparent English

equivalent as represented in writing.

The result is that Irish and Gaelic must be among

the least "phonetic" of languages. For example, the

sound represented in English (i) by the letter *Y*

appears here as initial slender *Dh* or *Gh*, and (as

nye) in *nd*;   (ii) *H* may be *sh* (but English *sh* is slen-

der *s*),*th*   (there is no English *th*:,*f* in *féin* ("self"),

and initial broad *ch* (broad medial and final *ch* repre-

sent the surd velar guttural); (iii) *V* and *W* appear

respectively as slender and broad *bh* and *mh* (and *W*

also as *Fh* in *ní fhuair* "I did not get"); (iv)

"chuintant" *J* (as in *judge*) appears as slender initial

D ;   (v) "chuintant" *ch* (church) as initial and final

slender *t* ;   (vi) *R* appears as *n* after initial *C*,

G, *M*, *T*. However (vii) English *F* may be said to appear

in initial *F*, in the medial *F* of the Future tense, in

the word *féin* after *cheana* (M. *hannah*), needed in

Irish for the meaning "already", and in aspirated p;

and (viii) Eclipse provides a normal hard B, D , G .

Equally disconcerting are (ix) the silent letters:

medial and final dh, gh, th, and initial fh; d

before L; n after L; s after prefixed t.

What words containing these sounds (or dropping

them) would look like if phonetically spelt, we can

see by juxtaposing them in their Manx orthography (as

we have done throughout this study); for this was

based on the English system:

	Irish[76]		Manx
(i)	dheanamh	to do	yannoo
	gheall	promised	yiall
	arna ndeanamh	done	er n'yannoo
(ii)	a sheasamh	standing	a hassoo
	seasamh	to stand	shassoo
	anois	now	nish
	thig	(will) come	hig
	fhéin	self	hene
	chonnaic	saw	honnick
(iii)	mo bhean	my wife	my ven
	A mhic!	O son!	vic!
	(mo mhac	my son	my vac
	mo bho	my cow	my vooa)[77]
(iv)	Dia	God	Jee
	tigharna	lord	chiarn

(v)	ait	funny	aitt
(vi)	mná	women	mraane
	cnoc	hill	cronk
(vii)	do phaidir	your prayer	dty phadjer
(viii)	ár bpaidjer	our prayer	nyn badjer
	ár dtalamh	our ground	nyn dhalloo
	ár gcinn	our heads	nyn ging
(ix)	beathaidheach	animal	bioagh
	beannughadh	to bless	bannee
	cheannaigh	bought	chionnee
	ithe	to eat	ee[78]
	blath	bloom	blaa
	fhuair	got	hooar
	d'fhreagair	answered	dreggyr
	Nodlaig	Christmas	N'Ollick
	olna	woollen	olley
	tsaoghal	world (dative)	theill

Not that Manx orthography is completely phonetic –
far from it. Sometimes *ghi-* is kept, though the sound
is *Y* (e.g. *ro-ghiare*, "too short"); and sounds peculiar to Manx seem not to have been given a phonetic
equivalent. Thus in the above list the double *S* of
(*s*) *hassoo* has nothing of the sibilant about it, being
more like a *Y* . A similar sound belongs to medial *sh*
in *toshaight*("beginning"; I. *tosach*) and *dj* in
credjal ("to believe"); broad initial *Ch* may represent the surd *velar* (as in *chammoo*"neither") or

H (as in *cha* "not"); *R* after *N* (e.g. *ynrican* "only")

sounds like a Z; *D* between slender vowels and medial

sh resemble the Z of *azure*; and not only final *T*

as in *aitt* above, but also final *D, N, L* seem to be

followed by a "chuintant" sound. The occasional sound

of a *D* before a final *N* and of a *B* before a final *M*

(e.g. *bedn* for *ben* "woman", *trobm* for *trome* "heavy")

is particularly interesting, because the same pheno-

menon appears in its Brythonic cousin (Late) Cornish

(e.g. *pedn* "head", *tabm* "piece")[79]. As for vowel-

sounds, *-ie-* represents *aï* in *mie* (i.e. agrees with I.

maith "good") and *hie* ("went") and *thie* ("house"),

and the trigraph *oie* represents *aï* in *soie* ("seated")

and *ee* in *oie* ("night" I. *oidhche*).

The Irish sounds discussed here belong to

Ulster (the "dialect" most akin to Scots Gaelic[80]).

Further south one will hear, for example, *raibh* ("was")

pronounced *rev* (not *ro*; cf. M. *row*), and a Z-sound

just audible after a final *R* (e.g. *air* when it is the

last word in the sentence), and not at first recognize

ithe ("ate") or *rith* ("ran") in the sounds *ic'he* and

ric'h.

Brythonic marks itself off at once by having its

stress on the penultimate syllable, to which it returned in the 11th century after five centuries on the
last syllable consequent on the loss of Case-endings.
Welsh is alone in having the difficult sound represented by double *L*, a new phoneme resulting from the
progressive loss of sonant quality in single *L* . This
must have happened later than the departure of the
Romans, because they would have needed a special
spelling-device to render it in their inscriptions;
and indeed not till the 11th century did Anglo-
Saxon attempt to render it (by *thl* and *fl*). *LL* had
become the symbol by the following century. The
original sound of *R* was also surdized, and since
the 16th century has been represented by *Rh* (for an
original *Hr*; cf. English *wh* for Anglo-Saxon *hw*,
as it is still pronounced.) Also peculiar to Welsh
is the prefixing of *Y* to words beginning with *sp*,
st, *sc*; e.g. *ysgrifennu* "to write" (C. *scryfa*, B.
skrivan), as Italian may prefix *i* after *in*. North
Wales even has a U-sound of its own. Welsh, however,
is certainly the most phonetic of the three and
therefore has no silent letters. It has more diphthongs (16) and 6 trigraphs.

Cornish, whose pronunciation was within an ace

of being lost[81] shares with Welsh both the voiced *th*

(represented however by *dh*, not *dd*) and the unvoiced

th, but pronounces double *L* as in English. One of its

U-sounds (represented by *ü*) resembles the French; and

the *A*-sound of "hay" is frequent, especially in mono-

syllables (e.g. *tas* "father" and *nef* "heaven"). There

are 11 diphthongs. Unlike Welsh, it has the letter *K*

used for the hard velar sound when final and before

e, *i*, *y* and consonants other than *L* and *R* ; other-

wise *C* (which, however, may stand for the sibilant in

loan-words such as *certan* "certain"). Intervocalic *S*

represents *Z* (hence *Penzance* for *Pen sans*, "Holy Head"

as does final *S* after a long vowel (e.g. *bos* "to be").

The letter *i* is not used, its sound being rendered

by *y*, which however is also consonantal (i.e. *yowank*

"young" alongside *skyans* "knowledge"). Silent are (or

tend to be) final *F*, final and, less often, intervocal

gh (cf. Goidelic), e.g. in the 2nd person plural endin

-ough, *-eugh*, *flogh* "child", and *byghan* "small".

Otherwise *gh* may represent the same velar sound as

Welsh *ch*, or, when intervocalic after *L* and *R* ,

an *H* ; e.g. *fleghes* "children", pronounced *flajhes*.

The diphthong rendered *ow* may be pronounced *oo* when
final (as in the plural of nouns) or cut to *o*' as
the Possessive Adjective or verbal particle. Unlike
Welsh and Breton, it uses *Qu* (cf. Manx).

Breton agrees with Cornish in not having the
sound of Welsh double *L*: but it has not the sonant
th (*dd*, *dh*) either (nor surd *th*, which they both have).
It is with Cornish again in writing *K*, which is the
third letter of its alphabet, since *C* appears only in
combination with *H*, either as chuintant (*ch*) or as
velar (*c'h*), which two letters come between *H* and *I*
in the dictionaries. Still with Cornish, it does not
sound the *h* in *bihan* "small" (sometimes written *bïan*)
but does not sound it in *ha* "and" either, where Cornish does sound it. *Y* is consonantal (and therefore
comes betweeen *I* and *J* in the alphabet and dictionaries). Unlike its sister-tongues, it has the letter
Z for the sound (sometimes written *zh*), though that
may represent an *H* or silence. Without *Qu* (replaced
by *c'hw*), it agrees with Welsh (where it is replaced
by *cw*), as it does with *gw-* (whereas in Cornish the
W is often slurred over). Before *e* and *i* W is pronounced *V* (as in Goidelic!), as it is also in the one

word *war* ("on") and its compounds. After a vowel fina

V may represent *O*; e.g. *bev* "alive" (cf. Cornish

beo). The letter-groups *GN* and *ILH* (never initially)

represent the French *mouillé* sounds (i.e. as in

peigner and Southern *fille*). Particularly distinctive

are the Breton nasal vowels (indicated by a *tilde* over

the *N* following the vowel): these are met above all

in the ending of the Infinitive (*-añ*, *-iñ* etc.), *emañ*

("is"), *heñ* ("he"), *bremañ* ("now"), etc., and before

V (e.g. *klañv*, "sick"). Once again, French influence

can only be suspected[82].

*   *   *   *   *

From this examination of the six languages it

emerges (i) that there is more homogeneity in the

Goidelic branch than in the Brythonic; (ii) that Manx

has diverged somewhat from the Goidelic norm and has

developed in the direction of simplicity[83]; (iii) tha

Welsh occupies a place apart in Brythonic; and (iv)

that the division between the two branches is not a

straight line but swerves to include one or the other

feature from either. The reason for all this is, of

course, historical: Goidelic is homogeneous because

Gaelic and Manx were carried from Ireland to Scotland

and Man by Irish emigrants; Welsh went its own way because the Saxon King Cewlin of Wessex defeated the
Britons at the Battle of Gloucester in A.D. 557 and
occupied this city, so that the 'Welsh' Britons were
separated from their kinsmen in the South; and these,
having in Cornwall no mountains to protect them, quickly
succumbed to the English, so that many of them emigrated
to the land opposite them, now called after them, Brittany. Here they may have found the old Gaulish tongue
still being spoken, and in any case were in contact with
a foreign people; and as they received further immigrants rather from North Wales than from Cornwall, their
language evolved into a form of Celtic now known as
Breton.

Such is the powerful instrument of human expression
created in its infinite variety by the Celts. Two
members have been for some time no longer a spoken
mother-tongue in the land of their peoples (Cornish for
200 years, Manx for 30), and they now maintain a precarious existence on the lips of local and other enthu-
siasts; the others, as we shall see, fight for survival with varying success.

C. Comparative Text

SIX CELTIC VERSIONS OF ST. MARK 4/13-20

English

13. And he said unto them, Know ye not this parable?
    and how then will ye know all parables?

14. The sower soweth the word.

15. And these are they by the way side, where the word
    is sown; but when they have heard, Satan cometh
    immediately, and taketh away the word that was sown
    in their hearts.

16. And these are they likewise which are sown on stony
    ground; who, when they have heard the word, immed-
    iately receive it with gladness;

17. And have no root in themselves, and so endure but
    for a time: afterward, when affliction or perse-
    cution ariseth for the word's sake, immediately
    they are offended.

18. And these are they which are sown among thorns;
    such as hear the word,

19. And the cares of this world, and the deceitfulness
    of riches, and the lusts of other things entering
    in, choke the word, and it becometh unfruitful.

20. And these are they which are sown on good ground;
    such as hear the word, and receive it, and bring
    forth fruit, some thirtyfold, some sixty, and some
    an hundred.

Irish

13. Agus deir sé leo: An bhfuil sibh-se aineolach ar
    an fháithscéal seo? Agus cad é mar bheas fios
    agaibh ar na fáithscéalta uilig?

14. An té a chuireas, cuirann sé an briathar.

15. Agus is iad seo lucht taobh an bhothar mar a
    gcuirtear an briathar, agus nuair a chluin siad, tig
    Satan láithreach agus beireann sé ar shiubhail

an briathar a cuireadh ina gcroidhthe.

16. Agus mar a gcéadna an lucht ina gcuirtear an síol
ar an talamh chlochach, is iad seo iad, nuair a
chluin siad an briathar, a ghlacas é láithreach le
lúthgháir,

17. Agus ní fhuil fréamh acu ionnta féin, ach tá siad
neamhbhuan; annsin, nuair a thig triobloid agus
géirleanamhaint mar gheall ar an bhriathar,
glacann siad scainneal ar an bhomaite.

18. Agus tá tuilleadh ann ina gcuirtear an síol frid na
dreasógai: is iad seo an lucht a chluin an briathar,

19. Agus tig cúraim an tsaoghail, mealladh an tsaidh-
bhris, agus dúil i neithe eile isteach go bplúchann
siad an briathar, agus bíonn se gan toradh.

20. Agus is iad seo iad i n-ar cuireadh an síol san
talamh mhaith, an lucht a chluin an briathar, a
ghlacas é agus a bheir toradh uatha, duine fá
dheich ar fhichidh, duine fá thrí fhichidh, agus
duine fá chéad.

Gaelic

13. Agus thubhairt e riu, Nach aithne dhuibh an cosamhlachd so? agus cionnus ma ta a thuigeas sibh
gach uile cosamhlachd?

14. Tha 'm fear-cuir a' cur an fhocail.

15. Agus is iad so iadsan ri taobh an rathaid, anns an
cuirear am focal, an déigh dhoibh a chluinntinn,
air ball a ta Satan a' teachd, agus a' togail leis
an fhocail, a shìol-chuireadh 'nan cridheachaibh.

16. Agus is iad so iadsan mar an ceudna a chuireadh
air fearann creagach; muintir, an uair a chluinneas
iad am focal, a gabhas e air ball le gairdeachas:

17. Agus cha'n 'eil freumh aca annta féin, ach mairidh
iad rè sealain; 'na dhéigh sin, 'nuair a dh'éireas
amhgar no geur-leanmhuinn air son an fhocail, air
ball a ta iad a' gabhail oilbheim.

18. Agus is iad so iadsan a chuireadh am measg an
    droighinn, an dream a dh'éisdeas ris an fhocal;

19. agus a ta ro-chùram an t-saoghail so, agus
    mealltaireachd saoibhreis, agus anamianna nithe
    eile teachd a steach, agus a'tachdadh an fhocail,
    agus nithear neothorach e.

20. Agus is iad so iadsan a chuireadh ann an talamh
    maith; an dream a chluinneas am focal, agus a
    ghabhas e, agus a bheir a mach toradh, cuid a
    dheich thar fhicead uiread, cuid a thri ficead
    uiread, agus cuid a cheud uiread as a chuireadh.

Welsh

13. Ac efe a ddywedodd wrthynt.   Oni wyddoch Chwi y
    ddammeg hon?   a pha fodd y gwybyddwch yr holl
    ddamhegion?

14. Yr hauwr sydd yn hau y gair.

15. A'r rhai hyn yw y rhai ar fin y ffordd, lle yr
    hauir y gair;   ac wedi iddynt ei glywed, y mae
    Satan yn dyfod yn ebrwydd, ac yn dwyn ymaith y
    gair a hauwyd yn eu calonnau hwynt.

16. A'r rhai hyn yr un ffunud yw y rhai a hauir ar y
    creigle;   y rhai, wedi clywed y gair, sydd yn
    ebrwydd yn ei dderbyn ef yn llawen;

17. Ac nid oes ganddynt wreiddyn ynddynt eu hunain,
    eithr dros amser y maent: yna, pan ddêl blinder
    neu erlid o achos y gair, yn y man y rhwystrir
    hwynt.

18. A'r rhai hyn yw y rhai a hauwyd ym mysg y drain;
    y rhai a wrandawant y gair,

19. Ac y mae gofalon y byd hwn, a hudoliaeth golud, a
    chwantau am bethau eraill, yn dyfod i mewn, ac yn
    tagu y gair, a myned y mae yn ddiffrwyth.

20. A'r rhai hyn yw y rhai a hauwyd mewn tir da;   y
    rhai sydd yn gwrandaw y gair, ac yn ei dderbyn,
    ac yn dwyn ffrwyth, un ddeg ar hugain, ac un dri
    ugain, ac yn gant.

Manx

13. As dooyrt eh roo, Nagh vel toiggal eu jeh'n
    choraa-dorraghey shoh? as kys eisht nee shiu dy
    chooilley choraa-dorraghey y hoiggal?

14. Ta'n correyder cuirr yn goo.

15. As ad shoh adsyn ta rish oirr y raad, ayn ta'n goo
    er ny chuirr, agh tra t'ad er chlashtyn, ta'n
    drogh-spyrryd cheet jeeragh, as goaill ersooyl
    yn goo va cuirt ayns nyn greeaghyn.

16. As ad shoh neesht yn vooinjer ta cuirt ayns thalloo
    claghagh, ta, erreish daue v'er chlashtyn y goo,
    chelleeragh dy ghoaill eh dy aggindagh:

17. Agh cha vel fraue oc ayndoo hene, as myr shen cha
    vel ad cummal rish agh son earish: ny lurg shen
    tra ta seaghyn ny tranlaase cheet orroo er coontey
    yn ghoo, chelleeragh ta nyn gredjue failleil.

18. As ad shoh yn vooinjer ta cuirt mastey drineyn:
    lheid as ta clashtyn y goo,

19. As ta kiarail y theihll shoh, as molteyraght berchys
    as saynt reddyn elley goll stiagh, as plooghey yn
    goo, as te cheet dy ve neu-vessoil.

20. As ad shoh yn vooinjer ta cuirt ayns thalloo mie,
    lheid as ta clashtyn y goo, as ta dy ghoaill eh,
    as gymmyrkey magh mess, paart jeih fillaghyn as
    feed, paart three-feed, as paart keead-filley.

Cornish

13. Leverel a wrug dhedha "A ny wodhough-why an parabyl-
14. ma? ytho, fatel woffydhough-why an parablys pup oll?
15. An haser a has an ger. Hag awatta'm re usy ryb an
    forth, le may ma hesys an ger; mes wosa y dh'y
    glewes, Satnas a dhe desempys, ha kemeres dhe ves
16. an ger o hesys y'ga holon. Hag awatta'n re-na
    kekefrysyu hesys yn dor meynek, kekemmys wosa y dhe
    glewes an ger, a'n degemer adhystough gans lowena;
17. mes y ny's teves gwrydhyow ynna'ga honen, hag yndella
    ny wrons pesya mes pols byhan; ena, pan dheffo
    anken ha tormentyans awos an ger, adhesempys codha

18 a denewan y whrons. Hag awatta'n re-na yu hesys yn
19. mysk dreyn;   neb a glew an ger, ha prederow an
    bys-ma, ha tenvos a rychyth, ha whans a bythow
    erel ow tos ajy, a dak an ger, hag y te ha bos hep
20. don frut. Lemmyn awatta'n re-na yu hesys yn dor
    mas, neb a glew an ger hag a'n degemer, hag a dhek
    frut, re dek warn ugans, re tryugans, ha re canspl⦁

Breton

13. Hag e lavaras dezho: "Ne gomprenit ket ar barabole:
    se? Penaos neuze e komprenfot an holl barabolenno

14. Ar Gomz eo an hini emañ an hader oc'h hadañ.

15. Ar re a zo a-hed an hent lec'h ma hader ar Gomz, a:
    re-se, a vec'h m'o deus he c'hlevet, e teu raktal
    Satan hag⦁e lam kuit ar Gomz bet hadet enno.

16. Hag en hevelep doare, ar re a zegemer an had war a⦁
    dachenn veinek eo ar re a zegemer ar Gomz gant
    levenez, kerkent ha klevet;

17. hogen n'eus ket donder enno; n'o deus ket dalc'-
    hegezh; ha pa zeu trubuilh pe wallgaserezh
    abalamour d'ar Gomz, raktal e kouezhont.

18. Re all a zegemer an had e-touez an drein, ar re-se
    eo ar re o deus klevet ar Gomz,

19. hogen prederioù ar bed, touell ar binvidigezh hag
    ar gwallc'hoantegezhiou all en em sil en o c'hreiz
    hag a voug ar Gomz ha difrouezh e chom.

20. Hag ar re a zegemer an had en douar mat eo ar re
    a glev ar Gomz hag en em zigor dezhi, ha frouezh a
    daolont, unan tregont, un all tri-ugent, hag un al:
    kant evit unan".

D. Notes to Chapter Eleven

1. So when we find that Latin has both *coquina*(cooking, adj.) and *popina* (eating-house), we deduce that the second word was borrowed from Oscan. (Celtic cognates are W. *pobi*, C. *pobas*, B. *poban* "to bake"). Cf. also the enclitic word for "and": Latin *-que* Umbrian *pe*, Gaulish *pe* (see n. 9), Greek *te*; and for "neither": Latin *nec*, Osco-Umbrian *nep*.

2. So if Welsh has a P where Irish has zero, the word must be a later borrowing; e.g. "plane-tree": Latin (from Greek) *platanus*, Irish *leathan*, W. *planwydden*. Having lost original P, retained original Q instead of changing it to P, and converted Latin P to Q in loan-words, Irish has a paucity of words beginning with P. This shows in dictionaries; e.g. in Dinneen's *Irish-English Dictionary* (1927), among the consonants, P has the least number of pages (except for N), namely 40, against 157 for C (exceeded only by S).

3. It is interesting that Armenian *hinq* ("five") shows Armenian resembling Celtic in losing initial P, but not belonging to the Q-group; cf. also its *hajr* ("father"), Latin *pater*, Irish *athair* (the pronunciation of which is indicated by the Manx *ayr*).

4. Suetonius, *Augustus*, 88.

5. D. Ellis Evans, *Gaulish Personal Names* , p.375.

6. Add to these contributions the system of vigesimal counting (already met in Cumbria and Wales).

7. It is not certain that the words *Sequana* (Nominative) and *Sequani* (the tribe of that name mentioned on p. 22) are related.

8. It was the study of these names which enabled C.W.G. Glück in 1857 to refute A. Holtzmann's preposterous theory, according to which the Continental Celts and the Germans were one and the same and had nothing to do with the Britons.

9. There may be an eighth Celtic language hidden in the
   40 inscriptions of the 2nd century B.C. attributed
   to what is called "Lepontic", the speech of a people
   centred on Lugano. There is nothing in the flexion
   of its Nouns that is not found also in Gaulish or
   Irish (e.g. Gen. Sing. in -*i*, Nom. Plur. in -*oi*);
   it has both the Weak and the Strong Preterite ending
   in E and U respectively; it has Proper Names
   similar to Gaulish ones: *Alkouinos* (*Alcovindus*),
   Eripochios (*Eribogius*), where *Eri* is an intensive
   Prefix); and it shows both loss of P (e.g. in that
   Prefix, *Eri-* and P for *Kw* (e.g. in enclitic *pe*;
   see n. 1). Besides this link with Osco-Umbrian it
   also has consonantal themes in -*ei*, and *as* for *ad*,
   as in the name *Askonetos*. For these reasons the
   author of the standard work on Lepontic, M. Lejeune, considers its Celtic parentage "probable".

   Examples : (i) The Latumaros Vase from the Tomb of
   Ornavasso: LATUMARUI SAPSUTAI PE UINOM NASOM ("To
   Latumarus and Sapsuta Naxian wine"); (ii) The
   Vergiate Stone (in Milan Archaeological Museum):
   PELKUI PRUIAM TEU KARITE ("Deo set up a bridge for
   Pelgo"). Cf. the Gallic town Samarobriva (Caes. *B.G.*
   5,24), i.e. "Somme-bridge" (now Amiens).

10. The Rel. Pron. is omitted before vocalic parts of
    Bos (see note 11).

11. See note 8. The Rel. Pron. is also omitted in Cornish
    before the vocalic parts of *Mos* ("To go"), in Breton
    before the Present *On* and *Emaon* of *Beza* ("To be")
    and all parts of *Kaoud* ("To have"), and in Welsh
    before *oedd*, *bu*, and *bydd* of *Bod* (the last two keep-
    ing their softened consonant; e.g. *Cymru fydd* "Wales
    (that) shall be").

12. In 1838 Franz Bopp first showed that the Mutations
    were caused by a preceding Def. Art. or other word,
    and the resultant indication as to the Case-endings
    of these preceding words proved that Celtic was
    as Indo-European in Declension as it was known to be
    in Conjugation.

13. Modern spelling omits most of these dead letters, with some loss to etymology.

14. How Welsh came to nasalize after "*fy*" (starting about A.D. 500) is not clear, especially since it does not require N to avoid hiatus before a vowel; e.g. *fy allwedd* "my key" (which may however be written "f'allwedd").

15. Believe it or not, *a* ("his") is the debris of the Indo-European word that produced Latin *eius*!

16. Becomes *yr* before a vowel original or after lost G.

17. According to the dictionaries, masc. in Irish and fem. in Gaelic. Yet Irish has respectively *pocán* and *gandal* for "he-goat" and "gander"! (But then *cailin*"girl" is a masculine Noun! - perhaps because of the suffix for diminutives -*ín*; cf. German *Mädchen*, neuter). Cf. the Gaelic words for *woman* (boirionnach), *cow* (mart), and *mare*(capall) - all masculine; and that for *farm-worker* (sgalag)-feminine.

18. SH represents the Goidelic pronunciation of S before a "narrow" vowel. (The Gaelic and Irish for "bee" is *beach*).

19. It has been stated that the Passive use arises from the ellipse of *cael* after *wedi*, i.e. that it is the normal Perfect Passive of the *cael*-idiom treated above. But if *cael* could be dropped without ambiguity, this is because the Verbal Noun is essentially neutral, neither Active nor Passive (cf. the Irish proverb quoted p.164); in which case *cael* was never necessary with *wedi*.

20. There is some doubt as to whether Gaelic *air* represents an original *iar* ("after") or is the modern Preposition *air* ("on"). Presumably the same doubt should attach to Manx *er*, especially as, like Gaelic *air*, there are occasions when it does not mutate (cf. p.164 "lost"); i.e. we are dealing with the fusion of two prepositions. The Object Pronoun in Manx follows the verb: *Ta mee er chionnaghey*

shiu. "I have bought you".

21. Both Cornish and Breton change their Particle to a
    Preposition before the Possessive Adjective.   Thus
    C. *ow* becomes *orth*, and B. *o* (*oc'h*) becomes *ouz*.
    (For Welsh *wrth* with the Infinitive see p. 219).

22. Not to be confused with *nee*, Interrogative and Neg
    tive of '*s*.

23. *Y* here is not the Relative Particle, but the relic
    of a *y* inserted for phonetic reasons before infixe
    m.

24. Strictly "among us" from the Preposition *mastey*.
    The Preposition *eddyr* "between" does not combine:
    eddyr shin "between us".

25. This word goes back to the Indo-European root that
    produced Latin *latus* and Welsh *lled* ("side").   Its
    development in Irish into a Preposition denoting
    the Agent ("by") shows that the modern use of
    seitens (lit. "from the side of") in a certain
    style of German is not such a "Sprachdummheit" as
    W. Schulze makes out in his book of that name (p.
    340).   After thousands of years the same metaphor
    at work again.

26. This Prepositional Pronoun is colloquially used ir
    Breton as the Direct Object of a Verb (cf. Welsh
    mohonom etc., as in the example on p. 171).   Thus
    the phrase on p. 171   12, no. viii, "If he sees
    me", could be: *Ma wel ac'hanon.*

27. The 2nd Person forms in P are condemned by some ε
    incorrect.   Their literary equivalents are *ac'h eι*
    and *hoc'h eus.*

28. Hundreds of years later the need to distinguish
     two kinds of Being was felt again, when Spanish aι
     Portuguese were evolving out of Latin, and *está*
     from *stat* was used for impermanent state in oppo-
     sition to *es* (*é*) from *est*.   Can this common featuι
     be a relic of the Celtiberi, the mixed race who

inhabited part of Hispania (Iberia) in and before
Roman times?

29. See § 25, p. 221.

30. If Latin *trux* is cognate, then an English contact
is *truculent*.

31. Also *labous*.

32. To this word Irish attaches the prefix *dear* (*deir*)
from *dearbh* "genuine", as also to "sister", and
other nouns (cf. Greek *autadelphos*).

33. Also *cona* and *cointe*.

33a. Having assumed the sense of "fellow clansman", it
was replaced in Classical times by the adjective
which often qualified it: *adelphos* ("from the same
womb"); cf. note 32.

34. This word shows that the cleavage between the two
branches continues. Irish sometimes uses its own
word, *aibhle* ("flying spark"). Cornish *tredan* is of
course a *calque* on the Welsh, like several others
undocumented in Middle Cornish (the form of the
language chosen for resuscitation). Gaelic has
gne dealanaich ("a sort of lightning").

35. Manx has for "without" also *fegooish*, which has the
peculiarity of combining with a prefixed Possessive
Adjective; e.g. *m'egooish* "without me", *dt'egooish*
"without you", *n'egooish* "without him", *ny fegooish*
"without her", *nyn vegooish* "without us, you, them".

36. A reminder that, in Goidelic, only Irish has preserved a second Conjugation with Future and Conditional in *-eoch-* as opposed to *-f-*. Incidentally,
it is odd (and a breach with Italo-Celtic unity),
that Goidelic evolved a Future and Conditional pair
in both its Conjugations, just as Romance did in
all of them.

37. Gaelic changes the Future Termination to (*e*)*as* after
mâ.

38. The Celtic infinitive is really a Verbal Noun; whi
    probably means, not that Celtic *lost* its Infinitiv
    (as Greek did), but that the Verbal Abstract Nouns
    from which the Infinitive in Indo-European eventu-
    ally developed kept in Celtic their nominal
    character.

39. Irish for Goidelic, Welsh for Brythonic, except
    where stated.

40. Cornish and Breton insert N before their word for
    20 after the Preposition *war* ("on"); e.g. C.
    war n-ugans, B. *war n-ugent*.

41. I.e. "the fortress of Lug"; cf. the Irish hero
    Lugh and the Welsh hero Lleu. Unfortunately,
    there is a Middle Welsh word *lleu* (Modern *goleu*)
    meaning "light", which agrees with a 9th century
    translation of *Lugdunum* as "mons lucidus". An
    even earlier derivation is from *loûgos* "raven"
    (Ps. Plutarch *de fluviis* 6,4); and modern ones
    link it with Gk. *loûgeon* "marsh" or early Irish
    lugh "lynx". But why not invoke Irish *lugh* "small
    the fusion of adjective and noun being characteris
    of Gaulish? Cf. *Noviodunum* (Nouan) "New Town" and
    Noviomagus (Nijmegen and Neumagen) "New Field".

42. Cf. Breton *Diziou* "Thursday". (After the Definite
    Article *Ziou* becomes *Yaou*).

43. Cf. Romagnol *San Grugnon* ("Saint Sulker") from
    grugno "snout", "pout": "Ash-Wednesday".

44. So too in Romontsch ("Calondas").

45. Sometimes Manx uses the Preposition *jeh* ("of") (cf
    the quotation on p. 199).

46. Manx uses the Latin loan-word *cabbyl* (gen. *cabbil*)
    though it shares *eagh* "steed" with I. and G. *each*
    (gen. *eich*), and the root *markee* "to ride". The
    gearran is strictly a gelding, as the root shows.

47. Collective; but *ones* for *lambs* separately. Cf.
    Italian collective fem. plurals of masculine nouns,
    e.g. *lenzuola* "sheets" (on a bed), *lenzuoli* "sheets"
    (in a cupboard).

48. Cf. the disagreement over gender among Romance
    languages with words derived from Latin Neuters.

49. J.J. Kneen, *An English-Manx Pronouncing Dictionary*
    (*Mona's Herald*, 1953), p. viii.

50. Cf. the Goidelic root *abr* appearing in certain
    parts of their verb "to speak".

51. Gaelic *sgilling* means "penny" (a premonition of
    times to come).

52. See p. 166.

53. Cf. *e ker* "in (to) town" without mutation, For *ker*
    see p. 186 .

54. Representing Irish *Ma's áil libh* ("If it's pleasing
    with you").

55. For *Dew re-dallo*.

56. Cf. Welsh *trugaredd*, Cornish *tregereth* "mercy" from
    Latin *mercedem* "reward", later "favour" and so
    "grace", when it took over from the Latin *gratiae*
    that prevailed elsewhere. Irish uses the word for
    "blessing" (*beannacht*) in greetings and farewells,
    the sense varying with the Preposition:*Beannacht
    leat* "farewell".

57. Cf. *an t-ath-la* "the morrow", *cur ar ath-la* "post-
    pone", *ath-uair* "again", *san ath-bhliain* "in the
    New Year", *ath-dhiolta* "second-hand" (resold). So
    too Gaulish *Ate-* as in the name *Atespatus* (cf.
    Welsh *ateb* "answer").

58. So: *comhdhail* "convention", "meeting" and Gaulish
    com(*b*), e.g. in the name *Combiomarus* (Livy 38,19,2).
    It may be intensive like Latin *cum-* e.g. *comhlionadh*
    "to fulfil" (cf. *complere*)

59. Cf. Gaulish *Voteporix* (p. 46), the *mons Vosegus* (*Vosg*
    of Caesar, *B.G.* 4,10, and the legate of the 22nd
    legion in A.D. 69, Vocula (Tacitus, *Hist.* 4,24).

60. Cf. W. *gor* in *gorwaith* "over-work", C. *gorfalster*
    "superabundance", B. *gorre* "surface", and the
    Gaulish Prefix *Ver-* as in *Vercingetorix*, *vertragus*
    "hound" (used by Martial, 14,200).

61. In its form *fir* it may represent *fear* "man" (Gen.
    sing. and Nom. plur. *fir*). Hence the equivalence
    of the Gaulish Prefix *vir-* is not certain, e.g. in
    the name of the Lusitanian chieftain whom the
    Romans could beat in 140 B.C. only by treachery,
    Viriathus.

62. Also *freas*, e.g. *freas-ghniomh* "opposition". In
    Gaelic *frith* indicates a lower degree; e.g. *baile*
    town, *frith-bhaile* "village" or "suburb". Manx
    uses the Adverb *noi* (lit. "against him").

63. For relationships "in-law" Irish either translates
    that phrase (*i ndlighe*) or adds *ceile* ("spouse")
    e.g. *mathair ceile* "mother-in-law". The real
    sense of *leas-* is "deputy" e.g. *leaschathaoirleach*
    "deputy-chairman".

64. The first *leath* is a noun "half", the second exist
    only as a Prefix meaning "lateral", "on one side".

65. Cf. the name of the Gaulish chieftain Tarcondimotu
    from whom Cicero received a letter on his way to
    Cilicia in 51 B.C. The Cornish for "tomcat" is
    gourgath ("man cat"; cf. W. *cath gwryw* and for
    "tabby" *cath fenyw*). Manx for "tom-cat" is
    collagh-kayt, from *kellagh* "cock" used particularl
    for the male of fowls.

66. In Gaulish, when prefixed to Adjectives, it is in-
    tensive; e.g. the Personal Name *Admarus* ("Very
    great"). Welsh and Breton also use the Ordinal
    ail ("second") (B. *eil*)as a prefix in the sense
    of repetition; e.g. W. *ailadrodd*, B. *eilgerian*
    (corresponding to Welsh *adeirio*)"to repeat". This

ail must be cognate with Old Irish *aile* and Latin *alius*, and reappears in the Gaulish Prefix *Allo-*. as in *Allobroges* ("from another land"; cf. *bro*, and Welsh *allfro* "foreigner").

67. Cornish uses also *tebel* ("wicked") as a prefix in this sense; e.g. *dyghtya* "to treat", *tebeldhyghtya* "to maltreat".

68. Cognate with Irish *so* and, via Greek, with English "hygiene". For the parallelism *s/h* see p.182.

69. Also in "nick-name" (*llysenw*, B. *lesanv*) as in Irish (*leas-ainm*); but for "vice-(president" etc.) W. uses the word *is* "lower". The Prefix is therefore Common Celtic. It enables Breton, unlike French, to distinguish a step-mother from a mother-in-law, called *mamm-gaer* like *belle-mère*. For step-mother Welsh has also *mam wen* (lit. "fair, or blessed, mother"). Cornish, though having the old words *whygeran* and *wheger* (Latin *socer* and *socrus* (s/h again!) for father- and mother-in-law, also uses *syra* and *dama* qualified by *da* "good"; so too *brodor-da* "brother-in-law, as an alternative to the trans-lation of the English "in-law" by *dre lagha*, which is the norm for "sister-in-law" (*whor dre lagha*). For son-, daughter-in-law, it has special words: *düf* (plur. *devyon*) and *gühyth* (plur. *gühydhow*). For relations by marriage Welsh follows the English throughout, though having *chwegrwn* and *chweger* (cf. Cornish above) for "father- and mother-in-law" as alternatives to *tad* (*mam*)*yng nghfraith*.

70. Its Indo-European cognate is *amb-*, *ambi-*, *amphi-*, *am-*. Cf. Old Irish *im-* (*iom-*), as in *imguin* "slay each other", *imsoi* "turns" (intransitive). In the Welsh form *am-* and in Gaulish it can serve as an intensive.

71. Goidelic prefixes *árd* ("high") as in *ardeaglais* "cathedral" (M. *ardchiamble*).

72. Goidelic is also not at one: Gaelic shares *iontach* ("wonderfully") with Irish, but prefers *gle*, while

Manx uses *feer* ("truly"); and all make much use o
their intensive prefixes.

73. For Goidelic equivalents see p. 227.

74. See *An t-Ultach*, February 1966, p. 9, and April
    1967, p. 7.

75. Before *th* and in final unaccented syllables such
    as *-án* and *-óg* the *síneadh* is kept although the
    vowel is pronounced short!

76. Spelling reform has changed the appearance of some
    of these words, especially where fossil letters ha
    been eliminated. Thus we now see in books: *tiarna*
    beathach, beannú, tsaol.

77. For final broad *mh* as *W* cf. *yannoo* above and *marro*
    (I. *marbh*, W. *marw*). But Manx has the letters *Qu*
    and *W* to represent these sounds where necessary;
    e.g. *quaail* "to meet", *my whaail* "to meet me".
    Gaelic *bh* and *mh* represent *V* except after a broad
    vowel followed by *L, R,* or *S*; e.g. *samhla* "likenes
    samhradh "summer" (M. *sourey*).

78. As the Future 3rd sing. ends in *ee* and "she" is *ee*
    "she will eat" would be *eeee-ee*, had not recourse
    been had to the Relative Future, *eeys.*

79. Manx may also sound G before final *ng*; e.g. *lhogn*
    for *lhong* "ship". For the opposite insertion of
    M before B cf. *tombaghey* "tobacco". (Cf. the
    notorious Greek Verb *blosko*).

80. And perhaps to Manx.

81. The sounds of Cornish were first described in 1707
    by the Welsh antiquarian Edward Lluyd, and are sai
    to be still influential in the pronunciation of
    English by genuine Cornishmen.

82. Breton, having no natural barrier such as a
    mountainous area (like Wales and Scotland) or a
    river (like Cornwall), was particularly exposed to

the infiltration of French sounds and words from
an early stage. Hence the presence of French
chuintants as in *jod* ("cheek") and *chom* ("to stay");
and thus *L* before *T* became *O* (e.g. *aotrou* "mon-
sieur", from *alltraw*; cf. Cornish *altrow* "stepfather", *geot* "grass"; cf. Welsh *gwellt*), while
conversely the final *L* of Old French was preserved
(e.g. *mantell*) just as *S* was before *T* (e.g. *mestr*
"maître"). Some of the thousands of Old French
loan-words later vanished from French; e.g. *paotr*
"boy" from *peautraille*. Modern borrowings are
sometimes disguised by adaptation to Celtic
phonetics; e.g. initial *V* becomes *GW* as in
gweturiou "voitures" (but *vélos* gives *beloiou!*).

83. It therefore has a strong claim to be the inter-
Celtic "lingua franca" sought by the Celtic
Languages Conference in Ireland in 1976. One of
the proposals, however, was for Cornish, as being
the weakest.

E. Linguistic Index to Chapter 11 pp.144-267

12. THE DECLINE OF CELTIC SPEECH

How much Celtic is spoken today? Let the statistics speak for themselves:

Language	Population 1971	Proportion of Celtic speakers					Total speakers 1971
		1901	1931	1951	1961	1971	
Welsh	2,731,204	50%	37%	29%	26%	20.84%	542,402
Irish[1]	4,514,313	28%	22%	23%	27.2%	28.3%	772,929
Gaelic	5,228,965	4.3%	2.7%	1.8%	1.6%	1.8%	88,892
Breton	1,500,000		75%	33%		44%	600,000
Manx	56,289	8.4%	1%	Below 1%	—	—	300*
Cornish	379,892	—	—	—	—	—	200*
Total	14,410,663						2,004,723

* (Self-)taught

To these figures must be added the native speakers
living outside their "national" borders, such as the
Welsh-speaking settlers in Patagonia now numbering a
few thousand, i.e. about the same number as speak it
in London and other English towns; the Scots of Nova
Scotia, and some Irish immigrants into the United
States: say 20,000 in all.

It is the percentages that matter, not the totals;
for it may well be the case that through the normal
increase of population there are more speakers of
Welsh, for example, today than ever before, but whereas
the earlier total represented the quasi-totality of the
inhabitants of the region, the present figures reveal
a steady lowering of the proportion, i.e. the gradual
submergence of the native language under that of the
newcomers, with the consequent threat to its survival
increasing with every generation. Between the beginning
and the end of the nineteenth century the proportion of
Welsh-speakers dropped from 90% to 54%[2], that of Irish-
speakers from nearly 75% to 28%. It has been calculated[3]
that if the proportion of Welsh-speaking children was
only 12% in 1977, then this number must be doubled by
1981 merely to keep the Welsh-speaking population stationary at 20%. Meanwhile the number of monoglots

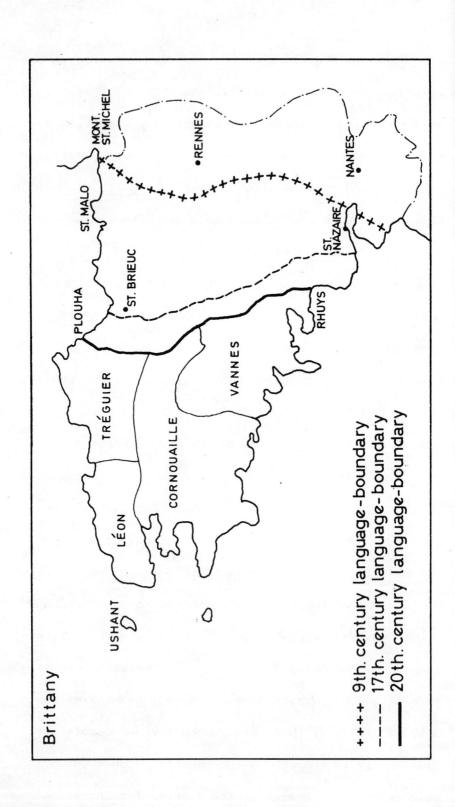

Brittany

USHANT

LÉON

TRÉGUIER

CORNOUAILLE

PLOUHA

• ST. BRIEUC

ST. MALO

MONT.
ST. MICHEL

• RENNES

NANTES
•

VANNES

RHUYS

ST.
NAZAIRE

+ + + + 9th. century language-boundary
– – – 17th. century language-boundary
—— 20th. century language-boundary

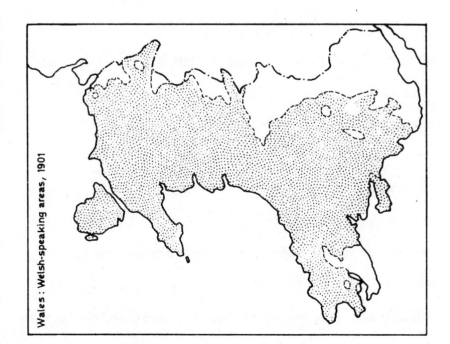

Wales : Welsh-speaking areas, 1901

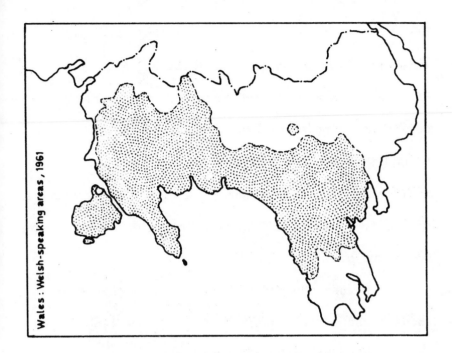

Wales : Welsh-speaking areas, 1961

steadily falls: between 1851 and 1891 the number of
Irish-speaking monoglots fell from 319,602 to 38,121
(5%) and is now estimated at zero; the number of
Gaelic-speaking monoglots in Scotland declined from
44,000 in 1891 to 2,178 in 1951, and to 974 in 1961.
(Brittany still claims 100,000). Thus the proportion
of Celtic speakers in the territory which they occupy
works out at 7.1%.

Even when the proportional figure (percentage)
shows a rise, one's satisfaction must be tempered by
the thought that the increased actual total recorded
in a census is based on self-assessment by those who
have learnt the language at school or in adult classes.
Thus the rise from 22% back to 28% in the number of
Irish-speakers between 1931 and 1971 is due in large
measure to the foundation of *Connradh na Gaeilge* (The
Gaelic League) in 1893 for the express purpose of
"reviving" Irish. In other words, these new speakers
are not necessarily using the language in the normal
routine of life; and in fact such non-native-speakers
were not even counted in earlier censuses. On the
other hand, they do supply the teachers necessary for
teaching the language in about half of Eire's Secondary

Schools and the 13,000 qualified to teach through

Irish in her Primary Schools. The Gaelic League has

therefore succeeded at least in keeping the language

alive; but that is not the same thing as restoring

it as the first language of the country.

Similarly with Gaelic: the last census-returns

show 6000 more speakers than in 1961, the first increase

since 1871, but for these new speakers Gaelic is now

their second language[4].

The truth of what has been happening to these

languages will perhaps make more impact, if proportional

figures are translated into visual terms. (See graph

on next page.)

There comes a point when, short of remedial meas-

ures, the decline accelerates, and the contrast between

the actual totals of native speakers at the beginning

and end of a given period makes   painful reading.

Between 1891 and 1931 the number of Gaelic-speakers was

nearly halved (from 250,000 to 136,000); twenty years

later it was down to 95,000. In 1971 the number of

Gaelic-speakers in Argyllshire had dropped by 2000 in

ten years (to 7825, of whom only 375 were under 14)[5].

Canada had 30,000 Gaelic-speakers in 1931; twenty

WHAT THE LAST 70 YEARS HAVE SEEN

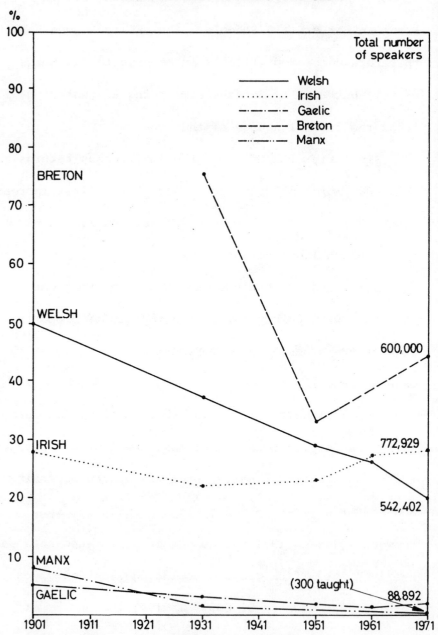

years later there were only 6,789. Between 1952 and

1974 the number of Breton-speakers fell from around

one million to 700,000. In 1901 there were 977,000

speakers of Welsh; in 1911 there were 929,000 - a loss

of 48,000 in ten years. Let Manx show how quickly a

language precipitates to extinction, when the terminal

phase has been reached. From 12,000 speakers of Manx

in 1874 and 4419 in 1901 (when something effective

could have been done) the number had fallen to 915 in

1921; to 529 in 1931; to 20 in 1946; to 10 in 1950[6];

to 2 in 1960, and to 1 in 1962, when the language as a

mother-tongue survived only in the thoughts of Ned

Maddrell, who took it to the grave with him in 1974 at

the age of 97. As a matter of fact, the language had

had only the twilight existence of unspoken thoughts

for at least the previous twenty years; for the sur-

viving speakers lived far apart and there was thus no

conversation. The latest date at which we can find a

Manx-speaking community in action in 1920 in the town

of Cregneash.

Thus anyone over four today will be able to tell

his children: "In my lifetime one of the mother-

tongues of the British Isles ceased to be"; and if

the child feels that the death of a language is as
much an ecological disaster as the extinction of a
species, he will ask: "Was nothing done to save it?"
And the answer will be: "Nothing". Although the doom
of the language had been proclaimed as early as 1859[7],
the falling of the last speakers one by one passed
unnoticed outside the pages of *Coraa Ghailckagh*: Sept.
1952 - Mrs. Watterson, aged 92 ("she loved the old
language, and it's many a tale she told of the old
days"); Feb. 1953 - Henry Boyde ("we can still hear
his voice, because he recorded his stories"); Apr.
1953 - John Kinvig, aged 93 ("he helped us to speak
Manx and was glad to see it revived"); Oct. 1954 -
Mrs. E. Karran ("she remembered the old days when one
could hear Manx spoken in every house in Cregneash");
Apr. 1956 - Thomas Leece, aged 96 ("a real Manxman").
Thus tolled the bell for Manx - unheard.

How can one now open a Manx book and not exclaim:
"What! You could let all this die? You could refuse
to speak this language, though in it your mothers
nursed you, you played your earliest games, and said
your first 'I love you'?"

How many languages have fallen by the way in the

march of history! and not a tear shed. Sumerian,

Babylonian, Minoan, Assyrian, Lydian, Phrygian,

Etruscan, to name only the most ancient, have van-

ished; yet once they were the speech of proud nations,

the bearers of a culture, the vehicles of a literature.

Armies marched to orders barked in them; priests put

their words in the mouths of gods; poets used their

music for their hearts' outpourings: but the days came

when they stood like Manx on the brink of eternal

silence, and the last speaker died and the language

passed, unmourned, unheeded, undescribed.

How can one explain that the great thinkers of

antiquity, with their unquenchable thirst for knowledge,

nevertheless left language unexplored? Even the

"master of those that know", Aristotle, whose writings

constitute an encyclopedia of contemporary knowledge,

never learnt another language, let alone saw linguistics

as part of science in the widest sense. He could collect

all that was known about the reproduction of animals,

but the strange languages on the borders of the Greek

world did not excite his curiosity. He tells us in his

Ethics of the Celts' alleged lack of fear of earthquakes

and floods (which sounds like a rationalization of

Ephorus' peculiar statement, quoted by Strabo 7,293,

that "they take up arms against the waves"), whereas

what we would like to have is the complete conjugation

of one of their verbs or even just fifty common words.

He and Plato were indeed philologists, but the words

they loved were Greek. Could not Thucydides, who

had a Thracian mother and was singularly well informed

on Thracian affairs, have told us at least enough about

the Thracian language to reveal the degree of its

similarity to Armenian? When we do find awareness of

a foreign language, it is in a comedy: for Plautus

in his play *Poenulus* introduces a Carthaginian spouting

20 lines of Punic, which doubtless had the audience

rolling in the 'wedges' but which today is rightly

taken seriously as a useful contribution to Phoenician

studies[8]. Not a single grammar, phrase-book, or dic-

tionary of another tongue was published in Greek or

Latin throughout the whole period of their greatness!

(Babylonian had at least dictionaries of Sumerian and

Kassite). Can it be that their own stupendous langua

seemed to them to render other forms of speech not wo

learning? Or was the eventual disappearance of these

other tongues taken for granted as they saw their own

cultural and administrative sphere spread across the
world? For us, that would have been a reason for
recording them. Though educated Romans learnt Greek,
we hear of no Greek Grammar written for speakers of
Latin; presumably the method was strictly the Direct,
and Old Cato had the benefit of a Greek slave. On
their very doorstep was Etruscan, which they knew to
be ancient and the bearer of a civilization different
from their own; yet they watched it pass into oblivion
without the slightest attempt to record its mechanism
for posterity. The army of Julius Caesar in Gaul had
interpreters on its staff, but not one of them felt the
impulse to record Gaulish for us, so that we might have
had a seventh Celtic language for our study. The ancients seem to have felt no obligation towards posterity, thinking of it only as the time in which a man
might be famous; but in that case they missed a chance
here.

The Greek attitude appears indeed in the very word
which they coined for "foreigners": *barbaroi* they called
them, which is as though we called them "jabberers", as
indeed we sometimes do. One thing is certain: no language
ever died for purely linguistic reasons. Languages as

such cannot be ranged in an order of merit any more

than can the notes of music. Greek may be superior to

Hebrew as the language of philosophy, but the

Septuagint shows us what happened to it when it tried

to render the sublimities of religion. Latin may be

ideally suited to the formulation of law, but the

Vulgate shows that the time had come for its daughters

to take its place. As mechanisms of speech even Latin

and Greek must accept as equals the tongues of the

Bushman and the Aborigine. Why then do they perish?

Notes to Chapter Twelve

1. Eire: 2,978,248; N. Ireland: 1,536,065. Tomás Ó'
    Domhnalláin points out in his article 'Ireland: the
    Irish language in education' in *Lingvaj Problemoj
    kaj Lingva Planado (LPLP)*, 1, No. 2 (1977), p. 84,
    that the figures would be very different if native-
    speakers only were counted. The 1946 census showed
    that native speakers in the Gaeltachtaí (parts of
    7 out of 32 counties, as against parts of 23 coun-
    ties in 1851) had decreased by 10% (to 192,963) in
    ten years. In *Meascra Uladh* ("Ulster Miscellany"),
    1974, *Gaeilge na hAlban - Gaeilge gan ghluaiseacht*
    ("The Gaelic of Scotland - Gaelic without a move-
    ment"), p. 90, Colm O'Baóill estimated the number
    of Irish-speakers in the Gaeltacht at about 30,000
    compared with 80,000 "self-styled" Gaelic-speakers
    in Scotland, and he added a graph to show how much
    faster the number of Ireland's native-speakers had
    fallen to this 30,000 from 680,245 than Scotland's
    250,000 had fallen to 80,000 in the same sixty
    years between 1891 and 1951, despite the difference
    in government-support between the two countries.

To quote Professor Brian Ó'Cuív of University
College, Dublin (*Documents on Ireland* No. 15, p.
6), "nobody can tell today (1960) how many of our
people are really Irish-speakers", and "probably
no more than 35,000 persons use Irish as their
ordinary medium of speech".

2. C. James,'Welsh Bilingualism - Fact or Friction',
   in *LPLP*, 1, No. 2 (1977), p. 7.

3. Meic Stephens, *Linguistic Minorities in Western
   Europe* (1976) p. 185.

4. R.E. Wood, 'Linguistic Organization in Scotland' in
   LPLP, 1, No. 1 (1977), p. 44. He points out that
   the imposing figure of 11,179 Gaelic-speakers in
   Glasgow (one-seventh of the Scottish total) seems
   less strong when contrasted with the million inhabitants of the city, whereas the mere 2540 speakers on the Isle of Harris constitute 94% of its
   population.

5. *Y Ddraig Goch*, Tachwedd 1978, p. 7.

6. Dr. Glanville Price correctly points out in *The
   Linguist* of Jan. 1960, p. 14, that "the (official)
   figure of 355 Manx-speakers in 1951 is quite
   unrealistic". For one thing, members of *Yn Cheshaght Ghailckagh* had tracked down only 20 in 1936
   (*An t-Ultach* Jan. 1977, p. 16 and March 1967, p. 5),
   which makes the earlier figures also suspect, and
   in 1947 had found only 10 for their desperate campaign of tape-recording (ibid. Jan. 1977).

7. "Manx is rarely now heard in conversation, except
   among the peasants. It is a doomed language."
   (A writer of 1859 quoted in *An t-Ultach* of March
   1967, p. 6).

8. M. Sznycer, *Les passages puniques en transcription
   latine dans le 'Poenulus' de Plaute* (1967).

13. THE CAUSES OF DECLINE

No single cause can explain the loss of a languag
by a people for whom it was once the badge of their
identity. There are many causes, political, economic,
psychological, closely interconnected and possessing
cumulatively such an irresistible force that we feel
inclined to say, It could not have been otherwise. Bu
could it? Let us examine each cause:

1. DISUNITY:

*Britanni . . . tandem docti commune periculum
concordia propulsandum*[1]: so wrote Tacitus as he prepa
to describe the Battle of the Grampians of A.D. 83, at
which the united Caledonians made their last desperate
stand against the might of Rome. How else could Rome
explain a Pictish army of 30,000 men? But it was certainly not a Celtic effort; for in the preceding sentence we are told that Agricola's army included regime
of Britons 'tested by a long peace', i.e. Brythons frc
the South, after only 40 years romanized enough to fig
for Rome.

In dealing with Celts Rome had no need to employ
policy of 'divide and rule': the divisions were alrea
there. She did indeed confer 'most favoured nation'
status on one of the Gallic peoples, the Aedui, but

this was a reward for Aeduan support against the Arverni

and Allobroges in 122 B.C. Thus when the Romans in-

vaded Gaul in 58 B.C., it was by invitation of the

Aedui, who had appealed for help against the Helvetii -

a fact of which the Roman general, Petilius Cerialis,

reminded the Gauls of a later generation, in A.D. 69,

when he crushed the last flicker of Gallic independence

proudly called the *Imperium Galliarum*[2]. The Aedui could

no more foresee that they were signing the death-

warrant of Gaulish than the King of Leinster could think

that he was putting Irish at risk when he called in the

English.

There could, of course, no more have been Pancel-

ticism at this date than there could have been Panhelle-

nism in Greece before Gorgias proposed it in 392 B.C.

It is doubtful whether the various Celtic peoples were

as conscious of having a common descent, language, reli-

gion, and culture as the Athenians were when, according

to Herodotus (8,144), they assured the Spartans in 480

B.C. that on this ground alone they could never ally

themselves with the Persians against Greeks. To be sure,

we have one clarion-call for Celtic unity in a violently

anti-Saxon poem from the Welsh *Book of Taliesin* of the

10th century, the *Armes Prydain* ("Prophecy of Britain'

It catalogues the misdeeds of the Saxons and, after

calling for

> an agreement of the Welsh with the men of
> Dublin, the Irish of Ireland, the men of
> Anglesey, the Picts, the men of Cornwall
> and of the Clyde,[3]

foresees the day when the united Britons will rule "fr

the Isle of Man to Brittany", i.e. when Britain is a

Celtic island again. But there was little chance that

such a dream would be realized, when each component

people was fragmented into a number of tribes or clans

under chieftains, princes, or kings, extending their

power at each other's expense and often combining in

groups against the threat of one of them become too

great, just as we see the Greek city-states doing in

their wars, alliances, and Amphictyonies. Even if a

powerful ruler succeeded in welding a number of prince

doms together, as Rhodri the Great did in A.D. 872,

when he ruled all Wales except part of the South, ther

could be no permanent cohesion as long as custom requi

a man's territory to be divided at his death among his

sons; and Rhodri had eight. The disastrous results c

such a custom appeared clearly in 1192 when King Rhys

was prevented by a quarrel among his sons from capturi

Swansea and thus adding to his realm the Deheubarth[4]

("the Southern Part"), as the region was called, a name

implying awareness that Wales was properly a single

country. "If they had stood together," says the hist-

orian[5], "the history of Wales would have been different

and certainly happier." What happened in 876 was that

South Wales allied itself with King Alfred of Wessex for

protection against Rhodri. Similarly, Rhodri's grand-

son, Hywel Dda, was King of all Wales except the south-

east in 942; but his title of "Good" was probably be-

stowed on him by the pro-English party of South Wales,

which desired union with England under Athelstan. In

the next century Gruffudd I conquered the Deheubarth and

formed a confederation of princedoms, but there could

be no permanency in such a system. Fortunately, Saxon

kings were also fighting among themselves at the same

time, and in 1055 Gruffydd became the ally of Aelfgor

of Mercia against the Saxons of Hereford and Gloucester.

The abandonment of the title "King" after 1157 was per-

haps a tacit recognition that unity could not be imposed

by conquest so long as there was a powerful neighbour

to divide and rule.

In Scotland the clan-system led not only to disunity among Highlanders, but also to enmity between

Highlanders and Lowlanders. When they did unite for

the War of Independence, England had become too strong

to be defeated. Hereditary feuds were handed down from

generation to generation, preventing the formation of

a Highland League; and when Montrose arose in support

of the Stuarts, one of the incentives used by the High-

land Chiefs to stimulate recruiting was the possibility

of plundering the Lowlands. In their turn the Lowland

barons were constantly intriguing with English kings

and their relations with Henry VIII formed, it has

been said[6], "a peculiarly discreditable page of history.

At the Battle of Culloden in 1746, there were Scottish

regiments on both sides, the issue being, not how

Scottish Scotland was to be, but how Catholic, and

whether the monarchy was to be autocratic or constitu-

tional.

What happened in Ireland we have seen: Strongbow'

invasion was the direct result of Irish disunity; and

since his army was probably half-Celtic by this time,

it was also another case of Celt against Celt. In fact

the Welsh could be said to be returning the compliment,

because there had been a time, as we have seen, when th

Irish had seemed likely to take possession of their coun-

try. There was nothing new in calling in a foreigner for

support. After all, if we can trust Giraldus Cambrensis

(*ca.* 1147- *ca.* 1220), it was a romanized Briton, Vorti-

gern[7], who first invited the Saxons into Britain.

The struggle with England was, therefore, in these

early centuries not a national one at all, and it was no

conscious treachery to a Welsh cause when a certain Cad-

waladr collaborated with the Normans against his brother

Owain, Prince of Gwynedd, in 1138, joined in England's

civil war in 1141, and fought in Henry II's army against

Wales in 1157. That is why he was eventually accepted

back by his brother and was able to end his life as a

"nationalist". Even Rhys II helped Henry II against his

rebellious sons in 1173, and Owain Glyndwr fought in

Richard III's army against the Scots in 1385. Welsh

soldiers fought for Henry II in France in 1188 and for

Henry VII in the last years of the Hundred Years' War.

All these might theoretically have appealed to King

Arthur's fighting against the Brythons of Strathclyde

or the Scots of Dalriada in the 5th century.

It is the same story in Brittany: all efforts to

unify the country under one strong ruler were frustrated

by the rivalry of its kings and their vassals; and
though we do not hear of Bretons fighting on the side
of Normans or French against Bretons, we see them in
Norman William's army at Hastings and appointed to
posts in Wales by the Normans (like the Bishop of Bangor in 1092). In fairness, however, it must be said
that we also see them trying to help Owain Glyndwr
with an expedition in 1405, though, as Frenchmen were
also doing so, this could have been due to French
Realpolitik against England rather than to a sense of
Celtic brotherhood. The same consideration must affec-
our appreciation of the Duke of Brittany's giving sanctuary more than once to Henry Tudor and supplying him with
an army of 5000 Bretons for his first vain attempt to
invade Britain in 1483.

The Isle of Man was not too small to know intesti-
strife. Olaf I was murdered by his nephew in 1153, an-
we have seen North and South take different sides in a
quarrel between Reginald I and his brother Olaf in 122-
but it was friction between the intervening King Godr-
II and the Chiefs of the Isles (Lewis, Skye, Mull and
Islay) which led to the loss of Mull and Islay in 1156
and thus eventually to the end of Man's rule outside h-

narrow bounds, which Godred put under the protection

of Henry II. What exactly this meant is not clear,

but it invited interference.

Cornwall, though bigger than Man, had no protec-

tive moat; and even unity could not have kept the

conquerors out. It is true that Cornishmen once

joined the Danes in the Invasion of Wessex, but they

were defeated by King Egbert the Great (802-839) and

lost their independence. Anglicization then proceeded

so apace that before they knew what was happening,

Cornish expatriates were defending Englishmen against

the Norman-French.

Disunity of course had roots that went deeper than

the rivalry of kings. It is enough to consider the

difference in the rules of succession to the throne to

perceive that the Celtic amalgam was composed of elements

as diverse as the Hellenic. In Pictavia succession

was through the female; in Dalriada and Brythonia

through the male, he being however a brother or nephew

in the former, and a son in the latter. It took parti-

cular circumstances to bring forth the sense of kinship.

2. LOSS OF STATUS:

Conquest alone is not enough to destroy a language;

it is the immediate consequence of conquest that proves
fatal. If the conquered show willingness to co-oper-
ate in the administration, they are exposed to contact
with the language of the conqueror. Merely to perform
their duties, they must speak it; and by speaking it
they inevitably some in some sort to identify themselves with their rulers, to feel as they do, and even
finally to be proud of speaking their language.

The speed with which Anglo-Norman language and
institutions spread over the Lowlands of Scotland is
remarkable. The way had been prepared by the Saxons,
whose influence had been boosted by the marriage of
Malcolm III to Margaret, the sister of Edgar Atheling,
in 1070. Their son David I made "Scotland" a feudal
monarchy. Anglo-Norman commanders were given baronies
in the country; parishes, shires, and the King's
justice arose on the English model; and the Highland
Line became a division between two civilizations, of
which the southern one was considered, and was in fact,
superior. Now occurs the real disaster for a language,
when it is associated with a lower status.

We see the same thing in Brittany: "Its aristocracy
attending its Princes in romanized circles, underwent

the ascendancy of an incontestably more developed

civilization, whose customs and language it quickly

adopted... It is well known that once a language

has been abandoned by its élite, it will sooner or

later be rejected by the middle classes, and this in-

evitably means relegation to the lower ranks of society"[8].

That is what the Irish found. When the dust of

the centuries-old struggle for independence had settled

and the Irish Republic had come into being (1947), the

enormous contrast between the condition of English and

that of Irish was seen more clearly than when the

dream of a Gaelic Ireland was part of the motive force

animating patriots. English had become a world-language

enjoying great prestige and allowing communication with

other nations on the widest scale. It had also become

the language of Shakespeare and an awe-inspiring liter-

ature. It was in every way what the Irish name for it

implies: *An Bhearla* "The Language", *sc. par excellence.*

And what had happened to Irish? It had become the lan-

guage of the countryside; and country-folk could not

be expected to know that it possessed a literature of

venerable antiquity, and that scholars all over the

world found its oldest documents a valuable source of

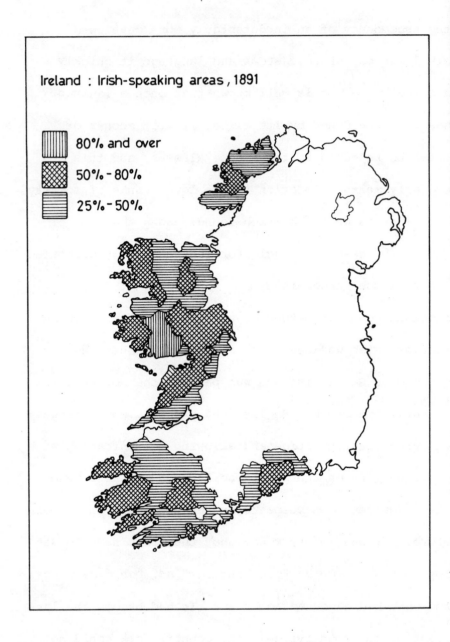

Ireland : Irish-speaking areas, 1891

80% and over

50% - 80%

25% - 50%

Ireland : Irish-speaking areas, 1961

80% and over
50% - 80%
25% - 50%

knowledge about the Indo-European family of languages.

They could see only that the more prosperous townsfolk

spoke English. Then the worst happened: they became

ashamed of their mother-tongue. In June 1951 a writer

in *An t-Ultach* ("The Ulsterman"), describing the native

speech of County Tyrone, stated frankly: "Irish is

spoken in the part of the country referred to only on

the following occasions: (i) to greet a fluent fellow-

speaker; (ii) at work on a farm when two men are

friends or relations; (iii) to express certain emotions

(iv) in reference to old traditions or local proverbs,

especially if humorous. Even on these occasions it is

usual to change to English in the course of the conver-

sation. The reason is not only a possible lack of

vocabulary, but the fear of mockery and the country-

man's inveterate desire not to attract attention . . .

Some are even reluctant to admit that they can speak

it . . . For some, Irish is synonymous with poverty

and social inferiority . . . It sometimes happens that

a child is beaten at school for using Irish and then

again at home for using English. This makes him hate

Irish . . . Young people think it is a sign of social

inferiority if their parents speak Irish, especially in

the presence of a stranger. Hence old people tend to
keep Irish to themselves as a kind of secret language.
People think that to give up using Irish is equivalent
to turning their backs on the visible and audible signs
of poverty and backwardness". Thirteen years later the
same magazine told us that "people in the Gaeltacht
(Irish-speaking areas) think they have risen in your
esteem when they speak English".

In the Isle of Man English was the language of the
gentry in the 17th century; and in the 18th a Manx
bishop, commenting on the unwillingness of certain
clergymen to preach in Manx, had stated his belief that
"this is the only country in the world that is ashamed
of, and even inclined to extirpate, if it could, its
own native tongue". The publication of Cregeen's
Dictionary of the Manks language in 1835 did nothing to
restore their pride; for George Borrow, visiting the
island in 1856 in order to learn Manx, had the impression
that "many people were ashamed to speak Manx", though
an old fisherman told him "that no Manxman need be
ashamed . . . and that Manx would be spoken as long as
Man floated"[9]. *Sancta simplicitas!* He had evidently
not heard of John Wesley's attitude to the language.

Wesley had visited the Island in 1777 and 1783 and
been pleased with what he found; but as for Manx, "we
should do everything in our power to abolish it from
the earth," he wrote to a friend in 1789. The only
remark comparable to this is that of the Earl of
Cromarty after the union of the Scottish and English
Parliaments in 1707: "May we be Britains, and down go
the old ignominious names of Scotland and England!"
How this remark was greeted, we are not told; but
there was uproar when it was echoed 272 years later,
on 6 February 1979, in a Glasgow Town-Hall by a
speaker who, according to the next day's *Daily Tele-*
graph, said "that he regarded himself as a Briton rathe
than as a Scot, adding that to call oneself a Scot
amounted to racialism".

In this exclamation we see the word "Britain" used
not in the old sense of Britannia, the Celtic Island,
but in its new legal meaning of the land of the Britis
and although this implies a recognition that Scotsmen
and Welshmen belong to a different race, and cannot
therefore properly be called "English", the fact remai
that it is difficult to adopt another language without
assuming another nationality. What makes Englishmen i

English. The process of anglicization had gone on apace

wherever English arms had penetrated and English fami-

lies settled. When the Welshman, Henry Tudor, ascended

the throne of England, it did not mean that the pendulum

had swung back and that the process of the celticization

of England was about to begin. England was already one

of the most powerful states of Europe, and Henry certain-

ly did not feel himself called upon to preside over the

dissolution of the empire of Edward I. Consequently

this apparently flattering choice of a Welshman to rule

England was really a blow to Welsh individuality. It

obliterated the distinction between Wales and England,

it consolidated the position of English as the language

of the governing class, in short, it established

Prydeindod as opposed to *Cymreictod*. (Centuries later

the choice of Lloyd George as Prime Minister was equally

flattering, and equally negative in its effect on

Cymreictod). By the 19th century Welsh politics were

so far identified with English that the radicalism of

their most vocal politicians never awoke, and was never

intended to awake, a stir of national consciousness;

and when the Education Act of 1870 dealt a mortal blow

to Welsh, especially in Glamorgan, not a voice was

raised in protest by the 'great Welshmen' of the time.

Yet, one must ask, what was a man to do, when, like

the poet H.E. Lewis (Elfed, 1860-1953), he loved both

Wales and Britain?

Nothing reveals more convincingly the depth to

which anglicization has gone in all the Celtic peoples

of the British Isles than their response to the common

danger in time of war. In 1914 England's difficulty

did give Ireland her chance and Kitchener did refuse

the offer of Irish Nationalists to serve oversea; but

the highest percentage of volunteers was Irish and 50,0C

Irishmen fell on the Allied side. In Wales the veteran

socialist, Keir Hardie, was shouted down when he made

a pacifist speech in August 1914, and more than 280,000

Welshmen joined the Armed Forces, - the highest propor-

tion of all the members of the United Kingdom; and the

result of the war for Wales was that the concept of

Prydeindod was further strengthened. Not only was

solidarity reinforced by joy in a common victory but

many of those who died were Welsh-speakers, whose passi

from the scene tore a great hole in the fabric of

Cymreictod. As for Scotland, the wisdom of the Elder

Pitt in allowing Highland Regiments to be raised after

the end of Jacobitism was amply proved on many a battle-
field. In 1939 war welded the British of the British
Isles together again; and it is difficult to imagine
a situation in which a threat to one would not be a
threat to all, or what would happen if one member
either opted for neutrality or openly sympathized with
an aggressor. Presumably it is supposed that each
country will be a member of a wider alliance such as
N.A.T.O., contributing according to its means and
joining in any common effort without loss of identity.

Things were no different when the opposing language was French: 250,000 Bretons fell in the first
World War - one quarter of Brittany's manhood; and
this figure is not only an indication of the region's
identification with France, but means, as with Welsh,
a weakening in the position of the language. For one
thing, it cost Breton one of her great poets, J.D.
Callac'h.

The loss of a father can be a tragedy for a language
too. It may mean that a family will not be brought up
to speak the mother's tongue, and thus the loss of
speakers in one generation is carried on, multiplied in
geometrical proportion, into the next. In any case the

attitude of parents to the native speech is crucial.

Paitchyn jiu, ashoon mairagh, as the old Manx proverb

puts it: "Children today, a nation tomorrow"; which

on the linguistic plane means that if children do not

speak it, a language will have been lost in a few

generations. Whether it will then still be the same

nation, is a moot point; according to another Celtic

proverb, Cornish this time, *Den hep tavas a-gollas y*

dyr: "A man without a language has lost his country."

  Things were no better in Cornwall. English became

the official language there in 1362, when it was de-

creed that the language of the courts should be, not

Latin and Norman French, but English. At once it be-

came a material advantage to know English, and Cornish

began to be deserted, first by the gentry, then by busi-

nessmen, until in the 17th century even bilingual coun-

try-folk began to bring up their children with English

as their mother-tongue. Nicholas Bosen, who lived then

and to whom we owe some of extant Cornish literature,

confessed that his mother refused to speak Cornish to

him; and a certain William Rowe of Sancreed never

spoke Cornish to his children[10]. A traveller in those

parts foresaw what the end would be: "The language is

⅃ike in a short time to be quite lost".

In Scotland "the majority of Gaelic-speaking parents are averse to the speaking of Gaelic to their children" [11], and this confirms the experience of a recent visitor who found a mother speaking Gaelic to her neighbours, but not to her son. In Brittany in 1974 out of 360,000 children under 14 only 18,000 could speak Breton. Irish parents who bring up their children to speak Irish as a mother-tongue are celebrated on both sides of the border as exceptionally patriotic. Only in Wales is it still natural for Welsh-speaking parents in areas free from *Seisnigrwydd* (Saxondom) to bring up their children as Welsh-speakers; but even so, as we have seen, these number only 12% of the total. How could it be otherwise when from Tudor times the Welsh *uchelwyr* ("gentry") had their sons educated in English schools and people, as someone wrote in 1585, began to "neglect and despise the Welsh tongue"?

Once English gets a toe-hold, the native speech is threatened. As a Report on Gaelic in the Hebrides put it in 1959 [12], "The process of anglicization begins around the centres of transport opposite the mainland. Thereafter an English "Pale" develops inland . . .

What happens is that localities traditionally

Gaelic . . . become anglicized for various local

reasons . . . and then the whole front proceeds to

break up." The chief of these local reasons is the

necessity of speaking English in order to do business,

so that success is associated with ability to speak it.

Then, to use the language of sociology, "the speakers

of the weaker language are reduced to those who are

less typical of the society as a whole", or, not to put

too fine a point on it, to a rustic, stagnant, and

often unlettered community. Oddly enough, the same

phenomenon appears in the lost status of Lowland Scots

since the union of the Crowns in 1603. The accession

of a Scotsman to the English throne was as fatal to

"Inglis" as that of a Welshman had been to Welsh:

"English became associated in the minds of Scots with

what was solemn and dignified, while the native tongue

was reduced to everyday, familiar, emotional, and comic

purposes"[13]. One is reminded of Romagnol, especially

since, like Scots, it was later purged of its less

dignified associations by the works of a great poet, Ald

Spallicci, the Burns of Romagna.

It is tempting to accuse parents of snobbery; and

certainly there was an element of this in the first

hobnobbing with the conquerors; but can parents be

blamed if, seeing that the way to get on in life is to

know a certain language, they desire their children to

be able to speak it? Indeed, if there is any snobbery,

it is more likely to be found in the children; wit-

ness the Irish children already mentioned and the Italian

child who burst into tears when her father spoke in

dialect in the presence of her friends.

Lest it be thought that such an attitude is pecu-

liarly Celtic, let us hear the complaint of a Friulan

patriot: "As long as a people . . . maintains its

language, it is a sign that it has not lost its per-

sonality, that it is not a mixture, that it is not bas-

tardized, that it has not disavowed itself . . . and

when it allows its language to die, it is a people in

dissolution, a mass of faded people without cohesion,

without strength, without an aim. When a people ad-

vances, its language develops, is stretched, articulated,

perfected; when it declines, its language also shrinks,

is contaminated and filled with foreign words and forms[14]".

It may be also a wry consolation for Celts that

the same human weakness killed Anglo-Saxon. Let the

historian Trevelyan state it: "In the 12th century

English snobbery was already at its beneficent task,

unending down the ages, of spreading the culture of

the upper class outwards and downwards among the

people . . . A chronicler tells us that 'uplandish men

will liken themselves to gentlemen and strive . . . to

speak French' . . . The great wave of French poetry

and French narrative that was sweeping over Europe . . .

invaded and conquered England"[15]. But the job was

bungled: Anglo-Saxon ceased to be, but its place was

taken by its own offspring, the fruit of a unique lin-

guistic miscegenation, and a much more powerful

engine of destruction.

3. SHORTAGE OF READING-MATTER :

To say that there is a lack of reading-matter in

Irish and Welsh, which could boast literary works of

the highest quality long before the upstart languages

of Europe were even formed, is a paradox which requires

justification.

Irish literature indeed goes back 1500 years, and

histories of literature are unanimous in praising its

qualities of imagination and descriptive power. Unfor-

tunately, we are unable to judge for ourselves; for

when, our appetites whetted by glowing assessments and

brief extracts, we hurry to the book-shop, we find, not

just that the desired book is out-of-print, but that it

has never been printed! The manuscript has been

'lying under dust-sheets on the library shelves'[16] for

centuries, read only by the authors of the aforesaid

histories. Obviously, then, literature of itself does

not constitute reading-matter; this depends on avail-

ability, and in our context quantity is perhaps even

more important than quality.

The very quality of these early works may in fact

unfit them for the task of vying with the appeal of a

stream of books written in a tongue becoming steadily

less alien. Even Douglas Hyde[17] describes (*Early*

Gaelic Literature, 142) the authors of the *Irish Annals*

as "learned men writing for the learned" in an esoteric

language; and the knowledge that Irish bards practised

"nearly three hundred different metres" (*ibid.*, 173) of

great complexity is doubtful recommendation today. On

the other hand, many of the Romances and Sagas, espe-

cially such classics as the *Táin Bó Cuailnge* ("The

Cattle-raid of Cooley") and the *Scéla Mucce Meic Dathó*

"The Story of Mac Dathó's Pig") (both available in

learned editions) could well become popular among

modern readers on the mere merits of the stories. The

Old Irish in which they are written (and which makes

them so precious to the philologist) would of course

have to be modernized, being very much more remote

from today's Irish than Chaucer's English is from ours;

but the writer who pleads[18] for just such a programme

of modernization in order to supplement the output of

living Irish authors is not exaggerating when he des-

cribes it as a "question of national pride". Meanwhile

we gratefully accept Dr. Carney's edition of *Medieval*

Irish Lyrics.

As for modern works, the 1977 catalogue of An

Siopa Leabhar in Dublin lists about 1400 works, includ-

ing 32 translations from 8 European languages and, what

is more encouraging, a large number of modern Irish

novels (though how many of them are still in print is

another question). In an article reprinted in *Meascra*

Uladh ("Ulster Miscellany") of 1974 Nollaig Ó hUrmoltai

presents an impressive list of these modern novels,

proving that it is not fair to say that Ireland's

mastery lies in the short story. Many have become

classics in their authors' life-time; for example,

Padraic O'Conaire's *Deoraidheacht* ("Exile") 1910, Seamas

O'Grianna (Maire)'s *Caisleain Oir* ("Golden Castle") 1924,

Seisamh Mac Grianna's *Mo bhealach fein* ("My own road")

1940, and Sean Mac Maolin's *Slis de'n tSaoghal* ("The Way

of the World") 1940.   Tomás Ó'Criomhthain's *An t-Oileanach*

("The Islander") has been translated into English. None

the less it remains true, as someone[19] has said, that

"there is not enough Irish prose in print today to enable

us to compare it with other literatures".

Some excellent poetry also appears in the pages of

An t-Ultach and elsewhere, much of it to be published

later in book-form; but the nature of poetry is such that,

if there were but one speaker of a language left and he

or she a poet, the poem would write itself down.

The ancient literature of Gaelic Scotland is

equally tantalizing in being mostly still in manuscript

in the National Library of Scotland. We should pro-

bably find, however, that in form and content it does

not differ much from contemporary writing in Irish,

since in both countries it proceeded from "a professional

caste writing for a feudal aristocracy"[20]. Much has

survived (potentially) in the "Book of the Dean of

Lismore", a manuscript of the first quarter of the 16th

century, which would be of particular interest for its
twenty or so 'Ossianic' poems. If the poems attributed
to this semi-mythical Irish bard (linked in Irish histo
with the Romances of the Fenian Cycle) had been in prin
by the 18th century, Macpherson, whose famous "Ossian"
electrified the nascent world of Romanticism, would not
have made such a muddle of the tales and his work would
have been sooner recognized for the counterfeit that it
is. Modern Gaelic poems are available in some abundanc
and the recent book, *Nua-Bhardacht na Gaedhilge* (1976),
provides them in a form that ancient works never knew a
seemingly never will. Meanwhile prose hardly ventures
beyond the essay and the short story.

Wales can be said to be best supplied with reading-
matter in our sense, because its long line of poets have
had the best of their work made available in one of the
prestigious 'Oxford Books of Verse'. Here we can see
that, starting like the others as a caste patronized by
an élite, Welsh poets (except their greatest, Dafydd ap
Gwilym, *ca*.1325-*ca*.1380) later played an important part
keeping alive the sense of nationality, and it can be no
coincidence that Welsh today is in a healthier state tha
its sister-tongues. Trevelyan is worth quoting again:

'The Welsh continued to elaborate their own bardic poetry
and music, destined in our own day to save Welsh intellect
and idealism from perishing in the swamp of modern cosmo-
politan vulgarity."[21] It has cherished too its ancient
masterpieces: one can walk into a shop and buy the
Mabinogion over the counter in Welsh or English. (Not
that one will always be so lucky, as he will find if he
asks for the *Anterliwtiau* (Interludes) of Twm o'r Nant
(1739-1810), though there is a good edition of his
Hunangofiant "Autobiography"[22]). Among modern works, in
Daniel Owen's *Gwen Tomos* (1894), it can boast a work fit
to rank with the great English novels of the 19th century;
and with the novels and short stories[23] of Kate Roberts,
Tegla Davies, Islwyn Ffowc Elis, Rowland Hughes, and
T.J. Morgan, and many others, some of whose works have
sustained the admirable series called *Llyfrau'r Dryw,*
anyone who would be well-read in Welsh prose today must
be ready to take time off from reading English. Yet that
remains the great temptation.

    Drama, like epic, is one of the literary genres, in
which Celtic has been deficient; but in this century
Welsh has gone far to supply the lack with the plays of
Saunders Lewis, J.G. Jones, H.W. Edwards, and Gwenlyn

Parry, and no doubt the scripts of many television-plays

are waiting to be published. Though drama is for the

spectator rather than the reader, its lack is serious when

another language holds the stage, especially if the book

of the play can afterwards be bought. Cornish has an

advantage here, in that its earliest surviving literary

remains are, as we have seen, a series of religious plays

in verse, and that extracts of these have been printed and

are available. Even so, the first reason for its decline

given by William Scawen in his *Antiquities Cornu-Britannic*

of 1680 was the lack of a literature and writers[24], and he

would hardly have modified this opinion, even if he could

have known that the Cornish patriot, Nicolas Bosen, had,

between 1660 and 1670, written for his children, among

other folktales, the interesting *Jowan Chy-an-Horth py*

An try Foynt a Skyans ("John of Chyanhorth or the three

maxims"), which it took the Welsh antiquary, Edward Lluyd

to publish in 1707 and which is today as useful for studen

as it was for Bosen's children and friends. Not until 19.

did Cornish receive its first printed book: R. Morton

Nance's *Lyver an pymp marthus Seleven* ("Book of the five

miracles of Seleven"): since when a Miscellany *(Kemysk*

Kernewek), a play in verse, *Bewnans Alysaryn* ("Life of

lysaryn"), by Peggy Pollard, the Gospel of St. Mark,

ome Psalms and Hymns, and the ambitious *Trystan hag Ysolt*

lready referred to, supplement the classical heritage and

llow more people to read Cornish today than were ever

ble to in the days of its strength.

The speciality of Manx took the form of carols

carvals). George Borrow thought that these "would be a

orthy though curious addition to the literature of

urope", but the book of them which was shown to him on

is visit was in manuscript[25], and as such it has remained.

he wonderful translation of the Bible was restored to us

n October 1979. Also on the credit side, Manx's first

rinted book, Bishop Wilson's *Principles and Duties of*

hristianity of 1707, has been reprinted in facsimile.

or the rest, the would-be reader of Manx must be content

ith a few tales published first in the columns of the

nx Star, among them some short stories by Neddy Beag

om Ruy, retrieved at last from manuscripts in the Manx

seum.

From our point of view it is unfortunate that often

e earliest printed works are of a devotional character.

at the Bible should come first, where it did so, was

ghly desirable, because thereby the language was

standardized and a norm was provided for subsequent

writers. It was followed, however, by a spate of devo-

tional works. In Irish the first printed book was a

translation of John Knox's "Liturgy" (published in

Edinburgh in 1567), and in the following century twenty-

two devotional works appeared (not counting the New

Testament)[26]. Even Keating, whose great *History of*

Ireland (1630) took the place of the Bible as the litera

norm, proceeded then to write two theological works. In

Scotland too, when the first printed books finally

appeared in Gaelic about 150 years ago, they were mostly

like Manx's first, devotional. As for Welsh, its very

first book (unless that be the collection of Proverbs,

Oll Synnwyr Pen, also ascribed to 1546) is a book con-

taining the Creed, prayers, and points of Catholic faith

(Yn y lhyvyr hwnn); and for the rest of the century

Protestants and Catholics vied with one another in urgin

Christians to devotion[27]. This did much for the languag

but it did not provide reading-matter for the 20th centu

Meanwhile English, not having had its literate class con

fined to the clergy[28] for generations, was producing wor

of abiding interest in philosophy (Locke) and drama

(Congreve etc.), not to mention poetry, thus gaining an

unfair advantage when the time for competition came.

Devotional too were the first printed prose works in Middle) Breton, from 1530 onwards; and the famous *matière e Bretagne* came to the world through the Anglo-Normans and the Franco-Bretons, Brittany itself leaving no literary memorial of it, any more than did Cornwall, its home and theatre, though modern amends have been made in both[29]. Brittany's princes had been so gallicized that there was no-one to act as patron of vernacular literature; and it is to the *lais* of the Norman Marie de France (mid-12th century) that we owe our knowledge of what Breton lays and tales were or might have been. Many Breton works share the Celtic fate of languishing in manuscript on library shelves; but even if these could be published, they would certainly illustrate what has been the greatest obstacle to the early rise of a Breton literature, namely the multiplicity of dialects (e.g. 22 variations of the Verb *anavezout* ("To know") and 27 of the word for "today", *hiziou*[30].No doubt it was similar dialectal differentiation that prevented the rise of a literature in ancient Gaul and thus hastened the extinction of Gaulish. The translation of the Bible came in the 19th century,too late to create a norm. This is gradually being achieved today through an output of novels, short

stories, plays, and of course poetry. (A recent

catalogue lists 33 prose titles, including two plays).

The problem with reading-matter is that it needs

readers; but a man speaks before he reads, so that in

the last analysis literature depends on the restoratio

of the language, not conversely. Provide the speakers

and the demand for books will follow. And writers thr

on demand.

4. LACK OF INSTRUCTION IN SCHOOL AND UNIVERSITY:

It is not enough for children to learn a language

at their mother's knee: they must be taught through it

and about it in school; otherwise it will be submerged

under the language of instruction and be quickly lost

when the child leaves school and enters a non-Celtic

world. Education Acts of 1892, 1901, and 1908 made no

reference to Gaelic, with the result that children fro

Gaelic-speaking homes began to lose touch with their

native culture, often abandoned the Highlands to be

assimilated into the English-speaking Lowlands, and le

Gaelic to the crofters.

The English Education Act of 1870 was an equal

disaster for Welsh. The guarantee of literacy which i

arried applied only to English; since there was to be

o teaching of or in Welsh, going to school and being

ducated meant for Welsh-speaking children the enforced

eprivation of their native tongue. They were punished

ike those Irish children we have already met, if heard

peaking Welsh in school. Thus without needing formally

o prohibit the use of Welsh, England had taken the sur-

st step towards achieving the ideal of all unitary

tates - an ideal which even Matthew Arnold supported[31],

amely, to eliminate anything that hinders the extension

f a single national language.

So too in Ireland: "It was the educational system

rom the 18th century onwards which had the most

ernicious effect on Irish in Ulster"[32]. In 1960 only

000 pupils were learning it in Ulster Grammar Schools,

nd it was a compulsory subject only in Catholic schools.

n 1968 it was being taught in only 151 schools out of

,332. As for the rest of Ireland, it has been said[33]

hat "with the help of famine and emigration the National

oard of Education founded in Ireland in 1831 succeeded

n getting rid of millions of Irish-speakers". Today in

ire the language is taught in all schools, primary and

secondary; but it is used as a medium of instruction only

in Irish-speaking areas (the *Gaeltachtaí*), and in about

4% of primary and 8% of secondary schools elsewhere. It

is interesting that while the number of such schools her

fell from 168 to 157 (with a loss of 342 pupils) between

1972 and 1974, it rose in English-speaking areas from 23

to 28 (with an increase of 250 pupils)[34]. The results,

however, according to Colonel Eoghan O'Neill in the

Celtic Annual of 1968, p.58, have not been entirely

satisfactory: "Irish has often been taught as a dead

language...The courses have concentrated too much on

grammar. The result has been that many leave school wit

out the ability to speak the language". This view was

confirmed in 1976, when the Committee on Language

Attitudes reported that only 9% of the population have

"high verbal competence"[35]. The fact is that once schoo

become islands in an ocean of English-speakers, an

essential ingredient is missing; for the link between

school and life is broken. Separate schools for each

language are certainly not the answer. Words from anoth

linguistic context are relevant here: "There is a danger

in having separate schools, one Friulan and one Italian,

because the greater prestige of Italian would result in

parents' sending their children to the Italian schools,

as happened in Switzerland with German schools (as

pposed to the Romontsh). Both languages should be

aught on equal terms in a single school."[36]

The fatal effects of a general educational system

mposed on a linguistic minority which it ignores can

est be seen in the results of its temporary suspension.

ne of the side-effects of the French Revolution was the

bolition of the educational system devised by the Church.

vernight the francization of Brittany ceased, and a new

eneration of Breton monoglots grew up which doubled the

umber of Breton-speakers by the end of the 19th century.

his was not at all what the Revolutionaries wanted; be-

ween 1880 and 1887 free, compulsory education through

rench was reintroduced, and as in Ireland and Wales

hildren were punished in school for speaking their

other-tongue.

. LOSS OF THE LANGUAGE IN RELIGIOUS LIFE:

The beneficial effect of its preservation in the

hapels of Wales is the measure of what the loss of its

anguage has meant to the other Celtic lands. The

ational feeling that survived in Wales through the

enturies was clearly linked with its religion. In 768

ales was the last of the Celtic communities of Britain to

abandon the old Celtic Church and conform to Rome
(after Iona and Strathclyde in 718, Devon and Cornwall
in 705, N.Ireland *ca.*700, S.Ireland in 625-638). When
the Welsh Church was disestablished twelve centuries
later, it was well said that the act was "Welsh
nationalism in religious dress".

What makes this religious success a more impressiv
achievement is that it was the recovery of lost ground.
By the middle of the 16th century Church-services in
Wales were entirely in English, as were the Courts and
local administration. Then came in quick succession th
translation of the Book of Common Prayer, of the Psalms
of the New Testament, and as a crowning triumph, of the
whole Bible, published in 1588 in the splendid language
of Welsh princes and poets. It is amusing that the
reason why Elizabeth I allowed these translations to be
used was the belief that they would speed up the learni
of English by a comparison "of both tongues together"[37]
and one might almost see in this the argument of some
cunning Welshman, were it not that the Queen applied th
same policy to Ireland. In 1602 she commissioned and
even supplied the types for an Irish translation of the
New Testament, and expressed her approval of ministers

could speak Irish. The results were beneficial to both languages: the English in Dublin, as Lord Chancellor Gerarde
complained, spoke Irish "with delight", and a great stimu-
lus was given to Irish prose-writing; while Welsh was saved
from deterioration, and when Methodism came, there was a
religious language ready for use; and today, if one wishes
to hear Welsh in an anglicized town, one goes to chapel.

Closest to Wales in this context is Lower Brittany,
where 75% of all parishes use Breton in sermons and cate-
chisms, and this though the Bible in Breton did not appear
till 1868. (A new translation has recently appeared). On
the other hand, the Catholic religion, unlike the Noncon-
formist sects of Wales, has a Mass, and when the use of
Latin in it is waived, the language that floods in is not
Breton, but French. There was only one Breton bishop in
Brittany in 1967, and their bishops have even been called
"artful instruments of francization", who refuse to say
Mass in Breton and see no connection between this attitude
and a decrease in the size of their congregations[38].

In N. Ireland the Catholic priests are the mainstay of
Irish. They are active in running the Summer Schools in the
Gaeltacht, and four of their bishops are Irish-speakers.
Only in Catholic schools is the language compulsory, and

the largest Gaeltacht in the whole of Ireland is said t
be Belfast; but they have only one service in Irish eve
Sunday, and Irish-speaking preachers in some other town
only once a month. A little over a century ago it was
the Presbyterians who were the more enthusiastic for
Irish. (After all, the Ulster Gaelic Society had been
founded by Protestants). Then came talk of Home Rule,
Irish became identified with Republicanism and Catholic
ism, and Protestants turned their backs on it. In what
was to be the Republic, Irish was not as fortunate as
Welsh in the support given to it by the Church. The
Penal Laws between 1695 and 1727 amounted almost to the
proscription of Catholicism, and would have meant, "if
they could have been carried out in every corner of the
country, that within one generation there would have
been no priest left alive"[39]. Thus when the situation
improved, the number of Irish-speaking priests had been
drastically reduced. The Catholic hierarchy were
impressed by England's foundation of Maynooth College i
the education of Catholic seminarists, and their bishop
favoured the idea of union with Great Britain, because
they believed that Catholic Relief would follow, as the
younger Pitt had implied, while they were cool towards

revival of Irish, because it did not seem likely to
further the cause of the Church. To the Elizabethan
Irish New Testament of 1602 the Old Testament had been
added in 1685, but neither enjoyed the wide reading usual
in Protestant countries, so that the Irish Bible did little
or nothing to link people's nationalist sentiments with
their religion and to keep the language alive in church
against the day when it could emerge into the secular
world. The impact of an Irish Bible was lessened also
by the fact that the disappearance of the bardic schools
in the 17th century removed the stabilizing influence of
a literary language, so that inherent tendencies were
given full play and Irish split up into the dialects of
Ulster, Connaught, and Munster. Ulster had to wait till
1942 for its Gospels and Acts, beautifully translated by
Canon Kerr. Then in 1964, as though the language had not
had enough to contend with, comes the abrogation of the
Latin Mass and the compulsory use of the vernacular. What
is Ireland's vernacular? It is certainly not yet that
which the Latin root of the word implies[40]. "A general
change to Irish would have been a fitting gesture of
gratitude towards the language which largely insulated
the Catholic Church in Ireland from any mass conversion

to the Reformed Faith," is one aggrieved comment[41]. As
it is, English is now heard even in the Gaeltacht's
chapels, and Dubliners must make do with one Irish Mass
in each church on Sundays. So, when *An t-Ultach* of
November 1978 joyfully announced the appearance, three
centuries late, of an Irish Bible for Catholics, one
hopes that it can yet make its contribution to the
survival of the language.

In Scotland it cannot be said that the Church contri-
buted much to the survival of Gaelic. In the Middle Ages
it was overtly hostile to Gaelic, and though there were
Gaelic-speaking clergy and the Catechism and Psalms had
been translated, the first Gaelic Bible had been no more
than a transliteration of Bedell's Irish version and
would have been unintelligible even to literate Gaels.
The SPCK had therefore some excuse for trying to propagat
Christian knowledge by the spread of English; but
Dr. Johnson had some reason to protest in 1766 against
some "who thought it reasonable to refuse Gaels a
version of the Holy Scriptures". Thus prodded, the SPCK
produced first the New and then in 1801 the Old Testament
in Gaelic, and allowed religious instruction to be given
in Gaelic in its schools[42] - an aim for which the

Edinburgh Society for the Support of Gaelic Schools had
been founded in 1811. A further advance came in 1843 when
the Presbyterian Church of Scotland, tainted by its
support of the Clearances (the expulsion of Highland
villagers for the sake of afforestation) in 1782, which
did as much harm to Gaelic as the Famine of 1847 was to
do to Irish, and, suspect on account of its link with the
land-owning class, was ousted in the highlands by the
Free Church, which soon established 712 schools with
Gaelic as the first language.

That the Catechism was the first religious work to
appear in Manx as it was in Gaelic is a sign that there
were plenty of Gaelgach/Gaidhlig-speaking children about
at that date (1707). Bishop Phillips (a Welshman!) had
translated the Book of Common Prayer in 1610, but it was
not printed until 1894. The first part of the Bible to
appear in print was St. Matthew's Gospel, in 1749; but
when Bishop Wilson and his Vicars-General were in prison
in Castle Rushen in 1722, they beguiled the time by
translating the Gospels[43]; and presumably it was these
translations that were taken up into the Manx Bible
commissioned by Wilson in 1748 and completed by a team of
parish clergymen under the supervision of Bishop Hildesley,

who lived just long enough to see its last pages in
print in 1772. Sermons continued to be made in Manx until
well into the 19th century. *An Coraa Ghailckagh* prints
one written in 1744 or earlier on the text of Joel 2,12-
13; and in 1947 the Manx Society published *A Sermon in
Manx Gaelic*, which could be as late as 1832. Perhaps we
should have had more of them, if Manx clergymen had been
more sensible of the distinction conferred on the languag
by the possession of its own Bible. This is not a slavis
translation of the Authorised Version, but thanks to the
reviser of the manuscript, the then Headmaster of Douglas
Grammar School (Rev. P. Moore), it incorporated the dis-
coveries made since 1611, while the style and language we
checked by his pupil John Kelly, later to be the author c
two Manx Dictionaries and a Grammar. It is excellent th
such a literary treasure has just been reprinted in our ow
day,   after   our appetites have been   whetted by an
edition of St. John's Gospel.

While Manx was being enriched by a Bible, Cornish
was in its terminal phase. It is certainly lamentable
that a 17th century plan to translate parts of the Bible
into Cornish did not get further than the Book of Genesis
that even this was never printed, and that the manuscript

is apparently lost. Whether a Cornish Bible could have
staved off the end, is uncertain; but that was not the
only religious lack. There was no Catechism and no Book
of Common Prayer; all they had (if they could find it)
was a translation of the Creed and the Lord's Prayer
printed in Dr. John Davies's translation (1632) of the
expurgated Protestant version of a Jesuit work, "A
Christian Directory", which had appeared in 1583 (the
Llyfr y Resolusion). There could therefore be no
church-services in Cornish; and it was lack of these
which Scawen considered another reason for its disappearance. It was indeed a serious error of judgment when
objectors to the Reformation in the 16th century rejected
the right to have the Prayer-Book in Cornish. This would
have brought back Cornish to the churches and might have
led to the translation at least of the New Testament.
When Wesleyism arrived, it was too late.

5. IMMIGRATION:

It so happens that the Celtic lands contain some of
the finest scenery in the British Isles, and being the
furthest point to which the Celts could retreat before
the Saxon drive westwards, some of its finest beaches.
The result has been a steadily increasing annual influx of

visitors, and the rise of tourism. On the material plane
this has been of immense benefit, and has allowed the
indigenous population to find employment on its own ground
To Man, which had 618,847 tourists in 1947, tourism has
brought "wealth undreamed of", as Kinvig[44] puts it; and
as its language was by then already in its death-throes,
no linguistic harm was done. The same of course may be
said of Cornwall.

Some of these visitors, however, come to settle in
the envied land, which can result in a change in the
ethnic composition of the inhabitants. In Man, where
there is the added attraction of low income tax, only 35
of the population is today ethnically Manx. In Cornwall,
as the genuinely Cornish desert the country for the town
so retired people come from across the Tamar to settle in
rural peace, so that the population has increased since
1957 and people of Cornish stock are now in the minority

When immigrants settle in an area of native-speaker
the long-term threat to native blood is not so important
as the immediate danger to the language. The man who se
the pernicious example of planting foreigners in Celtic
areas was Henry I, who in 1107 settled Flemings in South
Pembroke and Gower; and if the original motive was to le

them quarrel with their Welsh rather than with their

English neighbours, the fact remains that these areas of

Wales have been a "little England beyond Wales" ever since.

The Scottish king, James VI, deliberately planted Lowlanders

in the Highlands in order to effect the change from Gaelic

to English which was believed to be essential to the pro-

cess of civilization; and after becoming James I of

England in 1603, he applied a similar policy to Ireland,

having more success in Ulster than Queen Mary and Queen

Elizabeth had had in other parts of the country, where

the settlers were driven out or absorbed by the Irish.

Inevitably, part of Cromwell's vengeance took the form of

settling 40,000 Puritans on the lands of Irishmen trans-

planted to the western counties.

The worst threat to the Irish Gaeltacht proceeds,

oddly enough, from the very measures taken to protect it.

As we shall see, a language can flourish only if its

speakers need no other language in order themselves to

flourish; in other words, there must be local industries.

But industry involves a technical vocabulary, and Irish

emerged from suppression into the scientific age without

having "produced vernacular names for scientific,political,

banking, engineering, or mathematical terms"[45]. So "one

Minister for the Gaeltacht after another expresses his

anxiety over the fact that English is spreading through-

out the shop-floor in the factories set up by the

authorities. Perhaps no-one has told the workers the

Irish for their new tools and materials"[46]. Even greater

is the danger from another type of visitor: the very

pupils who go to Summer Schools in the Gaeltacht to learn

the authentic language and to "put the flavour", as they

call it[47], on their speech are "responsible for the spread

of English; for the local people have to step down to their

level, to speak bad or simple Irish or a mixture of Irish

and English so as to be understood, and the pupils teach

English to the children"[48]. In other words,as an earlier

writer, in *An t-Ultach* of January 1977, put it: Irish is

weak in the Gaeltacht...because it is being corrupted by

learners of the language...The majority of those who go

there go round speaking English the whole time... Every

year several people are there (i.e. in the Summer Schools

who do not know Irish well enough to sustain a conversa-

tion in it. Consequently they oblige others to speak to

them in English. These people have a pernicious influence

on the children of the Gaeltacht. One often sees children

going around trying to imitate them... Fortunately, an

attempt is being made to solve this problem by grading the
Summer-schools according to ability and by having an
entrance exam". Once again we see the impact of one
language being fatal to another through the voluntary
choice of the losing side.

In Wales there have been no deliberate plantations,
but a steady flow of English settlers over the centuries,
many attracted by the possibilities of employment in the
industrial zones; and if they were not all English, like
the 100,000 Irishmen who settled in Glamorgan between
1900 and 1920, they brought English with them. There is,
however, a new type of semi-settler, who constitutes a
particular threat to Wales: the Englishman who purchases
a house for occupation in his summer-holidays. This not
only brings an English family into what may be part of
the Welsh-speaking heartlands, but creates a depopulated
area for most of the year, while it reduces the number of
houses available for the Welsh. The same phenomenon is
now reported from Glencoe in Scotland.

7. EMIGRATION:

Part of the territory occupied by settlers has been
vacated by those who have left the country. The harm
done to a language by emigration depends to some extent on

the date when it occurred. If enough of the emigrants
are not Celtic-speaking, it can actually improve the
relative position of the native-speakers. This, however,
would probably not apply to Irish emigration, which has
drained away its native speakers for many centuries. Some
political action can have an immediate effect on emigration: when the introduction of Free Trade in 1846
deprived Ireland of protection against American wheat,
there followed a mass emigration to the U.S.A. and Canada
The failure of the potato-crop a year later produced
another outflow of emigrants, some of them reaching Canad
only to die, 5000 of them in Montreal alone. Fewer Welsh
men went to the States but the number was still high:
35,000 in the first sixty years of the 19th century, of
whom, between 1831 and 1860, five thousand went from
Cardiganshire. The harm was done in the 20th century,
when unemployment forced nearly half-a-million Welshmen
to seek work in England. In Cornwall the decline in
population due to emigration during the copper-slump in
1866, to cheap American wheat in 1874, and to competition
from English fishermen,could not reduce the number of
native-speakers below its wretched zero, but in so far as
it weakened the native stock, it prejudiced the chances

of revival. So too in Man: economic conditions at
various times in the 19th century led to considerable
emigration, and if there can have been few Manx-speakers
among the emigrants, the loss of even one was by then a
serious matter. Breton emigrants after 1763, when
conditions deteriorated, made for Canada, perhaps because
of the part Bretons had played in the French occupation
of Quebec in earlier centuries. Later emigration, however, sprang not from lack of employment, but from
missionary fervour: since the first oblate missions to
Canada in 1841 Brittany has done much with her monks and
nuns for the conversion of Eskimoes and Indians to
Christianity; which is why one finds lakes, rivers, and
villages, especially in Manitoba and Saskatchewan, bearing Breton names (e.g. St. Brieuc, Folgoet, Kermaria).
In 1913 a Breton from Gourin actually founded a 'Gourin
City' in the parish of Plamondan near Edmonton, Alberta,
and the village was still in 1947 mainly Breton, at least
in origin and character, if not in language. The
Unvaniezh Bretoned ar C'hanada ("Breton Union of Canada")
in Montreal had 1000 members in 1968. As in Wales, however, the dangerous drain is across the border of Brittany
into France proper, where the possibilities of employment

are greater and professional salaries higher. It is

ominously significant that the French Fifth Plan fore-

saw in 1966 that by 1985, whereas the population of Franc

will have increased by 45%, that of Brittany will have

remained stationary.

These economic facts will remind us that sentiment

is not enough for the salvation of a language. Those who

speak up in defence of a threatened tongue are in danger

of forgetting that a people's language is not a frill,

to be donned or doffed by an act of will or imposed by

some external authority. It is an essential part of

every individual and inseparable from his conception of

reality. As the German said: "Wir nennen es Wasser, und

es ist doch Wasser."[49] In it each one lives and moves

and has his being. It is as natural to him as the air he

breathes. Language is thus part of a milieu, and it is

this milieu that has to be protected in the first place.

"This is why, in Scotland as well as in Ireland and Wales

the economic survival of the vernacular-speaking areas is

so important."[50] Breton, for example, has for long been

chiefly the language of the countryside; consequently,

when the number of Breton farms fell from 250,000 in 1955

to 180,000 in 1970 (a decrease equivalent to the loss of

half-a-million workers on the land)[51], a deadly blow was
struck at the language. To bring back the language
means bringing back the agriculture or local industry that
was the economic basis of its presence, or providing an
alternative suitable to local conditions and ethnic
character. This is what Eire has set out to do for the
Gaeltachtaí by the creation of the Board called
Gaeltarra Eireann (Irish Goods). Its task is to make the
Gaeltachtaí economically viable, which means the creation
of jobs for all by 1980 (i.e. 12,000 jobs a year) with the
help of subsidies and tax-concessions to companies either
brought in from outside or founded by the Gaeltachtai
themselves (e.g. for processing fish). When it became
clear in 1974 that neither of these was achieving the
desired result (probably because of the rural Irishman's
dislike of factory-life), it was decided to concentrate
on the farming of fish, oysters, lobsters, and mussels
(which has involved the building of two new harbours) and
on the improvement of agricultural techniques. Such
strictly economic measures are a vital element in the
struggle for the preservation of a language[52].

8.   THE IMPACT OF NEWSPAPERS, CINEMA, RADIO, AND
     TELEVISION :

When the number of native-speakers falls, the
potential readership of a newspaper in the native
language falls also; which is to say that such a readership never comes into being. There has never been a
daily newspaper in any of the Celtic languages. It is
already a triumph, if a weekly or even a monthly can
survive, as they do in Eire, where two subsidized
weeklies, *Inniu* ("Today") and *Amarach* ("Tomorrow") contend for a maximum readership of 50,000 and are now
having to consider amalgamation[53]. The native-speaker
must be bilingual, if he wishes to read the news, and
this means, not only loss of status for his "first"
language (and consequently its soon becoming his second),
but also a decline in the need for literacy in it.

The cinema poses an even greater threat, because it
caters less for man's thirst for knowledge than for his
desire to be entertained, and it appeals as much to
children as to adults. There could be Welsh on the stage
and a Welsh theatre could survive on a small budget; but
the cinema requires huge sums to support it, and it is not
surprising that exponents of Celtic speech have never been
able to produce films of any length or importance. The

only counter-measure (and it is now being adopted in parts of Wales) is to dub the film in Welsh and supply English sub-titles.

As though the fatal effects of 100 years of journalism and 50 of the cinema were not enough, along come first radio, and then television, to bring the official language of the State into every home in the last strongholds of native speech. To enjoy and exploit the new medium, English must be learnt, unless the native-speakers are to be content with the meagre listening and viewing time allotted them: the Gaels of Scotland with $3\frac{1}{2}$ hours a week (if they have VHF sets), a religious service of half-an-hour on Radio 4 on Sunday afternoons and 20 minutes of Gaelic from a new station at Stornoway but no regular Gaelic programme on television; the Gaels of Man with five minutes of news at 9 o'clock on Sunday mornings (broadcast by members of the Manx Language Society); the Welsh with 26 hours a week by BBC Wales and about 11 hours a week on television (times that exceed those for English on the same wavelength); the Bretons with 3 hours a week on radio and 24 minutes weekly on television (1978)[54]. The Northern Irish and the Cornish rarely, if ever, hear their language on the air. In the Republic of Ireland, where Irish is one of the

State's official languages, the situation is complicated

by two factors: the dialectal differences between Ulster

Connaught, and Munster; and by the ability of the easter

part of the country to receive the programmes of the B.B

the consequent dissatisfaction of the rest at having onl

the one channel of the State Radio-Television Service

(RTE), and the difficulty of the only solution, to provi

a second domestic channel, in that the question immediat

arises, How much Irish shall it have? Opinion-polls hav

produced conflicting results: one showed a majority for

an all-Irish TV-station; in another the demand was for t

relay of the B.B.C. or of other foreign stations[55]. Mea

while, viewers have two Irish programmes a week and a

daily 1¼-minutes news bulletin; and the Gaelic League

(Connradh na Gaeilge), thinking what the injection of

English from the screen is doing to the Gaeltacht, feels

so strongly about it that it has gone over to militancy

and asked its members to refuse to pay their television-

licences[56]. It is a disquieting phenomenon when Welsh

and Irish, so differently placed in relation to their

Governments, are found having to employ the same tactics

9. LINGUICIDE:

It will have been seen that there was never an overt
campaign to destroy any of the Celtic languages. It
merely happened that the measures taken by each Government
in what it presumed to be the interests of a unified state
were such as to bring each language to the verge of extinction. The drafters of the Act of Union between
England and Wales, in stating what it intended "utterly
to extirpate" took care to refer only to "the sinister
usages and customs" of Wales without referring specifically
to the previously mentioned "speche nothing like ne
consonant to the naturall mother-tongue used within this
Realme". Paradoxically, it was when the Government thought
it was acting most philanthropically that it was doing the
most damage. Literacy is desirable in a civilized state,
and the Bills introducing general education at the end of
the last century guaranteed an ability to read and write to
every child in the country; but the language taught was
English in the British Isles and French in Brittany, and
the more they became literate respectively in these, the
less they became in their mother-tongues. Or let us
suppose that the Governments were well aware that this
would be the result: they genuinely believed that the

substitution of English and French for Celtic was
necessary to the full development of their citizens'
faculties. How else could sane men believe that "the
Welsh language is a vast drawback to Wales and a manifold
barrier to the moral progress and commercial prosperity
of the People" (Report of 1847); and that "the prevalence
of Welsh and the ignorance of English...exclude the Welsh
people from the civilization of their English neighbours"
(*The Times, ca.*1870); and that "the people of Wales
laboured under a peculiar difficulty from the existence of
an ancient language" (a Welsh M.P. in 1846). How else
could Matthew Arnold feel as he did? It never occurred to
them to ask how it came about that the Welsh, who had once
been more civilized than the Anglo-Saxons and the Anglo-
Normans, were in their day, in material standards, behind
the English. For them, if they had enjoyed the permissive
latitude of today's speech, Welsh was just the "bloody
language" that Lord George Brown has testily called it[57].

England saw itself as the propagator, not only of
civilization, but of civic liberties. "Your ancestors did
not churlishly sit down alone to the feast of Magna Carta,"
said Burke in his great speech, *Conciliation with the
Colonies*, in the House of Commons on 22 March 1775: "Irela

was made immediately a partaker... The refusal of a

general communication of these rights was the true cause

why Ireland was five hundred years in subduing...It was

soon discovered that nothing could make that country

English, in civility and allegiance, but your laws and

your forms of legislature. It was not English arms, but

the English constitution, that conquered Ireland."

Passing to Wales, he points out that the attempt "to sub-

due the fierce spirit of the Welsh by all sorts of rigorous

laws" merely meant that "Wales rid this kingdom like an

incubus; that it was an unprofitable and oppressive

burden", and that only when at last men saw "the ill-

husbandry of injustice" and finding "that laws made

against a whole nation were not the most effectual methods

for securing its obedience", they then "gave to the Welsh

all the rights and privileges of English subjects..., from

that moment, as by a charm, the tumults subsided..., peace,

order, and civilization followed in the train of liberty."

If the purpose was to snuff out the Celtic languages,

Machiavelli could not have prescribed a better policy. It

was indeed a prescription for anglicization which led to

wholesale desertion of these tongues, the one and only

barrier to the complete take-over of their countries. We

have seen what *Prydeindod* signified for Wales: Welshmen

embraced their liberties without seeing that they were

hugging their chains.

If governments did not proclaim their policies,

individuals appointed by them were less inhibited. This

was particularly true of France, where after the Revolutic

anything un-French was viewed with suspicion and the Bretc

language seemed to reflect a permanent flaw in the solid

structure of the state. Consequently we hear such extra¬

ordinary statements as that of Barrère in 1794: "Among a

free people language must be one and the same for all", as

though the existence of a linguistic minority somehow

affected the liberties of the rest (instead of conversely)

or that of the Prefects who in 1831 said: "The Breton

speech must be absolutely destroyed"; or that of the Sub-

Prefect who in 1845 told teachers: "Remember that you have

been set up only in order to kill the Breton language";

and as recently as 1925 a Minister of Education can say:

"For the unity of France the Breton language must die".

At least the Bretons have been forewarned; and if their

language is still threatened today, its condition is

mostly due to the other causes which we have mentioned.

Gaelic has been in a peculiar position, because the

earliest attacks on it did not come from England. It was

a Scottish Government which in 1616 passed a Statute en-

joining "that the vulgar Inglishe toung be universalie

plantit, and the Irish language (sc.gaelic), which is one

of the chief and principall causes of the continewance of

barbaritie and incivilitie amongis the inhabitants of the

Iles and Heylands, may be abolishit and removit". The

result was that Gaelic ceased to be an essential element

in the composition of Scottish nationalism and that

animosities were created between Highlanders and

Lowlanders. It must not be forgotten, however, that there

are 'colonies' of Gaels in the Lowlands amounting to

38,000 Gaelic speakers (half of them in Glasgow)[58].

Notes to Chapter Thirteen

1. "The Britons, taught at last that a common danger must
   be repelled by unity." Similarly Trogus (p.15) 20,5,7,
   attributes the Gallic invasion of Italy of *ca.*400 B.C.
   to *intestina discordia et adsiduae domi dissensiones.*

2. Tacitus,*Hist.*4,73: *terram vestram ceterorumque Gallorum
   ingressi sunt duces imperatoresque Romani nulla cupidine,
   sed maioribus vestris invocantibus, quos discordiae usque
   ad exitium fatigabant.* (It was not out of greed that
   Roman generals and commanders entered your (Treviran and
   Lingonian) territory: it was in response to the appeal of
   your ancestors, who were being driven to the brink of
   ruin by their quarrels).

3. Translated by Gwyn Williams, *An Introduction to Welsh
   Poetry,* p.63. He reminds us that "the men of Dublin"
   were the Danes.

4. Not from Late Latin *dextralis* (sic) *pars* ("right-hand",
    i.e. "southern") "part", but a hybrid compound of
    partem and W. *deheu* "south".

5. Gwynfor Evans, *Aros mae*, p.146.

6. R.S. Rait, *History of Scotland*, ch.2, p.66.

7. Sometimes believed to be a title including the Irish
    word for 'lord', *tighearna*; but the *G* could not lose
    its aspiration (and consequent silence),and the *T*
    would be aspirated after the prefix *fior*. The word is
    the same as Welsh *Gwrtheyrn* from *Guorthigirn*, Old
    Breton *Gurtiern*.

8. F. Gourvil, *Langue et littérature bretonnes (Que sais-
    je?*527) 1960, p.63.

9. From Borrow's notes for a book to be called "Red Path
    and Black Valley", quoted in *Mona Herald* about 1965.
    The MS is in the Manx Museum Library.

10. *An Lef Kernewek* No.130 (1976/2), p.6.

11. From a Report quoted by Meic Stephens, *op.cit.*, p.65.

12. Meic Stephens, *op.cit.*, p.61.

13. Meic Stephens, *op.cit.*, p.81.

14. Josef Marchet, 'Un element fondamental dal Moviment
    autonomistic' in *La Patrie* (1976), p.15.

15. *op.cit.*, p.143.

16. Micheál Ó Mairtin, 'Seanlitriocht na Gaeilge', in
    An t-Ultach, Feabhra 1978, p.8. "If the Irish manu-
    scripts (on the shelves of the Royal Irish Academy,
    of Trinity College, of the British Museum, Maynooth
    College, of the Bodleian, and elsewhere) were all
    printed, they would probably fill 1,200 or 1,400
    octavo volumes, perhaps even more." (Douglas Hyde in
    the first of the two books referred to in the following
    note, p.xxii).

7. Eire's first President, founder of *Connradh na Gaeilge*, and author of *The Story of early Gaelic literature* (1895) and *A literary history of Ireland* (1899).

8. M.Ó. Mairtin, *loc.cit.* His example, a version of *Táin Bó Fraich* ("Fraoch's Cattle-raid"), was not followed up. As a matter of fact, Anrai Mac Giolla Chomhaill in *An t-Ultach*, Mean-fomhair 1968 had published some extracts in modern spelling from works of the 15th century; but what was to have been a series soon petered out, the more regrettably since his *Díolaim Próis* ("Prose Selection") *1450-1850* is now out-of-print.

9. Donn Piatt in *An Glór*, 18adh Iul, 1942 ('Litridheacht na Gaedhilge').

0. J. Marx, *Les Littératures celtiques* *(Que sais-je?*, No.809, 1967), p.122.

1. *op.cit.* (1948!), p.210.

2. The *Interludes* can be read in Swansea Public Library, in that splendid Rotunda which war and even the developer have spared.

3. A useful collection is in *Ystoriau Heddiw* (ed. T.H. Parry-Williams, 1964).

4. G.H. Sutton, *Konciza historio pri la kornvala lingvo kaj ĝia literaturo* (1969), p.5.

5. Mona Douglas, *The Romany Rye in the Isle of Man* (The Isle of Man Weekly Times, 1966).

6. They are listed by D.Ó Doibhlin in *Meascra Ulaidh*, pp.95-6.

7. Exactly the same thing was going on at the same time in the Romontsch zone of Switzerland: 1665 *Spieghel de devotiun*; 1690 *La consolaziun de l'olma devotiusa*, etc.

8. Not for nothing has the word *clerical* its two senses.

29. Breton now offers *Tristan hag Izold*,"réédition du
     célèbre roman de Xavier de Langlais".

30. G. Gourvil, *op.cit.*

31. "The lower part of this school," he reported in 185?
     "might with advantage have more done to anglicize tl
     and in 1855 he said: "The difference of language be-
     tween England and Wales will probably be effaced...,
     an event which is socially and politically so desira

32. Meic Stephens, *op.cit.*, p.126.

33. G. Evans, *op.cit.*, p.280.

34. T.Ó Domhnalláin, *op.cit.*, *LPLP* 1, No.2, p.89.

35. *ibid.*, p.84.

36. G. Sobiela-Caanitz, speaking on 'Ladin in Swiss
     Universities' to a Friulan audience on 19 March 197'
     (*Int furlane*,Mai 1977, p.4).

37. The words of the Act of 1563 were echoed with a dif
     erent emphasis in the 18th century by a monoglot
     Englishman who had to justify his appointment as vi
     in a Welsh-speaking parish: "By Act of Parliament a
     English Bible is to be kept in all the churches in
     Wales, that by comparison of that with the Welsh th
     may the sooner attain to the knowledge of the Englis

38. *Celtic Annual*, 1967, p.90.

39. P. Mac Giolla Cheara (Canon Kerr), *Sceal na hEirean*
     cuid a do, p.47, (1939).

40. A *verna* was a home-born slave, and *vernaculus* meant
     "indigenous".

41. *Celtic Annual*, 1966, p.56.

42. Colm Ó Baoill in *Meascradh Uladh*, p.90.

43. *An Coraa Ghailckagh*, Laa Souney, 1956.

44. *A History of the Isle of Man*, 1950.

45. Douglas Hyde, EGL pp.xix-xx, pointing out that "in its power of forming word-combinations Irish scarcely falls short of Greek and German".

46. Muiris Ó Droigheáin in *An t-Ultach*, Deireadh-Fómhair 1978, p.16.

47. Using the word *blas*. It is interesting that St. Patrick, in his *Confessio* (9), uses the Latin word *saliva* for the "flavour" of his Latin *scriptura*. One is tempted to think he is translating the Irish *blas*, but alas! the same phrase *saliva scripturae* occurs in St. Jerome's Letter to Pope Damasus (366-384).

48. *An t-Ultach*, Deireadh-Fómhair 1978, p.13: *Saothar na gColaiste Samhraidh an fiu é?* ("Is the work of the Summer Schools worth-while?"). This was the prize-winning essay of a student written after attending the Summer School in Rann na Feirste (near Bunbeg in Co.Donegal). In the number of the previous month (September) Maire Ni Ghogain had asked, *Cad is fiú na Colaiste Samhraidh?* ("What are the Summer Schools worth?"). She pointed out that the Eire Government makes a grant of £110 per pupil for a 3-week Course, spending probably £500,000 a year. In *An t-Ultach* of Meitheamh 1979, p.10, Proinsias Ó Miánam paints a gloomy picture of the decline of Irish in the Gaeltacht and puts the blame squarely on the industrial scheme known as *Gaeltarra Eireann*. Its staff prefer to speak English and are allowed to do so, contrary to the rules. In this they are only following the example of banks, shops, and public services such as the police. Letterkenny telephone-operators have been known to refuse calls in Irish.

49. "We call it water, and it *is* water."

50. J.R. Edwards in the review referred to in n. 3 , p. 367.

51. *Y Ddraig Goch*, Chwefror 1978, p.9.

52. Pol Mac an Draoi, 'Gwaith yn y Gaeltacht', in *Y Ddr*
    Goch, Hydref-Tachwedd, 1977, p.9.

53. Pol Mac an Draoi, 'Gwasg sych. Picil paperau Iwerdd
    in *Y Ddraig Goch*, Ebrill-Mai, 1977, p.9.

54. Per Keribin, 'Bu gan Lydaw hefyd ei "Welsh Not"' in
    Y Ddraig Goch, Chwefror, 1978, p.9.

55. Pol Mac an Draoi, 'BBC i ni - dyna gri Gwyddelod',
    op.cit., Rhagfyr, 1977.

56. *id.*, *ibid.*, Mehefin, 1977, p.8.

57. See p. 15.

58. See p. 283, n.4.

14. THE REVIVAL

We shall begin with the language that has been
brought back from beyond the grave: Cornish. How can a
language be resuscitated, especially if it died before
the invention of recording devices? It was touch-and-go
for Cornish. Fortunately, the Dolly Pentreath who died
in 1777 was not the last native-speaker, as reputed, but
the last monoglot. There was a John Nancarrow of
Marazion, called by the historian Barrington in 1779 "a
fluent speaker of Cornish" (and he could judge, because
he had interviewed Dolly in 1768), who was still alive in
1790. Next, one Bodenor, who wrote to Barrington in
Cornish, saying that he knew five native-speakers in
Mousehole, lived until 1794. With John Tremethack, who
taught his daughter Cornish, we reach 1852, and his
daughter, as Mrs. Kelynack, was still alive in 1875. We
can then reach 1891 with John Davey of Boswednack, whose
memorial plaque in a church at Zennor (set up in 1930)
states that he "was the last to possess any traditional
knowledge of the Cornish language". On this tenuous
thread was preserved the pronunciation, without knowledge
of which Cornish would have gone beyond recall.

The man, however, who gave Cornish the "kiss of life"
was Henry Jenner (1848-1934). Encouraged by a tour of

Cornwall in 1875, on which he "collected knowledge of the language" from various people, including Bernard Victor of Mousehole, who had learnt Cornish from his grandfather (possibly one of Bodenor's five speakers), he ceased to be a mere antiquarian philologist and embarked on the task of reviving Cornish as a spoken tongue. In 1903, after a century of silence, Cornish sounds vibrated on the air again, from his lips at a conference in Brittany.
Dictionaries, grammars, a magazine followed, the meritorious names being R. Morton Nance (1873-1959), A.S.D. Smith ("Caradar") (1883-1950)[1], and E.G.R. Hooper ("Talek"), Editor of *An Lef Kernewek* (fortunately still with us).
To Smith is owed the first part of the Cornish Bible to appear in print, St. Mark's Gospel (1936), to which St. Matthew's was added in 1977. Jenner and Nance translated a few of the hymns published with fourteen Psalms in a *Lyver Hymnys ha Salmow* in 1962. These, with *An Ordenal rag Gwesperow* ("The Book for Evensong") including 1 Corinthians 13, 1-13 have allowed services to be held in sufficient numbers to require an advisory group to be set up by the Bishop of Truro for the supervision of liturgical translation; and among the translators is the Bishop of St. Germans, the Rt. Rev. Richard Rutt, who is

he "first prelate to be able to speak Cornish in
:hurch-services"[2]. For what seems to be the first prin-
ed sermon in Cornish we had to wait for No.131 of *An Lef
'ernewek* (1977). Meanwhile the Cornish Language Board
ad been set up in 1967 for the purpose of having
:ornish taught in schools as an optional subject, so
hat every Cornish man and woman who so desired could
ave it as a second language. Thus does Cornwall strive
:o "win back what it lost partly through our own inertia",
s John Page confesses in *Cornish Life* echoing Scawen,
ho three centuries earlier had made apathy another of
he causes of decline. It has succeeded to the
xtent that more people know Cornish today than for two
undred years[3].

The Isle of Man's own Education Authority, recog-
izing public demand, allows the language to be taught as
n extra-curricular subject in about half the primary
schools and in one secondary school, and in 1975 provided
Manx classes at night schools for as many as 500 students.
he average Manxman, however, is more interested in his
ndependence of England; and though there occurred a more
serious confrontation than usual over the British Govern-
ent's ban on Radio Caroline North, it is doubtful whether

there would have been the same fuss if it had been
broadcasting Manx lessons instead of "pop" music.

Both Cornwall and Man have done something to remind
visitors of what could have been their heritage, and
that they are in what was once foreign territory. Signs
in Celtic on buildings and Post Offices, Celtic words on
table-napkins, Celtic greetings on cards, do after all
create a faintly exotic atmosphere that can appeal to
tourists so long as it does not embarrass them as does
ignorance of French in France. Particularly effective
has been the singing in Cornish of Brenda Wootton on
television and in clubs[4]. Popular reaction has been
"fantastic", she says, adding what we most want to hear,
that "people are ashamed that they do not know the
language of their own country". Thus, the shame that
was once felt by speakers of Cornish is now the lot
of those who cannot speak it. Well may she conclude that
"Cornish will never again be as dead as it was". Dorothy
Wordsworth, who visited the Isle of Man in June 1828, was
struck by the difference from England. She noted the
"women with round hats like the Welsh", and the "small
Manx ponies with panniers made of matted straw"; and the
"groups sitting about...chattering in Manx reminded her

of the continent". Today in Man the introduction of

Manx passports has created a demand beyond all expecta-

tion, and the visitor seeing a crowd outside a church

would be surprised to learn that there was no room for

them inside, where a service in Manx was being held. It

is now fashionable to give one's house a Manx name; and

if there is an element of snobbery in all this, so much

the better: snob-value is the best protector of a

language, and it would be fitting that what

snobbery helped to kill, snobbery should revive. At

least there can be no doubt about the correctness of the

pronunciation of Manx; for the language survived long

enough for the tape-recorder to be invented, so that

between 1929 and 1932, when its days were obviously

numbered, a complete phonetic rendering was recorded from

ten of the last native-speakers by Dr. Carl J.S.

Marstrander, Professor of Celtic in the University of Oslo;

and the five manuscript volumes were presented to the Manx

Museum in 1951 on behalf of the Norwegian Government[5].

In 1947 Eamonn De Valera visited Man as President of

Eire; and hearing that there were no adequate sound-

recordings of native-speakers, he spontaneously offered

to put at the disposal of the Manx authorities the mobile

recording unit due to be delivered to the Irish Folklore
Commission, which urgently needed it for its own tasks.
So for a fortnight in the spring of 1948 the brand-new
apparatus recorded sixty different items from eight
native-speakers, constituting four hours of material.
In July of the following year Professor F.J. Carmody of
University of California at Berkeley,who had already
collected much linguistic material in 1949[6], recorded
five informants for four hours. (In the previous month
E. Jolly had recorded some native-speakers for the B.B.C.
Further recordings were made by the Manx Folklore Survey
(Sept. 1949) and the Manx Language Society (in the early
'fifties). In 1950 Professor H. Wagner, now Professor
of Celtic at Queen's University, Belfast, compiled
phonetic lists of words and phrases from interviews with
six native speakers[7], and in December of that year
Professor K. Jackson of the University of Edinburgh
collected material in the same way for the Gaelic
Linguistic Survey of Scotland[8]. In 1972 and 1973 the
last interview was given, when David Clement of the same
Survey spoke with the last native·speaker, Ned Maddrell,
whom we have already met.

That such a situation should ever arise for Welsh

is inconceivable. Only the anglicized parts of Wales
need such attempts as we have mentioned to remind
Welshmen of their still existing heritage and to prevent
the visitor from taking the surrounding Englishmen for
granted. Even so, it is only in recent times that Welsh
towns have had bilingual street-names, that railway-
stations are named in Welsh as well as in English, and
that road-signs bear the Welsh as well as (if not above)
the English name of the town. All this has been the
result of the official status won for Welsh in the
'sixties; and that in turn was achieved thanks to the
possibility of waging the campaign for the rights of
Welsh simultaneously on two fronts, the political and
the linguistic. While the Welsh Nationalist Party (Plaid
Cymru, The Party of Wales) gained positions of influence
in central and local government, the Cymdeithas yr Iaith
Gymraeg (Welsh Language Society), by militant action often
landing its members in court and even in jail, has since
1962 directed the attention of the authorities to areas
where the language was not receiving its due. Equally
important is the work being done to raise a generation of
Welsh-speakers through all-Welsh Nursery and Primary
Schools, and its Youth Movement (Urdd Gobaith Cymru).

A similar operation of aims is seen in Cornwall and
Man: alongside Mebyon Kernow (The Sons of Cornwall) there
has been since 1967 the Kesva an Tavas Kernewek (The
Cornish Language Society); alongside Mec Mannin (The Sons
of the Isle of Man) is Yn Cheshaght Ghailckagh (The Manx
Gaelic Society), founded in 1899. Wales has shown them
how political and linguistic gains react favourably on
each other.

In Brittany the two fronts of the struggle, the
cultural and the political, are less clearly divided:
the Parti National Breton, (Strollad ar Vro, The
Country's Group) founded in 1919 with the slogan "With
France if possible, without France, if necessary", ushered
in a great blossoming of Breton literature. Subsequent
organizations were more militant, but prone to a continuous fission as emphasis shifted to one or other of
current ideologies. In 1962 the Mouvement pour l'Organi
sation de la Bretagne lost its youthful left-wing
membership when these formed their own Union Démocratiqu
Bretonne, which demands only Home Rule and eschews
violence, but is more interested in Socialism than in th
language. The word "démocratique" means for them "anti-
capitalist", it being believed that capitalist France is

responsible for Brittany's condition. Least

sympathetic of all to the Breton cause is the Communist

Party. The attempt to persuade the French Left that one

can be both socialist and pro-Breton seems to have been

successful at first; for in local elections in 1977 the

U.D.B.'s candidates were on the same list with those of

the Left and won 37 seats[9]. In 1978, however, they won

only 4% of the votes, two markedly more militant

organizations having meanwhile arisen: the Front de

Libération de la Bretagne and the Armée Révolutionnaire

Bretonne, which together maintain a liaison mission in

Dublin, the A.R.B. having even borrowed the motto "Sinn

Fein" (On-unan)[10]. At about the same time there came

into being another organization, Sav Breizh ("Arise,

Brittany"), avowedly nationalist and progressive, but

rejecting violence and committed to a Breton-speaking

Brittany.

Other organizations fight for more specialized aims

such as having Breton in schools both as a medium and as

a subject of instruction: Ar Falz (The Sickle) and Ar

Brezhoneg er Skol (Breton in School). In 1951 a law was

in fact passed to allow the optional teaching of Breton

on a par with forestry[11]. In 1967 a petition for more

effective teaching of Breton was signed by one-and-a-half million people.

All this political activity must have had something to do with the progress evident in the cultural field, with the sale of books on the increase, twenty periodical wholly in Breton, a literary review (*Al Liamm*, "The Bond" sponsored by a publishing house of the same name, and numerous magazines on political and other specialized subjects. An interesting move is the attempt of the magazine *Gwalarn* ("North-east") under the editorship of the writer Roparz Hemon to avoid traditional Breton themes in favour of translations from foreign works, which involves the adaptation of Breton to the life of the urban middle class. Confidence in the future is shown by the work done on the provision of a scientific vocabulary. The Church too has reversed the trend away from Breton, and the clergy now have their own Society, Kenvreuriezh ar Brezhoneg ("The Brotherhood of Breton").

It must be remembered that it is Lower Brittany where Breton is spoken, the language having retreated from as much of Upper Brittany as it ever penetrated and never having been spoken in the south-east of the region. In this, Brittany is in the same position as Scotland, which has not been a monolingual

country since the Picts faced the Romans across or north

of Hadrian's Wall. Since the arrival of the Anglo-Saxons

through Northumbria Scotland has in fact been trilingual:

first Welsh, Pictish, Anglo-Saxon, and finally Gaelic,

English, and Scots, whose status as language in its own

right cannot be denied when in it wrote one of the

British Isles' greatest poets, Burns, and which very

properly has its own chapter in Meic Stephens' book,

Linguistic Minorities in Western Europe. It is against

this background that the present position and prospects

of Gaelic must be considered. In the first place, the

language clearly plays a lesser part in nationalist

thought; indeed, it can be said[12] that Gaelic is a

language "without a Movement". The recently founded

Comunn na Canain Albannaich ("Scottish Language Society"),

most of whose members are not native-speakers, aims to

get Gaelic spoken throughout Scotland, a position which,

as we have seen, it has never enjoyed. Thus the

only road-signs in Gaelic are those set up in 1973 by one

of the few landlords interested in the language[13]. On

the other hand, in all linguistic questions Gaelic is well

looked after by *An Comunn Gaidhealach* ("The Gaelic

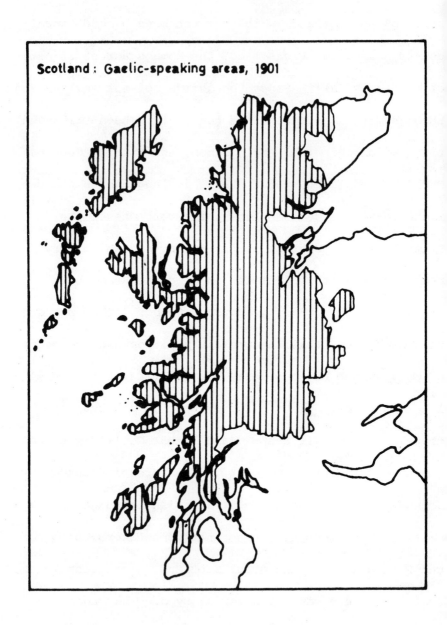

Scotland: Gaelic-speaking areas, 1901

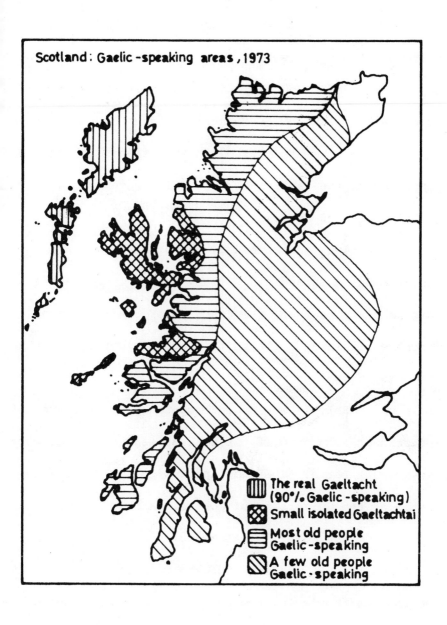

Scotland: Gaelic-speaking areas, 1973

The real Gaeltacht
(90% Gaelic-speaking)

Small isolated Gaeltachtai

Most old people
Gaelic-speaking

A few old people
Gaelic-speaking

Society"), which was founded around 1890 with largely

cultural aims; witness the annual *Mod*, their equivalent

of the Eisteddfod and the Oireachtas. It has an inner

group called *Clann an Fhraoich* ("Children of the Heather"

which avoids the use of English in its work[14]. Publishe

supported by the Gaelic Books Council, have raised the

annual number of titles to around forty; and a future

readership seems guaranteed by the use of Gaelic for

instruction in Infant and Primary Schools. So far as

survival is concerned, the teaching of Gaelic in two

Teachers' Training Colleges is of more significance than

its being taught as part of the Celtic Courses in three,

where presumably it would continue to be studied even if,

and perhaps even more if, it were as dead as (or no more

alive than) Latin. The same applies to the Courses in

Breton at the University of Rennes. Much of course depen

on local County Councils. Those of Ross and Inverness ha

appointed special advisers for their schools charged with

the task of increasing the use and teaching of Gaelic. I

1963 one of them reported: "The language is being used in

much wider context than was formerly the case. More

emphasis is now being placed on the teaching of Gaelic as

a subject, and in certain schools a limited use is being

made of Gaelic as a medium of instruction... The attempt
to introduce a scheme of exclusive Gaelic teaching for
Gaelic-speaking children has not been abandoned."

In Northern Ireland the old language of Ulster is
kept alive by the efforts of *Comhaltas Uladh* ("The Ulster
Committee"), sc. of *Connradh na Gaeilge*,
publishes a monthly, *An t-Ultach* ("The Ulsterman"),
maintains a network of branches ("*craobhacha*") throughout the Province, and organizes Summer Schools for
children and adults in the various *Gaeltachtaí*, especially
that in Rann na Feirste, County Donegal. Most of these
children have probably learnt the elements in a school run
by the Christian Brothers, and they must promise not to
speak a word of English as long as they are in Irish-
speaking Ireland. Unfortunately, the situation in the
six Counties is such as to distract attention from the
fate of the language.

In Ireland proper (if one may so put it) the struggle
might be thought to be over and Irish out of danger; but
what has happened holds a warning for all champions of
suppressed languages. The fatal difficulty for Irish is
that the rival tongue happens to be a language in world-
wide use, knowledge of which confers a distinct advantage

in an era of multinational organizations. (Significantly
and logically, Ireland waived her right to have an Irish
translation of all documents issued by the Common Market,
contenting herself with an Irish version of the Document
of Accession).[15] This advantage is particularly felt by
members of the Government, who are in constant touch with
their European colleagues; and the result is that the
use of Irish by Government and its officials has not
evolved as expected. The lead that should have been
given to the country and the consequent rise in the status
of the language have not been forthcoming. Thus Fine
Gael, when in opposition in 1966 (as it is again today),
proposed to abolish the requirement of Irish for entry
into the Civil Service and to make Irish optional in
secondary schools. It may have been influenced by the
formation in that year of the Language Freedom Movement,
which aimed to restrict Irish in schools to the status
of cultural subject, to abolish the bilingual requirement
for public servants, and even to limit aid to the
Gaeltacht. (Similar rumblings of discontent have recently
been heard in Wales).[16]

The struggle for the language is over, and that is
just the danger. It is no longer linked to a political

campaign; it is no longer a part of patriotism: it must
stand or fall now, not on its own merits, but on the
degree of the people's conviction that Irish is
necessary to Ireland. A single example will show what
the country is up against.   It happened in Bunbeg in the
heart of the Donegal Gaeltacht: "I went to the Police
Station in Bunbeg recently," writes someone to *An
t-Ultach* in June 1977, "to ask for a Driving Test form.
The Sergeant brought out a great bundle of forms, but
there was not so much as one of them in Irish. He told
me in English (all the policemen in Bunbeg speak English)
that I would have to write away for one. I told him
'Write away for it yourself. You ought to have Irish
forms in the heart of the Gaeltacht'. 'Gaeltacht be
damned,' was his reply." No wonder a writer in the
Celtic Annual of 1969 cannot contain his bitterness:
"The revival of Irish has always been applied in a
half-cock manner," he says; "denied any community-life,
denied any snob-appeal from the example of the National
Assembly, it has never been able to develop the momentum
to carry it forward. Unless there is a radical change,
Irish has no future".

It is incredible that this can be said when nearly

all Primary School teachers are bilingual, when down to
1973 a pass in Irish was necessary for matriculation, and
when the Census-figures of 1971 show a rise in the number
of Irish-speakers; but the Irish-speakers in the
Gaeltacht (i.e. the majority of the native-speakers in
the country) have shrunk from 85,547 in 1956 to 55,550 in
1971, only 40% of Secondary School teachers consider them
selves fluent enough for teaching through Irish, and
Galway has the only University providing degrees in Irish
taught subjects (of which there are sixteen)[17]. Moreover
what has been achieved is the result of a policy imposed
on the country by its Government, and "however much an
authority supports a language, if the population has not
the will to learn, there is not much sense in it"[18].
Indeed, harm is done to the language, because compulsion
rankles. Children in other countries can fail in their
language-studies without detriment to their careers, but
in Ireland failure to pass an examination in Irish used
till recently to close the door to the Civil Service.
This has made the language unpopular. Efforts have even
been made to simplify it by jettisoning 'dead' syllables
and (alas!) abandoning the Roman script that was
its glory; but the only way to make a language easy is to

place the learner in a community that speaks that language, and that community cannot be created until enough learners have already learnt it. So today, after fifty years of freedom to do what she liked with her language, Eire finds that all that has been achieved so far is that its decline has been arrested.

We now find ourselves right up against the crucial question: What does saving a language mean for these countries?[19] For Ireland it once meant restoring Irish as the language of the whole country, to be "a normal means of conversation and communication among Irish people".[20] But did that mean that it was to supplant English? If not, then the aim was preservation rather than restoration; or, in other words, the country was to be bilingual. Bilingualism, however, is an ambiguous term. A person is bilingual when he or she speaks two languages with equal facility, having been brought up to speak both; but a country is bilingual when, as in Belgium, two languages are spoken within its borders with an equal degree of recognition as an official language. The first sense imposes on every citizen the necessity of knowing the two languages of the country, which in practice means the learning of one of them; and here the problem begins.

The two linguistic communities may not be equally moti-
vated: Celtic-speakers have more reason to wish to learn
the language which opens the door on international inter-
course than English-speakers have for learning a language
which closes it; and Celtic-speakers have also the easier
task, because if English is the language of administratio
they will see and hear it all around them. In other word
one language would predominate over the other. An
independent Government would then have to decide between
compulsion, which would be regarded as discriminatory,
and optionality, which would mean the end of complete
bilingualism as a practical policy. Then any insistence
on the merits or necessity of knowing the "weaker" langua
becomes a source of friction, as Welsh-speaking Welshmen
(*Cymry Cymraeg*) have found; but if Welsh were not made
compulsory for entry into Government or Civil Service,
then from the start all such activities would involve the
apparatus of simultaneous translation and the duplication
of documents and all the expense thereof. Presumably the
same problem would face autonomous Brittany.

Bilingualism raises also the problem of ensuring tha
there is no damage done to a child's intellectual growth
as shown in its power of expression. Unfortunately, ther

is evidence to suggest that the bilingual child may be
at a disadvantage. An investigator[21] found that "Irish
children from English-speaking homes were considerably
behind British children in achievement in English, and
similarly behind Irish-speaking children in achievement
in Irish." English-speaking children taught arithmetic
through Irish were also retarded in "problem arithmetic".
Similarly, an investigation into the teaching of English
in Wales to children between the ages of 8 and 11 reveals
that many so-called 'bilinguals' in Wales end up with a
Welsh-English hybrid[22]; and if this would surely be the
result of wrong methods rather than of any inherent flaw
in bilingualism itself, it remains true that to bring up
a child to speak two languages is a task requiring the
greatest care.

In Scotland, despite the activities of *Comunn na
Canain Albannaich*, which, as we have seen rejects the
distinction between Highlands and Lowlands and works for
the restoration of Gaelic as Scotland's national tongue,
there can be no question of organised bilingualism for the
whole country, still less of using Gaelic in any national
Assembly as the normal language of debate. The Scottish
National Party made no mention of Gaelic in its
policy-statement of 1964, and this too though it had

approved a policy of preservation in areas where it is

still spoken (an approval repeated in the House of Commons

in 1968). Nor are the Gaels the more vociferous part of

the Nationalists: they do not claim to be more Scottish

than monoglot English-speaking Scots, and they do not as

a whole struggle for the return of Gaelic speech to the

north-east and centre of Scotland from which it has

retreated. All they want is to preserve what they have,

and the recognition of their language as an essential part

of the Scottish heritage, to be treated with respect and

fostered by any Government in Edinburgh. Thus Scotland

would be a bilingual country in the same way as Belgium is

with the difference that personal bilingualism would be

limited to the Gaels; and indeed it is for this that the

Highland Society is fighting, and has to fight even harder

now, because the new Regional Boundaries drawn in 1978

have diluted some Gaelic areas; e.g. by including the

Perthshire Highlands in the central Region[23]

This concern is an encouraging phenomenon. While in

Eire, Wales, and Brittany, Celtic is to have a role in

government, in Scotland, Man, Cornwall, and Northern

Ireland as at present constituted, Celtic is to be kept

alive simply "because it is there": the question has

become a humanitarian one. The modern world has advanced at least so far that it will no longer stand aside and see a language, any more than a species, disappear. Much, however, depends on Celtic-speakers themselves. Let them reflect that languages are not killed: they commit suicide.

Notes to Chapter Fourteen

1. Obituary in *Coraa Ghailckagh*, Laa Souney, 1952.

2. *Daily Telegraph*, 3 March 1975, and *Sunday Telegraph*, 11 April 1976.

3. J.R. Edwards, reviewing P.B. Ellis's *The Cornish language and its literature* in *LPLP* 1, No.2 (1977), p.98.

4. Similarly popular are the Irish groups, 'The Chieftains' and 'Bothy Band', the Welsh 'Mynediad am ddim', and the Breton 'Ar Log' (The Cell).

5. Dr. Marstrander was not the first foreign scholar to to be interested in Manx. In 1851 Lucien Bonaparte (nephew of the former Emperor and a well-known phillogist) came to the island on the first of several visits. A Briton, John Rhys, wrote the *Outlines of the phonology of Manx Gaelic* in 1894.

6. See the *Zeitschrift für Celtische Philologie* Vol.24, pp.58-80 for his article 'Spoken Manx'.

7. These two tape-collections, as copied by the School of Scottish Studies in 1973, were made available in 1978 on a gramophone record (with accompanying booklet) produced by Mr. George Broderick for Resound Ltd., Sale, Cheshire.

8. Published in the *Linguistic Atlas and Survey of Irish Dialects*,Vol.IV (Dublin, 1969).

9. Per Keribin, *Y Ddraig Goch*, Mehefin 1977, p.9.

10. *Daily Telegraph* of 21 May 1978 and *Sunday Telegraph Magazine* of 11 June 1978.

11. *Y Ddraig Goch*, Ebrill 1978, p.7.

12. And has been said by Colm Ó Baoill in his article quoted on p.282, n.1.

13. *ibid.*, p.91.

14. R.E. Wood, *op.cit.*, in *LPLP*, 1 No.2 (1977), p.45.

15. Since then, however, several documents have been published in Irish by the Council of Europe and the European Communities. An article in *An t-Ultach* of Sept. 1978, p.6, lists 21 of them.

16. See p.364.

17. Tomás Ó Domhnalláin, *loc.cit.*, *LPLP* 1, No.2 (1977), pp.89-93.

18. L. Pietersen, 'Die Zukunft des Friesischen', *LPLP* 1, No.3 (1978), p.147.

19. It is significant that the B.B.C. in its weather-forecasts now uses the phrase "taking each country in turn, starting with England".

20. quoted by Moshe Nahir, 'The five aspects of language-planning', in *LPLP* 1, No.2, p.110, from the report of a commission set up in 1964.

21. J. MacNamara, *Bilingualism and Primary Education* (1966 quoted by Patricia Nichols, *op.cit.* in *LPLP* 1, No.1, (1977), and T.Ó Domhnalláin, *op.cit.* in *LPLP* 1, No.2, p.86.

22. C. Treharne, a Research Fellow, discussing an investi-gation directed by D. Sharp of University College, Swansea (C. James in *LPLP* 1, No.1, p.79).

23. John van Eerde, 'Gaelic in Scotland', in *LPLP* 1, No.1, (1977), p.35.

BIBLIOGRAPHY

1. History

Chadwick, Nora.   The colonization of Brittany, from
                     Celtic Britain (British Academy
                     Lecture, Oxford Univ. Press, 1967).

"   "   Celtic Britain (London: Thames &
                     Hudson, 1964).

Dillon, Myles and   The Celtic Realms (London:
Chadwick, Nora.   Weidenfeld & Nicolson, 1972).

Evans, Gwynfor.   Aros mae (Swansea: John Perry,1971).

Garnier, C.-M.   Eire, Histoire d'Irlande (Paris:
                     Aubier, 1939).

Hanson, R.P.C.   St.Patrick, his origins and career
                     (Oxford: Clarendon Press, 1968).

Herring, I.J.   History of Ireland (London:
                     J. Murray, 1937).

Kerr, P.M.(Canon).   Scéal na h-Éireann (2 vols.) (Eire:
                     Dundalk Press, 1938-1939).

Kinvig, R.H.   A history of the Isle of Man
                     (Liverpool: University Press, 1950).

Ó Cuív, B.   A view of the Irish language
                     (Dublin; Statistical Office, 1959).

Powell, T.G.E.   The Celts (London: Thames & Hudson,
                     1960).

Rait, R.S.   History of Scotland (London:
                     Thornton Butterworth, 1930).

Salmon, Mary.   A source-book of Welsh history
                     (Oxford: University Press, 1927).

Stephens, Meic.   Linguistic minorities in Western
                     Europe (Llandysul, Dyfed: Gomer
                     Press, 1976).

Trevelyan, G.M.   History of England (London: Longmans,
                     Green, 1948).

2. Language

a. British Latin

Hamp, E.P.   *Social gradience in British spoken
                     Latin* (Reprinted from *Britannia,*

Vol.VI, 1975) (London, Society for the Promotion of Roman Studies).

Mann, J.C.   *Spoken Latin in Britain as evidenced by the inscriptions* (in *Britannia*, Vol.11, 1971) (London: Society for the Promotion of Roman Studies).

Shiel, N.   *The coinage of Carausius as a source of Vulgar Latin forms* (Reprinted from *Britannia*, Vol.VI, 1975) (London: Society for the Promotion of Roman Studies).

b. Pictish

Tucker, C.   The Orphans of History, No.1 The *Leid* of the Thistle; No.2 The Pictish Chronicle (Kirkcudbright: The author, 1977-8).

c. Brythonic

Jackson, K.H.   Language and History in Early Britain (Edinburgh: University Press, 1957) (with full bibliography).

d. Welsh

Betts, C.   Culture in crisis: the future of the Welsh Language (Wirral: Ffynnon Press, 1976).

Council for the Welsh Language   A future for the Welsh Language (Cardiff: H.M.S.O.,1978).

Finch, P. (ed.)   How to learn Welsh: a guide book for adult learners. (Swansea: Christopher Davies, 1978).

Lewis, H.   Datblygiad yr Iaith Gymraeg (Cardiff: Welsh University Press, 1931).

Stephens, Meic.   The Welsh Language today (Llandysul: Gomer Press, 1973).

Williams, W.O.   The survival of the Welsh Language after the Union of England and Wales: the first phase 1536-1642 (*Welsh History Review* 2 (1964), pp.67-93).

e. Cornish

Dexter, T.F.G.   Cornish Names (London: Longmans,
                    Green, 1926).

Ellis, P.B.   The Cornish Language and Literature
                    (Henley-on-Thames: Routledge &
                    Kegan Paul, 1974).

Evans, D.S.   The history of Cornish(in *Studies*
                    (Dublin, 1969), pp.293-309).

Smith, A.S.D.   The story of the Cornish language:
                    its extinction and revival (Camborne:
                    Camborne Printing Co., 1947).

Sutton, G.H.   Konciza historio pri la kornvala
                    lingvo kaj literaturo (London:
                    British Esperanto Assoc.,1969).

White, G.P.   A handbook of Cornish Surnames
                    (Camborne: G. Pawley White, 1972).

f. Breton

Falc'hun, F.   Histoire de la langue bretonne d'après
                    la géographie linguistique.
                    /Doctoral thesis/ (2nd ed. 1963).

Gourvil, F.   Langue et littérature bretonnes (*Que
                    sais-je?* Paris: Presses
                    Universitaires de France, 1960).

g. Gaulish

Ellis Evans, D.   Gaulish Personal Names (Oxford: Clar-
                    endon Press, 1967) (with full
                    bibliography).

Lejeune, M.   Lepontica (Paris: Société d'Éditions
                    "Les belles lettres", 1971).

Whatmough, J.   The dialects of ancient Gaul (1970)
                    (with full bibliography).

h. Irish

Athbheochan na   (Dublin: Stationery Office, 1965).
Gaeilge

Greene, D.   The Irish language (Cork: Mercier
                    Press, 1972).

i. Gaelic

MacKinnon, K.   The Lion's tongue (Inverness: Club
                       Leabhar, 1974).

                       j. Manx

Thomson, R.L.   The study of Manx Gaelic (Oxford:
                       University Press, 1971).

                       3. General

Daniel, E.C.   The linguistic role of the Breton
                       Marches (*The Linguist*, 1960, pp. 294-
                       5 and 330-1; 1961, pp. 16-7).

Edwards, J.R.   Report of the Committee on Language
                       Attitudes Research (Dublin:
                       Government Stationery Office):
                       reviewed in *Lingvaj Problemoj kaj
                       Lingva Planado*, 1, No.1 (Den Haag:
                       Mouton,1977).

"   "   /Review of/P.B. Ellis, The Cornish
                       language and literature, in *LPLP* 1,
                       No.2 (1977).

Eerde, J. van.   Gaelic in Scotland (*LPLP* 1, No.1,
                       1977)

James, C.   Welsh Bilingualism (*LPLP* 1, No.2,
                       1977).

MacNamara, J.   Bilingualism and Primary Education
                       (Edinburgh: University Press, 1966).

Meillet, A.   Les dialectes européens (Paris:
                       Librairie E.Champion, 1922).

Nichols, Patricia   Ethnic consciousness in the British
C.   Isles (*LPLP* 1, No.2).

Ó Cuív, Brian.   The Irish Language and Literature
                       (Documents on Ireland No.15), (Dubli
                       Department of External Affairs, 1960

Ó Domhnalláin, T.   Ireland: the Irish Language in
                       Education .(*LPLP* 1, No.2).

Price, Glanville.   Breton (*The Linguist* 1956, pp.295-6
                       and 43-4).

Price, Glanville.	Gaulish (*ibid.*, 1959, pp.44-5 and 72).
" "	Manx (*ibid.*, 1960, pp.14-5, 40-1, and 71-2).
" "	Scottish Gaelic (*ibid.*, 1961, pp. 156-6 and 191-2).
Thurneysen, R.	Die Keltischen Sprachen (Die Erforschung der Indogermanischen Sprachen, Strassburg; K.J. Trübner, 1916).
Watkins, C.	Italo-Celtic revisited (Ancient Indo-European Dialects, ed. Birnbaum & Puhvel, pp.44-8, 1966).
Williams, *Sir* Ifor.	Enwau lleoedd (Liverpool: Gwasg y Brython, 1969).
Wood, R.E.	Linguistic Organizations in Scotland (*LPLP* 1, No.1, 1977).
" "	/Review of/ Meic Stephens, The Welsh Language today (*ibid.*).
Articles in	*An Lef Kernewek, Coraa Ghailckagh, Y Ddraig Goch, an t-Ultach, The Isle of Man Weekly Times,* as quoted in the text.

4. Literary History

Gourvil, F.	(See above under Language, Breton).
Hyde, D.	The story of early Gaelic Literature (London: Fisher Unwin, 1895).
" "	A literary history of Ireland (London: Benn, 1967, reprint of 1899).
Marx, J.	Les littératures celtiques (*Que sais-je?* Paris:PressesUniversitaires de France, 1960).
Parry, Thomas.	Hanes Llenyddiaeth Gymraeg hyd 1900 (Cardiff: University of Wales, 1944).
Sutton, G.H.	(See above under Language, Cornish).

5. Grammars and readers

a. Irish

Christian Brothers.	First Irish Grammar (Dublin: M.M. Gill & Son,pre-1941).
MacGiolla Pádraig, B.	Réidh-Chursa Gramadaighe (Dublin: Brun agus Ó Nuallain, 1939).
MacNamee (Mac Con Midhe), P.	An bealach úr (4-part beginner's reader) (Belfast and London: O Fallúin, 1969).
Ó Creag, Séamus.	Irish Grammar and Composition (Derry: Craig & Co., 1926).
Ó Domhnalláin, Tomás.	Buntús Cainte (First Steps in spoken Irish, Parts 1 and 2 of recorded course)(Dublin: Oifig an tSoláthair, 1967).
Ó Searcaigh, Séamus.	Coiṁreir Ghaedhilg an Tuaiscirt (Belfast: Oifig an tSoláthair, 1939).
Pokorny, J.	A historical reader of Old Irish (Halle: Max Niemeyer, 1923).

b. Gaelic

Gillies, H.C.	The elements of Gaelic Grammar (London: D. Nutt, 1902).
MacFarlane, A.	Handbook of Gaelic Phrases and Sentences (Edinburgh: J. Grant,1939).
Macfhionghuin, L.	Leabhar IV (Glasgow: Blackie, 1946).

A wide range of textbooks is always available from An Comunn Gaidhealach, Abertarff House, Inverness.

c. Manx

Gell, J.	Conversational Manx (Douglas, I.O.M. *Mona's Herald*, 1954).
Goodwin, E.	First Lessons in Manx *(Yn Cheshaght Ghailckagh,* 1947).
Kneen, J.J.	Manx Idioms and Phrases (Menston, Yorks.: Scolar Press, 1938).

Stowell, B.   Gaelg trooid Jallooghyn (*Yn Cheshaght Ghailckagh*, 1947).

d. Welsh

Morris Jones, J.   An elementary Welsh Grammar, Part 1 (Oxford: Clarendon Press, 1926).

Richards, M.   Cystrawen y ffrawddeg Gymraeg (Cardiff: Welsh University Press, 1938).

Smith, A.S.D.   Welsh made easy
(Caradar)   (Wrexham: Hughes and Son, 1933).

e. Cornish

Hooper, E.G.R.   The Commentary on *Gwryans an Bys* of
(Talek)   A.S.D. Smith (Camborne: *An Lef Kernewek*, 1962).

Morton Nance, R.   Cornish for all (Marazion: Federation of Old Cornwall Societies).
  "   "   "   "   "   "   " (3rd edn., 1958).

Smith, A.S.D.   Cornish Simplified (Camborne: *An Lef Kernewek*, 1965).
  "   "   Supplement to the above, Part II, 2nd edn. (1966).
  "   "   Supplement to the above, Part IV, The Cornish Verb BOS (1963).
  "   "   An examination of the functions of forms of the Cornish Verb BOS (Reprint from the *Journal of Celtic Studies*, Vol.2, No.2, 1958).
  "   "   Lessons in spoken Cornish (Camborne: *An Lef Kernewek*, 1968).

f. Breton

Hemon, Roparz.   Marvailhou ar Vretoned (Brest: *Gwalarn*, 1941).

Seite, V. and   Deskom Brezoneg (Emgleo-Breiz, Ed. F.C.B
Stephan, L.   1957).

Vallée, F.   La langue bretonne en 40 leçons (Saint-Brieuc: A. Prud'homme, 1940).

6. Dictionaries

Anwyl, J.B.	Spurrell's English-Welsh, Welsh-English Dictionary (Carmarthen: W. Spurrell & Son, 1934).
Bhaldraithe, Tomás de.	English-Irish Dictionary (Dublin: Oifig an tSoláthair, 1959).
Cregeen.	Dictionary of the Manks Language, (Douglas, I.O.M., 1835).
Dinneen, P.S.	A concise English-Irish Dictionary (Dublin: M.H. Gill & Son, 1939).
Dinneen, P.S.	Irish-English Dictionary (Dublin: Irish Texts Society, 1927; reprinted 1975).
Dwelly's	Illustrated Gaelic to English Dictionary (Glasgow: Gairm Publications, 1971).
Erwan ar Menga.	Geriadur Esperantek-Brezhonek (Douarenez: Hor Yezh, 1978).
Fargher	English-Manx Dictionary (Onchan, I.O.M.: Shearwater Press Ltd., 1980).
Hemon, Roparz.	Dictionnaire Breton-Français (Brest: Al Liamm, 1964).
Kneen, J.J.	English-Manx Pronouncing Dictionary (Douglas, I.O.M.: Mona's Herald, (1953).
MacFarlane, M.	Gaelic-English Dictionary (Stirling: Eneas Mackay, 1953).
Morton Nance, R.	A Cornish-English Dictionary (The Cornish Language Board, reprinted 1967).
" "	English-Cornish Dictionary (Marazion: Federation of Old Cornwall Societies, reprinted 1969).
Wood, W.	Fockliooar Gaelg-Baarle, a short school dictionary of Manx Gaelic (Glasgow: An Cheshaght Ghailckagh, 1950).

7. Language-Learning Records and Tapes

BRETON

iinicassette longue durée *Kenteliou brezhonek*	37,50
All the texts of the Manuel *Kenteliou*	francs.
rezhonek, 17 francs)	
iinicassettes Philips, Cours élémentaire:	
leçons 1-12	37,50
leçons 13-25	37,50
	francs.

All available from: Mlle.J. Queillé, *Al Liamm*,
47, Rue Notre-Dame, 22200 Guingamp, Brittany.

rezhoneg...buan hag aes ("Breton...quickly
nd easily"): 2 cassettes or 5 records (33⅓RPM),
with illustrated manual of 256 pages and the
author's book containing translations of the
dialogues and versions of the exercises:

Price including manuals - records		91
	cassettes	100
		francs.

(Manual alone 18.50fr.; book alone 4.50 fr.)

Komzit ha skrivit brezhoneg ("Speak and write
Breton"): 2 cassettes with 98-page manual containing exercises from "Brezhoneg..buan hag aes".

Price - cassettes with manual	77
manual	13.50
	francs.

Kenteliou kentan e brezhoneg ("First lessons
n Breton"), an introductory course in "Common
Breton": 2 records (33⅓RPM) with booklet

Price	30
	francs.

(Note: The last three works, by Per Denez of the
University of Haute-Bretagne, Rennes, are obtainable from:
Editions-Disques OMNIVOX, 8, Rue de Berri, 75008 Paris).

CORNISH

L.P. Tape-Recordings, *Kernewek Bew,* available	
from Richard Gendall, Shaft Down, Hayle, Cornwall,	
on receipt of tape of 5¾ inches	50p.

Record: Side 1. Selections from the Ordinalia, etc.
        Side 2. The story of John of Chy-an-Horth
Crowdy Crawn, a collection of songs and prose in
Cornish, by Richard Glendall and Brenda Wootton.
(Sentinel L.P.)   post-free   ..   £2.76

   (Records available from: Mrs. S. Trenberth,
   Bronwith, Garkar Road, Trethwrgy, St. Austell,
   Cornwall).

                        GAELIC

Gaelic stories told by Peter Morrison: cassette
published by the School of Scottish Studies, and
accompanied by 16-page leaflet containing translations. (From Tangent Records Ltd).   ..   £4.35

   (Records and cassettes are available from
   An Comunn Gaidhealach, Abertarff House,
   Inverness).

                        IRISH

Linguaphone: 4 cassettes or 21 records, with
illustrated textbook, Course handbook, and
Study-plan   ..   £75

   (207 Regent Street, London W1R BAU)

Teach Yourself Irish: cassettes
Buntús Cainte ("Rudiments of speech"), a series
planned and written by Tomás Ó Domhnalláin, on
2 records, to be used in conjunction with Part I
of the book of the same name   ..

   (Ceirníní Gael Linn, 54 Sráid Grafton,
   Dublin 2, Eire).

Gael-linn Ceirníní Teagaisc (Educational Records)

   (26 Cearnóg Mhuirfean, Baile Átha Cliath 2, Eire).

CT 1/2 *Teach yourself Irish:* a set of two LPs by
native Irish speakers to accompany the book by
Professors Myles Dillon and Donncha Ó Croinin
published by the Irish Universities Press. This
course is suitable for those who wish to learn
Irish, but who might not be able to attend formal

classes.

    Price: (Ireland) £7.98 + postage (incl.VAT)
          (abroad)   £6.30 + postage (76p)

CT 5/6 *Buntús Cainte*: an easy conversational
CT 7/8 course based on the latest theories of
CT 9/10 language-teaching. Available on records or
       cassettes, this course is suitable for
       school-children, adult beginners, or those
       whose Irish is rusty from lack of practice.

    Price: (Ireland) £7.98 per part + postage (inc.VAT)
         (abroad) £6.30 per part + postage (76p)

MANX

Cassettes: *Bunneydys* ("Foundation"), a Course for
      learners, (the text of Book 1 of the same
      name, 65p. Book 2, unrecorded, is 80p) . . £3

      Conversational Manx (the text of the Neddy
      Beg stories, 35p)   . . £2.50

Record or Cassette: *Chengey-ny-mayrey* ("Mother-
      tongue"), the last seven native-speakers
      talk to their interviewers and to each
      other; with booklet containing the texts
      and notes by George Broderick.
      A recording made by Resound Ltd., Sale,
      Cheshire and published by Soras Mac Ruairi
      for Shearwater Press Ltd., Onchan, Isle
      of Man   . . £3.99

  All available from: An Cheshaght Ghailckagh,
Mrs. J. Bayliss, "Elmwood", Glencrutchery Road,
Douglas, Isle of Man.

WELSH

Linguaphone: 4 cassettes or 21 records, with textbook,
      handbook, and instruction-booklet . . £75
    (For address see under Irish)

B.B.C.: "Let's speak Welsh"
            Record 1   . .   £1.80 + VAT
            Cassette 1 . .   £2.90 + VAT
            Cassette 2 . .   £2.90 + VAT
    (Books 1 and 2, 55p each; Books 3 & 4, 35p each).

Cwrs Cymraeg Llafar: cassette from Christopher Davies,

INDEX

BOOKS   FROM   OLEANDER

Oleander Language and Literature

MARVELL'S ALLEGORICAL POETRY

Bruce King
Professor King, of the University of Missouri, has set
out to answer the central problems of Marvell criticism:
what kind of poet was Marvell and what are his poems
about.

US $8.95   ISBN 0 902675 60 5   UK £3.75

FRIULAN: Language and Literature

D.B. Gregor
The first English-language grammar of the Friulan langu-
age of north-east Italy is accompanied by an anthology of
the most important poems and prose texts to be written in
Friulan, with facing English translations by the author.
Card cover.

US $15.00   ISBN 0 902675 39 7   UK £5.00

ROMAGNOL: Language and Literature

D.B. Gregor   .
The first English-language grammar of the Romagnol language of central Italy is accompanied by an anthology of
the most important short poems and prose texts to be
written in Romagnol, with facing English translations by
the author. Card cover.

US $15.00   ISBN 0 902675 12 5   UK £5.00

MAD NAP: "PULON MATT"

D.B. Gregor
The poetic masterpiece of the language of Romagna, the
Italian region encompassing Ravenna, Rimini, Cesena and
Faenza. It is a burlesque based on the epic *Orlando
furioso* by Ariosto, but has never up to now been printed,
even in Italian. Here is the Romagnol original, with
versions in both modern Italian and English. Card cover.

US $15.00   ISBN 0 902675 37 0   UK £5.00

INDONESIAN TRADITIONAL POETRY

Philip Ward

An English-language anthology of texts with translations
and linking commentary from Javanese, Minangkabau,
Sundanese, Nias, Ngaju Dayak, Tolaki, and many other
tongues spoken by the 124 million people of Indonesia.

US $13.50   ISBN O 902676 49 4   UK £4.00

THE ART AND POETRY OF RAMUZ

David Bevan

This first major work on Ramuz in English, by David Bevan
of the University of Port Elizabeth, establishes the Swiss
novelist as one of the most significant literary figures
of our century. It demonstrates how Ramuz achieves in
his fiction a close interrelation between his message and
his style, finding in his best work the full internal
coherence characteristic of great art.

US $8.95   ISBN O 902675 47 8   UK £3.75

BIOGRAPHICAL MEMOIRS OF EXTRAORDINARY PAINTERS

William Beckford

The extraordinary writer and eccentric William Beckford
(1760-1844) is best known to English readers for his
oriental novel *Vathek* (1786), but he had already achieved
fame at the age of 20 by parodying the popular art books
of the day (and incidentally also the voluble housekeeper!
in this satire.

US $9.50   ISBN O 900891 13 O   UK £4.00

TRANSLANTIC CHINESE: A POEM BY TS'UI HAO

Wayne Schlepp

An American scholar of Chinese teaching in Toronto
illuminates a great eighth-century poem, with several
versions in English, French and German to demonstrate
the pitfalls. Paper cover.

US £1.25   ISBN O 900891 OO 9   UK 52p

JUST PICK A MURRICANE?

N.E. Chantz

A comic lexicon of American usage described by a newspaper as "ticklingly funny". Card cover.

US $1.25   ISBN O 902675 11 7   UK 30p

THE QUELL-FINGER DIALOGUES

The imaginary dialogues are now known to be based on the
thought of Dr. Reinhold Regensburger, founding president
of the Private Libraries Association, who died in
December 1972. Privately printed.

US $1.25   ISBN O 900891 01 7   UK 52p

THE SMALL PUBLISHER: A MANUAL AND CASE HISTORIES

Audrey and Philip Ward

How does one set up, run, and make a success of, a small
family publishing business without initial capital?
The Wards have been publishing for 20 years, and their
book uses the experiences of more than 50 other small
presses for background data.

US $22.50   ISBN O 900891 59 9   UK £8.95

ENLIGHTENMENT THROUGH THE ART OF BASKETBALL

Hirohide Ogawa

The Japanese 'inner game' of basketball explained with
wisdom and humour, and illuminated by the images
created for the book by Peter Nuttall. "You say
'enlightenment', and you say 'basketball', but one must
walk on both legs".

US $8.95 Hardback ISBN O 900891 36 X   £3.95
US $3.95 Softback ISBN O 900891 35 1   £2.50

DARTS: FIFTY WAYS TO PLAY THE GAME

Jabez Gotobed

A new darts game for every week of the year, together
with old favourites played by the champions, for the
7 million darts players in Britain alone. Variations on
many of the new games are offered.

US $9.95 Hardback ISBN O 900891 71 8   £4.20
US $4.75 Softback ISBN O 900891 72 6   £1.95

A DICTIONARY OF COMMON FALLACIES

Philip Ward

"One of the most entertaining reference books ever written" - Daily Telegraph.

"Fascinating" - Sunday Express. 2 vols.

THE GERMAN LEFT SINCE 1945

W.D. Graf

A detailed study of the socialist opposition in the Federal Republic of Germany since the end of World War II.

US $27.95 Hardback ISBN O 902675-54-O   UK £8.95
US $13.95 Softback ISBN O 902675-68-O   UK £4.50

Oleander Travel Books

BANGKOK: PORTRAIT OF A CITY

Philip Ward

A journey of fourteen chapters, stressing the enchantment of the most exotic city of the Orient: its temples and palaces, its rivers and canals, its music, sport, art and drama. With excursions to Ayudhya, U Thong, - and the Bridge on the river Kwai.

US $6.50   ISBN O-902675-44-3   UK £2.50

COME WITH ME TO IRELAND

Philip Ward

"Usefully straddles the fence between a guide-book and a personal record: discursive and anecdotal, it reveals the author's real feeling for people and atmosphere, and. the book is crammed with well-checked historical, literary and local information as well. A most admirable companion for an Irish journey, he leads you away from the highroads to the hidden treasures off the beaten track. A useful road map is included" - *Ireland of the Welcomes*. With town plans and many half-tone plates.

US $6.50   ISBN O-902675-36-2   UK £2.50

THE AEOLIAN ISLANDS

Philip Ward

The mighty Stromboli and legendary Vulcano are two of the
most impressive volcanoes in Europe. But what of the
other islands in the Aeolian group north of Sicily?
Philip Ward, who studied Italian in Perugia, describes
the ageless beauty of the Aeolians in their historical
setting and what has happened since the Archduke's time.
Illustrated with maps, drawings and photos.

US $6.50   ISBN 0-902675-43-5   UK £2.50

TOURING CYPRUS

Philip Ward

"This is a valuable book for those who want a brief guide
to Cyprus. It omits nothing and is sensibly arranged.
The information about hotels, methods of transport,
shopping and so on is accurate. Philip Ward, who has
long experience of Mediterranean and Middle East countries,
writes well and amusingly about the history of the island
and the many fine sights for the historically-minded to
seek out. He is particularly knowledgeable on the
Byzantine frescoes for which Cyprus is famous; most of the
best are in rather inaccessible spots and his advice on
how to find them is just what the tourist wants" -
Times Literary Supplement. With town plans and many
half-tone plates.

US $6.50   ISBN 0-902675-13-3   UK £2.50

Indonesiana

INDONESIA: A TRAVELLER'S GUIDE

Darby Greenfield

Travelling a quarter of a million miles in search of the
wonders of Indonesia, the British writer Darby Greenfield
spent eighteen months preparing this first ever *Baedeker*
to all twenty-six provinces of the emerald world of
Indonesia.

Vol.1 *Java and Sumatra*
US $9.95   ISBN 0 902675 46 X   UK £2.95
Vol.2 *Bali and the East*
US $9.95   ISBN 0 902675 48 6   UK £2.95

INDONESIA: A BIBLIOGRAPHY OF BIBLIOGRAPHIES

J.N.B. Tairas
A librarian working in the Jakarta Acquisitions Office
of the Library of Congress, Mr Tairas is in a unique
position to provide reference librarians and Indonesian
specialists with the first major checklist of national
source materials ever made publicly available.

US $13.50   ISBN 0 902675 50 8   UK £4.00

Arabia Past and Present

(in collaboration with The Falcon Press, Italy)

1. COLOURS OF THE ARAB FATHERLAND

Angelo Pesce
Ninety-nine magnificent colour plates portray the
unequalled beauty and variety of Saudi Arabia, with
27 pages of text, a select bibliography, and a full-
colour map.

US $39.95   ISBN 0 902675 18 4   UK £18.00

2. JIDDAH: PORTRAIT OF AN ARABIAN CITY

Angelo Pesce
The definitive scholarly work on the major Red Sea port
and at the same time a spectacular picture book, with a
foreword by Freya Stark. Forty-eight colour plates,
numerous maps, 148 pages of text, 33 pages of appendices,
and bibliography. Full cloth and pictorial jacket.
2nd edition 1976.

US $59.95   ISBN 0 902675 34 6   UK £27.75

3. ASIR BEFORE WORLD WAR I

Sir Kinahan Cornwallis
A reprint now first authorized, of the confidential Arab
Bureau of Cairo *Handbook to Asir* (1916). Even now the
most comprehensive study (and practical route-guide) to
this mountainous province of southwest Saudi Arabia, with
its capital at Abha.

US $13.50   ISBN 0 902675 57 5   UK £5.00

4. ARABIA IN EARLY MAPS

Gerald R. Tibbetts
The bibliography of printed maps of the Arabian Peninsula from the first attempts, based on Ptolemy, to the time of Bourguignon d'Anville and modern cartographic methods. With many illustrations and a historical essay on the development of Arabian cartography.

US $35.50   ISBN 0 902675 58 3   UK £15.00

5. DIARY OF A JOURNEY ACROSS ARABIA (1819)

George Forster Sadleir
The first reprint of the gripping chronicles of the first Westerner ever to cross Arabia from east to west. Lost for fifty years, the book first appeared in a small edition at Byculla, near Bombay, in 1866. With a new introduction by F.M. Edwards.

US $18.00   ISBN 0 902675 59 1   UK £8.00

6. REPORT ON A JOURNEY TO RIYADH (1865)

Lewis Pelly
Back in print for the first time in over a century, this classic of Arabian travel covers the trail from Kuwait to Riyadh, and back to Bahrain via Hofuf and al-'Uqair. 1978 reprint, with a new introduction by R.L. Bidwell, Secretary, Middle East Centre, Cambridge University. A companion volume to Sadleir's *Diary*.

US $16.00   ISBN 0 902675 64 8   UK £6.00

7. HEJAZ BEFORE WORLD WAR I

David George Hogarth
The Arab Bureau of Cairo's revised 2nd ed. of their Hejaz handbook (1917) is here reprinted with new colour covers and a new introduction by R.L. Bidwell. A companion volume to Cornwallis's *Asir*.

US $16.00   ISBN 0 902675 74 5   UK £6.00

8. TRAVELS IN ARABIA (1845 and 1848)

Georg August Wallin

The Finnish explorer Wallin published the results of his travels in Arabia in early volumes of the *Journal* of the Royal Geographical Society, here reprinted for the first time with introductions by W.R. Mead of University Colleg London, and M. Trautz.

US $22.50   ISBN O 900891 53 X   UK £9.00

9. THE GOLD-MINES OF MIDIAN

Richard Francis Burton

A classic of travel in Egypt and northwest Arabia in 1878, with the added excitement of mining for gold and other minerals. This new edition, by Philip Ward, is based on the author's own annotated copy in the Royal Anthropological Institute Library, London, and supersedes the original edition, marred as it was by hundreds of errors and misprints.

US $32.50   ISBN O 900891 50 5   UK £15.00

10. KING HUSAIN AND THE KINGDOM OF HEJAZ

Randall Baker

The first objective analysis of the formerly independent Arab State which now forms the western region of Saudi Arabia, with a penetrating study of Husain, Hejaz's first king who may have been misjudged by most Arab historians. By the Dean of the School of Development Studies, University of East Anglia.

US $29.95   ISBN O 900891 48 3   UK £13.50

11. THE LAND OF MIDIAN

Richard Francis Burton

The centenary edition of this classic of Victorian adventure, now in one volume as compared with the two-volume original edition of 1979, but unabridged. *The Land of Midian* is the sequel to Burton's famous *Gold-Mines of Midian* and takes the exploration of northwest Arabia to much greater lengths.

ISBN O 900891 55 6

12. MONUMENTS OF SOUTH ARABIA

Brian Doe
The archaeology of Oman, Hadhramaut, Yemen, and
southernmost Saudi Arabia is described in detail, with
numerous plans, maps, and photographs in both colour
and black-and-white. The scholarly apparatus is intended
for specialists, but the treatment of the material will
also appeal to the general reader.

Libya Past and Present

1. TRIPOLI: PORTRAIT OF A CITY

Philip Ward
'The Arab World' wrote of Philip Ward's *Touring Libya:
the Western Provinces* (Faber and Faber; reprinted): 'For
anyone who had already booked a trip to Libya or is
contemplating one, I strongly recommend they read
Philip Ward's book and keep it near at hand during their
visit'. This is a poet's evocation of the sights and
sounds, pleasures and surprises of the capital of Western
Libya. Map. Street plans of the old town and the new
city. 21 plates.

US $6.00   ISBN 0 902675 06 0   UK £2.50

2. SABRATHA: A Guide for Visitors

Philip Ward
The only book in print in any language on the most
charming city of Roman Libya. "Orderly and authoritative.
No one will want to visit or study this site without the
help of this model guide" - *Archaeology*. Superb photos
by Hans Lafeber.

US $6.00   ISBN 0 902675 05 2   UK £2.50

3. LIBYAN MAMMALS

Ernst Hufnagl
"This excellent field guide to the mammals of Libya...
(has)... a good key, many pen-and-ink sketches, and
notes on identification, habitat, behaviour, food and
distribution of the species..." - *Times Literary Supplement*. Drawings by Ed van Weerd.

US $13.50   ISBN 0 902675 08 7   UK £4.00

4. THE LIBYAN CIVIL CODE

I.M. Arif and Meredith O. Ansell

An authoritative English translation of the Civil Code
of Libya together with an expert comparison with the
Egyptian Code from which it was derived in extenso. A
significant addition to legal literature. A limited
edition.

US $45.00   ISBN 0 902675 00 1   UK £18.75

5. THE GARAMANTES OF SOUTHERN LIBYA

Charles Daniels

"Authoritative... A splendid introduction to a long-
standing historical mystery as well as a guide-book to
the archaeology of the Germa desert" - *Archaeology*.
Photos & drawings by the author.

US $6.00   ISBN 0 902675 04 4   UK £1.95

6. THE WAY TO WADI AL-KHAIL

Philip Ward and Ed van Weerd

Philip Ward's book on the prehistoric carvings of the
Little Valley of the Horses, southwest of Mizda,
describes the rock art most accessible from Tripoli, with
practical hints on obtaining a guide and the types of
country encountered on the way. Eddy van Weerd has provided stunning pictures in colour and monochrome.

US $1.75   ISBN 0 902675 17 6   UK 52p

7. APULEIUS ON TRIAL AT SABRATHA

Philip Ward

The great Latin writer Apuleius, born about A.D. 125,
who married a wealthy widow of Roman Tripoli, was tried
for sorcery in the law-court of Sabratha in 157 at the
height of his oratorical powers.

US $2.50   ISBN 0 9026675 09 5   UK 75p

8. MOTORING TO NALUT

Philip Ward and Angelo Pesce

"An excellent ... motoring guide and pictorial atlas of the Jabal Nafusa area and its contemporary inhabitants" - *Middle East Journal* (Washington).

US $1.75   ISBN 0 902675 03 6   UK 52p

9. THE LIBYAN REVOLUTION: a source-book of legal and historical documents
Vol.1: 1 September 1969 - 30 August 1970.

I.M. Arif and M.O. Ansell

Dr. Arif and Mr. Ansell have assembled English versions of the early laws and decisions which shaped the new republic. Part 1 translates the contents-lists of all official gazettes issued during the first year. Part II translates in full the key laws, such as the new Labor Law and major historical documents. Part III is a verbatim transcript of the Intellectual Seminar held in Tripoli, May 1970.
"For students of Near East politics this is an absolutely essential book" - *Book Collecting & Library Monthly*.

US $22.50   ISBN 0 902675 10 9   UK £6.00

Cambridge town, gown and county

I THE CAMBRIDGESHIRE COPROLITE MINING RUSH

Richard Grove
The first comprehensive account of the scramble for coprolite land in 19th-century Cambridgeshire, with contemporary illustrations.

US $4.25   ISBN 0 902675 61 3   UK £1.30

II RAILWAYS TO CAMBRIDGE, ACTUAL AND PROPOSED

Reginald B. Fellows

A full account of how the first railways came to Cambridge, and why others didn't.

US $3.25   ISBN 0 902675 62 1   UK 90p

III CAM BRIDGES

Richard J. Pierpoint
For beauty, utility, and historical interest, the
bridges over the Cam in Cambridge are second only to
those of London's Thames.

US $4.25   ISBN 0 902675 63 X   UK £1.30

IV LONDON TO CAMBRIDGE BY TRAIN 1845-1938

Reginald B. Fellows
A railway classic first privately printed in 140 copies
and now reissued with all the text and plates.

US $3.25   ISBN 0 902675 65 6   UK 90p

V CAMBRIDGE CASTLE

William Mortlock Palmer
Out of print for nearly fifty years and here reissued
with a new bibliography by M.J. Petty, F.L.A. Fully
illustrated.

US $4.25   ISBN 0 902675   UK £1.30

VI CLAY TOBACCO PIPES IN CAMBRIDGESHIRE

Robert John Flood
The history of local clay pipes, their manufacture, use
and virtual extinction by the spread of the briar.
Fully illustrated.

US $4.25   ISBN 0 902675 70 2   UK £1.30

VII PERSE: A HISTORY OF THE PERSE SCHOOL, 1615-1976

S.J.D. Mitchell
The major public school's biography, stressing the
W.H.D. Rouse years (1902-28). Hardback.

US $15.00   ISBN 0 902675 71 0   UK £4.95

VIII THE CAMBRIDGE THAT NEVER WAS

F.A. Reeve
Some of the abandoned proposals for 'beautifying'
Cambridge have been rational enough, but others have
been almost ludicrous, and F.A. Reeve (who served on the
County Council for thirteen years) has summarized the
most bizarre.

US $4.25   ISBN O 902675 72 9   UK £1.30

IX PREHISTORIC CAMBRIDGESHIRE

Alison Taylor
The County Field Archaeologist has written a succinct ,well-
illustrated account of Cambridgeshire's earliest settlements. For the specialist, the general reader and also
schools.

US $4.25   ISBN O 900891 05 X   UK £1.30

X DOVECOTS OF CAMBRIDGESHIRE

Peter Jeevar
An important survey of the 17th and 18th century pigeon-
houses with gazetteer, full-page drawings, and many plates.

US $4.25   ISBN O 900891 06 8   UK £1.30

XI ANGLO-SAXON CAMBRIDGESHIRE

Alison·Taylor
An up-to-date account of the Germanic invasions of
Cambridgeshire by the County Field Archaeologist intended
both for the general reader and for school use.

US $4.25   ISBN O 900891 07 6   UK £1.30

XII CAMBRIDGE NEWSPAPERS AND OPINION, 1780-1850

Michael J. Murphy
The impact on daily life of the city's early press,
shedding new light on aspects of local and national
politics and society. Hardback.

US $9.95   ISBN O 900891 15 7   £4.50

XIII ROMAN CAMBRIDGESHIRE

David M. Browne
A contributor to the new *Victoria County History* of
Cambridgeshire has condensed his material for the
general reader. Well illustrated.

US $4.25   ISBN O 900891   UK £1.30

XIV THE CAMBRIDGE NOBODY KNOWS

Frank A. Reeve
Seventeen byways (and subways!) of England's fairest city
which few have ever explored.

US $4.25   ISBN O 900891 lo 6   UK £1.30

XV MEDIEVAL CAMBRIDGESHIRE

Henry Clifford Darby
Professor Darby's first book after retiring as head of th
Department of Geography, University of Cambridge, distill
a lifetime's knowledge of the county in the Middle Ages.
For schools and the general reader.

US $4.25   ISBN O 900891 11 4   UK £1.30

XVI CURIOSITIES OF RURAL CAMBRIDGESHIRE

Peter Jeevar
Drawings and photos from the county's four corners to sho
such oddities as snow-ploughs, a ha-ha, pounds and lock-u

US $4.25   ISBN O 900891 12 2   UK £1.30

XVII VARSITY RAGS AND HOAXES

Frank A. Reeve
The uproarious pranks and hoaxes which made Cambridge
headlines over the centuries, including night-climbing an
the latest student rags.

US $4.25   ISBN O 900891 16 5   UK £1.30

XVIII GODMANCHESTER

Michael Green
Many years of excavation have given the author unique qualifications to describe this Cambridgeshire town from earliest times to the modern period.

US $4.25   ISBN O 900891 18 1   UK £1.30

XIX CAMBRIDGESHIRE IN EARLY POSTCARDS

Michael Rouse
An illustrated study of the 'Golden Age' of the Cambridgeshire picture postcard.

US $4.50   ISBN O 900891 23 8   UK £1.40

XX CAMBRIDGE CHARACTERS

Irene Lister
Portraits in word and picture of some of the most illustrious and eccentric men, women (and horses!) connected with Cambridge's university and city.

US $4.50   ISBN O 900891 25 4   UK £1.40

XXI CAMBRIDGE BUSES

Mark Seal
The story of omnibuses based in Cambridge from the early days to 1978, profusely illustrated.

US $4.50   ISBN O 900891 24 6   UK £1.40

XXII CAMBRIDGE STREET LITERATURE

Philip Ward
The founder of the Private Libraries Association describes the almanacks, ballads, chapbooks, playbills and posters printed in Cambridge.
soft covers
US $4.50   ISBN O 900891 21 1   UK £1.50
hard covers
US $8.95   ISBN O 900891 52 1   UK £3.95

XVIII GODMANCHESTER

Michael Green

Many years of excavation have given the author unique qualifications to describe this Cambridgeshire town from earliest times to the modern period.

US $4.25   ISBN O 900891 18 1   UK £1.30

XIX CAMBRIDGESHIRE IN EARLY POSTCARDS

Michael Rouse

An illustrated study of the 'Golden Age' of the Cambridgeshire picture postcard.

US $4.50   ISBN O 900891 23 8   UK £1.40

XX CAMBRIDGE CHARACTERS

Irene Lister

Portraits in word and picture of some of the most illustrious and eccentric men, women (and horses!) connected with Cambridge's university and city.

US $4.50   ISBN O 900891 25 4   UK £1.40

XXI CAMBRIDGE BUSES

Mark Seal

The story of omnibuses based in Cambridge from the early days to 1978, profusely illustrated.

US $4.50   ISBN O 900891 24 6   UK £1.40

XXII CAMBRIDGE STREET LITERATURE

Philip Ward

The founder of the Private Libraries Association describes the almanacks, ballads, chapbooks, playbills and posters printed in Cambridge.

soft covers
US $4.50   ISBN O 900891 21 1   UK £1.50
hard covers
US $8.95   ISBN O 900891 52 1   UK £3.95

XXIII POVERTY IN CAMBRIDGESHIRE

Michael J. Murphy
How legislation and social agitation have affected the
life of the poor in Cambridgeshire.

US $4.50   ISBN O 900891 29 7   UK £1.40

XXIV PETERBOROUGH: A HISTORY

H.F. Tebbs
The first comprehensive account of the city's development for 300 years.

US $16.50   ISBN O 900891 30 O   UK £6.50

XXV CAMBRIDGE COLLEGE WALKS

Frank A. Reeve
A new guide to 2-hour strolls, illustrated with rare earl
lithographs and engravings . 64 pages.

US $4.00   ISBN O 900891 42 4   UK £1.20

XXVI PROMENADES À CAMBRIDGE

Frank A. Reeve
An original French-language guide to the colleges.
40 pages.

US $3.50   ISBN O 900891 43 2   UK 95p

XXVII SPAZIERGÄNGE DURCH CAMBRIDGE

Frank A. Reeve
An original German-language guide to the colleges.
40 pages.

US $3.50   ISBN O 900891 44 O   UK 95p

XXVIII EARLY CAMBRIDGESHIRE

A hardback compilation of *Prehistoric, Roman, Anglo-Saxon
and Medieval Cambridgeshire* above.

US $15.00   ISBN O 900891 08 4   UK £4.95

XXIX CAMBRIDGE MUSIC

Frida Knight

Musicmaking in Cambridge from the Middle Ages to the
present day, with illustrations and a foreword by
Sir David Willcocks, formerly Director of Music at
King's College Chapel, and now Director of the Royal
College of Music.

US $16.50   ISBN O 900891 51 3   UK £6.95

Oleander Modern Poets

1. UNDERSEAS POSSESSIONS: Selected Poems

Hans-Juergen Heise

"Thematically adventurous... subtle and sensitive... he
can assimilate and juggle with the paraphernalia of
modern technology... but can still subordinate them to
the demands of his own fantasies..." - *Times Literary
Supplement.*

US $3.50   ISBN O 902675 33 8   UK £1.25

2. A HOUSE ON FIRE: New Poems

Philip Ward

A British expatriate writer responding here to Libya
(the sequence in *A house on fire*), to Malta (the sequence
in *Time's green touch*), and to Egypt (the sequence in
Like Hathor). Also available: *Seldom Rains* ($1.25 or
52p), *At the Best of Times* ($1.25 or 52p), and *Maps on the
Ceiling* ($1.25 or 52p): the Libyan trilogy by
Philip Ward.

US $3.50   ISBN O 902675 38 9   UK £1.25

3. THE HIDDEN MUSIC: Selected Poems

Osten Sjöstrand

Sjöstrand, the leading Swedish poet of his generation
with Tomas Tranströmer and Lars Gustafsson, has won the
Bellman Prize for Poetry, his country's premier award.

US $4.00   ISBN O 902675 35 4   UK £1.25

4. CONTEMPORARY AMERICAN POETRY: A Personal Anthology
Allan Burgis.
Out of print.

US $1.5O   ISBN O 902675 55 9   UK 52p

5. CONTEMPORARY GERMAN POETRY: A Personal Anthology
Ewald Osers
A winner of the Schlegel-Tieck prize for the best
published translation from the German (1970),
Ewald Osers now brings his intimate knowledge of new
German writing to an English-language audience with a
careful selection of fourteen major writers who have
emerged since World War II: Cibulka, Fried, Piontek,
Anders, Fritz, Becker, Hartung, Zornack, Kunze, Härtling
Schäfer, Leisegang, Delius and Theobaldy.

US $4.OO   ISBN O 902675 69 9   UK £1.35

6. THE SCANDALOUS LIFE OF CÉSAR MORO: Selected Poems
César Moro
The most important of the Peruvian surrealist poets,
Alfredo Quíspez Asín (known as 'César Moro') lived and
worked in the Paris of Aragon, Breton, and Éluard,
contributing to their review *Le Surréalisme au service
de la Révolution*. But his books were elusive, in
limited editions for bibliophiles, and this is the first
representative selection of his poems in French and
Spanish ever to be made available in English, presented
by Philip Ward, Editor of *The Oxford Companion to
Spanish Literature*.

US $3.25   ISBN O 902675 73 7   UK 9Op

7. IMPOSTORS AND THEIR IMITATORS
Philip Ward
Writing in *The Times Literary Supplement,* Gavin Ewart
said of these new poems: "Many of them deal with mind-
events and loneliness,some with small happenings and
mini-thoughts ("Refugee" - the pleasure of avoiding
poetry, "Misunderstandings" - international semantics).
It is for their wit and their sure technique, based on
complete avoidance of rhyme and rhythmical banalty, that
these poems are to be valued".

US $4.25   ISBN O 900891 22 X   UK £1.35